THE LAST YEARS
OF THE GENERAL

THE LAST YEARS OF THE GENERAL

KEN GLAZIER

Capital Transport

AUTHOR'S NOTE

Between 1930 and 1933 the foundations were laid for a revolutionary change in the organisation and operation of transport in London which would wipe out the traditional road transport operators and replace them with a unitary authority holding unprecedented monopoly powers. Yet in this swansong period the operators continued to show the same enterprise and care for their businesses and customers as had always characterised the best. In 1930 AEC had just introduced its new range of models and the LGOC, after several years of inactivity, was embarking on a massive fleet renewal, which together with the investment which the Independents had started to make several years before, marked the introduction of the first truly modern buses to the capital. The Underground Group also set out to modernise its tram operations, with the introduction of superb new tramcars and London's first trolleybuses, while the municipalities, notably the London County Council, also invested in fine new trams from a more traditional mould.

The same year saw the announcement by Herbert Morrison of his plans for a publicly owned Board with monopoly powers and responsibility for all forms of transport in a large area of greater London and the Home Counties. The new Board took control on 1st July 1933. Outside London, the industry was also being substantially reformed, with the passage in 1930 of the Road Traffic Act.

This book covers the history of the three-and-a-half years leading up to the formation of the Board and a further volume will deal with the first six years of the new authority. It is an extremely complicated subject and a fully detailed account could run into several volumes. I have therefore adopted a selective approach, using 'case histories' to illustrate particular threads of activity, while covering the main thrust of the story as fully as possible.

One important respect in which I have been selective is in the area covered. As far as possible, I have included all vehicle and major service developments in the old London Traffic Area, as defined by the 1924 Act, including the municipal tramways, and all matters affecting the Underground Group companies, irrespective of where they operated. The major exclusions, therefore, are the operators working outside the London Traffic Area. This was necessary because of the size and complexity of the subject which simply could not have been accommodated without compromising the comprehensiveness of the coverage.

Putting together an account such as this is only possible with the aid and support of many other people and I would like to take the opportunity to thank all those who have helped me in different ways. My special thanks go to Dr Andrew Gilks, who has generously made available many valuable vehicle records from the Chiswick archive, has untiringly and willingly answered all my questions and has devoted time to checking the end result. Ken Blacker, Hugh Taylor, David Ruddom, Reg Westgate, Malcolm Papes and Brian Bunker have all given generously of their time to carry out detailed checking of the text and appendices and to supply new, corrected or additional information. David and Malcolm have also helped considerably in locating suitable illustrations. Others who have supplied information and photographs are John Gent, George Robbins, who also kindly made available material from J.F. Higham's collection, the late Dick Turnbull, who threw useful light on the activities of East Surrey and LGCS and Martin Elms, who helped considerably with schedules information. The many photographers, who are acknowledged in the body of the book, also deserve special thanks as without their enthusiastic work this book would not have been possible.

I would also like to record my grateful thanks for his unfailing support and encouragement when my enthusiasm showed signs of flagging, to my dear friend Aspi Daver who sadly died while I was working on the draft. Although he had no interest in the subject, he never failed to take an interest in my progress and urge me on, even from a hospital bed during his final days. To him I dedicate this book.

London, August 1994

KEN GLAZIER

Title page The interior of the new Upton Park garage with a selection of the 157 LTs delivered there between November 1931 and February 1932, showing three different body styles. The complex roof structure which can be seen enabled the entire floor space to be free from pillars. *LT Museum U13138*

Opposite 'A warm welcome aboard' seems to be the message conveyed by the soft glowing light and deeply cushioned seats of this LGOC T type bus. The sense of luxury is further enhanced by the mirror situated between the bulkhead windows and by the smooth modern interior finish. *LT Museum U6081*

First published 1995

ISBN 185414 170 8

Published by Capital Transport Publishing
38 Long Elmes, Harrow Weald, Middlesex

Printed by Bath Midway Press
Holt, Wiltshire

CONTENTS

CHAPTER ONE

LONDON IN 1930

Above **George Street, Croydon, on a busy shopping day at the beginning of the 1930s. Both buses belong to the LGOC and are supplied by Elmers End garage, the elderly open-top K on the left operating on trunk route 12A, while the more modern covered top NS is working local route 178 to Addiscombe. The conductor of the K can be seen in traditional pose, supervising boarding from the head of the stairs, hand poised ready to hit the bell plunger which is just visible above the advertisement panel.** Handford Photography

Facing page **An early experiment with a roundabout at Cambridge Circus, replacing the straight crossing from its five inlets. Buses of three Combine associates are in the foreground, a BAT NS just edging in on the left, LGOC's LT 150 passing Alkit's Dress Hire shop in the centre and an Overground ST has turned into Charing Cross Road. In the distance are three more buses, including a covered top NS. Other traffic comprises almost exclusively taxis and commercial vehicles, with only one private car in evidence.** LT Museum U12061

By the beginning of 1930, helped by the impetus of improved public transport, London had already grown well beyond the Victorian and Edwardian built-up area which had set the boundaries to the better part of the bus and tram service network during the horse and early motorised era. Between the censuses of 1921 and 1931, the population of greater London grew from seven-and-a-half to over eight-and-a-quarter million, an increase of over nine per cent. By contrast, in the County of London, the population of around four and a half million declined by $2^1/_2$ per cent. The County of London at this time comprised the area more recently known as 'inner London', while the territory defined as 'greater London' covered an area rather larger than that of the GLC after 1964. Bus services had been spreading more and more into these newly developing suburbs during the 1920s, particularly in those neighbourhoods which had been opened up by Underground railway extensions and by the electrification of the Southern Railway's network in the south. Nevertheless, the greater concentration of services was still within the older developed parts of the metropolis, where the network covered more or less all the roads it was destined to do for the next thirty or so years.

Practically everybody who needed to travel did so by public transport, whether for business or pleasure and it was mostly only the privileged who used private cars, whilst the poorest travelled very little and much of what they did, they did either on foot or by bicycle. To meet the massive demand, bus and tram services were run at intensive frequencies over a quite complicated network. Then as now, Oxford Street was a major draw along which the London General Omnibus Company and its associated companies alone scheduled 330 buses an hour each way during peak hours (about one every second), with not all that much less at other times. Victoria Embankment, the main central London terminus for the London County Council's south London trams, enjoyed 423 trams an hour (carrying, incidentally, thirty-thousand passengers in the peak). Outside central London, Brixton Road between Kennington and Gresham Road had sixty-two trams and seventy-four buses an hour; and Green Lanes Harringay had fifty-eight trams and ninety-five buses. Such levels were repeated all over inner London, where the conductors' cry 'there's another one right behind' was still a statement of fact rather than the protective white lie it was to become half-a-century later.

At the other extreme, large areas of the inner home counties were still open country or, particularly in Middlesex, still covered by a market garden trade, although this was already going into decline. Once beyond old established centres like Hendon or Eltham, travellers would find themselves in green fields served by country lanes with much of the road system over which later generations of buses were to work, yet to appear. Although frequent bus services were operated over the main roads connecting these towns with their neighbours, much of the journey between many of them was spent passing through the countryside, sometimes along roads which would be barely recognisable to the modern eye.

Even in inner London, though, the road system still lacked some key links. Work had only just started on a new bridge to replace the 1862 structure at Lambeth, which had been restricted to pedestrians since 1910; planning for an improved layout at Vauxhall, including a new section of South Lambeth Road and a new road called Parry Street, was in its infancy; at Waterloo a hastily erected temporary bridge had been in use for traffic in one direction since the old one had subsided in 1923 and there was as yet no sign of any permanent replacement; the nineteenth century suspension bridge at Chelsea was unsuitable for modern traffic; and it would be the end of the decade before there was a bridge usable by buses at Wandsworth.

In many ways the roads were still in the earliest stages of coming to terms with the comparatively new phenomenon of motor traffic. There were as yet no illuminated traffic signals in London; all traffic control was done by police officers on point duty, a use of his skilled manpower not much liked by the Commissioner of Police. The first traffic lights were installed at Ludgate Circus only in July 1930 and the Treasury was reluctant to release money to pay for any more, despite the economies which the Police said they could make. An experiment with linked lights was carried out in Oxford Street in June 1931 and the success of this led to pressure from the Metropolitan Boroughs for more to be authorised. The Ministry of Transport at last gave the go-ahead for further schemes in June 1932. In such a state of backwardness, with roads made of materials which encouraged rather than prevented skidding, with tyre technology at its most primitive and bearing in mind that there was as yet no qualifying test for a driving licence, it is hardly a surprise that the accident rate was appallingly high. An average of four people a day were killed on London's roads in the three months from July to September 1930 (a total of 361) and 15,287 were injured. Of those killed, thirty-two involved buses and eight trams.

Traffic congestion as understood by later generations hardly existed outside the confines of the City and West End. With public transport so dominant it was as often blamed on buses and coaches as on other traffic but such regular congestion as did occur was beginning to become a threat to the reliability of those very services. Undoubtedly one major cause was the surprisingly large proportion of commercial vehicles which was still horse-drawn; in some areas it rose above half of the total. In inner London, if not in the leafier suburbs, as much as fifteen per cent of all wheeled traffic could be horse-drawn, with the startling proportion of thirty-five per cent being reached in the singular case of Tower Bridge.

When contemporary commentators or politicians referred to 'congested areas' they were usually talking about population over-crowding, which was a serious problem in parts of inner London and in the East End. This form of congestion was to some extent a boon to transport operators as it provided a densely packed source of business, easy to serve with the high frequency levels and close-knit route patterns common in such areas. On the other hand many people unfortunate enough to live in these places could not afford the luxury of travel. To ease their lot, the municipal undertakings, notably those in the East End with highly developed public service philosophies, offered special fare concessions to poorer residents, who generally lived in areas of unrelieved bricks and mortar, so that they could reach open spaces for recreation. An interesting example, which illustrates this well, was the special quarter rate tickets to Wanstead Flats issued to children from East Ham during the school holidays.

This Premier Dodson bodied Dennis 4-ton forty-eight seater was first licensed in November 1923 and as such represents the first generation of post-First World War Independent buses, many of which were replaced in the early 1930s. It was withdrawn in February 1930. Dennis Odd collection

Contrary to popular belief, the road transport scene in London at this time was remarkably stable, thanks to the operation of the London Traffic Act of 1924. Originally introduced as a control measure to put an end to the chaotic road conditions in London which was alleged to be caused by unfettered bus competition, it had placed unprecedented powers in the hands of the London & Home Counties Traffic Advisory Committee and the Metropolitan Police who ensured its stringent application through the Public Carriage Office. Through this procedure the Police determined not only the licensing of bus routes but also continued to exercise rigid control over the design and maintenance of buses which were allowed to ply in the Metropolitan Police District. This ensured much higher standards of safety in London than the rest of the country, where such controls barely existed, but, unfortunately, the Police apparently saw their role as passive and negative and made no direct contribution to the positive development of either route planning or vehicle design.

The route control provisions had more or less eliminated on-the-road competition on ordinary short stage bus services and between them and the tramways, which were afforded special protection under the Act through the medium of the 'Restricted Streets Orders'. These put a limit on the number of buses which could operate along specified roads where the police deemed that the limit of capacity had been reached. The restricted streets were by no means all tram routes but the Police did not exercise the same powers over the level of service provided by the tramway undertakings, so, where the orders were applied to tram routes, it was inevitable that the trams would benefit. Legal restrictions often lead to the application of subtle imagination to by-pass them and so it was in this case. Operators looked for ways of linking

key objectives by ingenious 'back-street' routes avoiding the restricted roads. Two famous examples were Birch Bros' route 231 between Hampstead Heath and Harlesden, linking Swiss Cottage, St Johns Wood, Maida Vale and Kensal Rise; and the 263 between Finsbury Park and Chingford, linking Highbury, Kingsland, Dalston and Hackney by a remarkably tortuous route, on which six operators ran at various times. Despite such resourcefulness, the general effect of the Metropolitan Police's stewardship was to ossify the route network.

The policy of the Metropolitan Police on the control of bus design was also notorious for its conservatism and is generally held responsible for delaying the introduction of improvements such as covered tops, pneumatic tyres, drivers' windscreens, drivers' cab doors and enclosed staircases. Width and length restrictions, over and above those applying in the rest of the country, also imposed unasked, for capacity constraints, as well as limiting the extent to which passenger amenities could be improved. By 1930, the battle for covered tops and pneumatic tyres had been won at last but the authorities were only just beginning to ease their attitude to drivers' windscreens and the enclosure of staircases, while cab doors and indeed saloon doors were to remain on the restricted list for many more years.

One of the best known, but perhaps not best understood, consequences of the 1924 Act was the control of route numbering by the Public Carriage Office. A system was invented by Chief Constable Bassom under which each route, including bifurcations from the main route, had its own individual number and every shortworking was identified by a suffix letter on the main number. Thus the number 25 applied to the full route from Victoria to Seven Kings, 'shorts' from Victoria to Aldgate were 25A, to Manor Park 25B and so on. Routes closely associated with each other were, wherever possible, given numbers one hundred apart, such as 125 from Ebury Bridge to Becontree Heath but this was sometimes varied, usually because the higher number was not available, in which case a consecutive number was used if possible (126

Victoria to East Ham). Suffix letters beyond F were not used, although in the initial draft allocation, route 59 was given suffixes up to N. Generally, however, if there were more than six shortworking variations, another number was allocated for the rest. As originally set up, routes between 1 and 199 were mostly LGOC and those between 200 and 299 were allocated to routes operated exclusively by Independents. Routes which ran into the London Traffic Area from outside were numbered between 300 and 399 in the north, 400 and 499 in the south and 500 and 509 in the west. By 1930, the system also encompassed the rest of the 500s and the 600s, which were mainly Independent and new suburban development routes and the neat division between the Combine and Independents had been dissipated by the acquisition of companies by the LGOC. In such a large area and with a changing network, it was inevitable that this attempt to apply logical principles was bound to produce oddities and also at times to be incorrectly applied. The famous example of the former is route 11 whose number applied to the route from Wembley to Liverpool Street, operated only on special occasions, while the daily operation from Shepherds Bush was numbered 11E. An example of incorrect application is route 303 from New Barnet to Hatfield, which had journeys to Potters Bar bifurcating from the main route down Church Road, numbered 303A instead of a different number. Other examples may be found in Appendix One.

Competition did not disappear completely for long but reappeared in a different form during 1926 and 1927. As a direct result of the restrictive nature of the 1924 Act, some coach operators introduced local fares on their longer distance services, paving the way for the proliferation of so-called suburban coach services from 1928 onwards. By the beginning of 1930, there was already an impressive network of routes serving Southend, Tilbury, Grays, Ongar, Bishops Stortford, Newmarket, Hertford, Welwyn Garden City, Baldock, Bedford, Luton, Dunstable, Leighton Buzzard, Kettering, Watford, Hemel Hempstead, Tring, Aylesbury, Amersham, High Wycombe, Maidenhead, Reading, Windsor, Guildford, Farnham, Sevenoaks and Tunbridge Wells run by nearly twenty-five different operators, with more already poised to join the multitude. These operators claimed to have found a loophole in the law but others, including the powerful London General Omnibus Company, believed that they were breaking the law and were able to succeed only because the traffic authorities turned a blind eye.

The LGOC held back at first, perhaps inhibited by the fact that its Managing Director, Frank Pick, was a member of the London & Home Counties Traffic Advisory Committee, although it was not idle. Its chosen course was to draw specific infringements to the attention of the Ministry of Transport in the hope that they would be stamped out. The LGOC was particularly put out by operators starting services along roads where the Combine had been forced to reduce bus frequencies as a result of the operation of Restricted Street Orders, like Battens along Barking Road, or where they had been specifically refused permission to put on more buses, as on routes 38 and 138 which were assailed by competition from coach operators working between Dalston and High Beach at weekends. By 1929, the competition was damaging longer distance bus services so much that the LGOC reckoned to have lost about a million passengers paying fares of over 7d. Finally losing patience, the Group decided that it too must break the law if it was to survive in that particular market. General's late arrival on the scene was evident from the fact that in January 1930 they were running only two routes, both from Watford, one to Golders Green the other to Charing Cross via Oxford Circus; yet this humble showing was to be the seed of a large and flourishing network.

The overwhelming majority of passenger journeys by public transport in the London area (over eighty per cent) were made by road and by far the greatest contribution to this was made by the motor bus. In fact buses accounted for fifty-three per cent of passenger carryings by all forms of local transport, both road and rail. All were supplied by privately owned companies but the days of fierce cut-throat competition had long since passed and there were now only fifty-eight companies operating principally in the London Traffic Area. Fifty-four of them were 'Independents', a term used in this context to mean an operator with no ties, either by ownership or agreement, to the so-called 'Combine'. This was the mildly pejorative term used to describe the group of companies owned by, or associated with, the Underground Electric Railways Co, the LGOC being the largest and best known.

The rest of the road transport was supplied by trams but here the ownership pattern was quite different. Most trams were owned and operated by municipalities and were therefore in what became known much later as 'the public sector'. The largest of these and indeed the largest in the country was the London County Council, which over the years had entered into operating agreements with other undertakings, both municipal and private, to forge a London-wide network of services. Other municipalities with their own tramway undertakings were the County Boroughs of East Ham and West Ham, Ilford Urban District Council, Walthamstow Council, Leyton Urban District Council (run on its behalf by the LCC), and the Urban Districts of Erith and Bexley (covering Dartford). Finally, there were the Croydon Corporation

Tramways, certainly within the London orbit but not considered by that proud borough to be part of the metropolis. There were also three privately owned companies, all subsidiaries of the Underground Group and therefore sister companies of the LGOC. The largest was the Metropolitan Electric Tramways Company Ltd, operating in Middlesex and Hertfordshire mostly as agents for the County Councils and therefore, in modern business jargon, running a 'joint venture'. Further west was the London United Tramways Co Ltd, covering an area roughly in an arc from Uxbridge Road to Tolworth and Wimbledon. Finally, the poor relation of the Group, the South Metropolitan Electric Tramway and Lighting Company Ltd, between Croydon and Crystal Palace, Penge, Mitcham and Sutton. The three companies operated under the umbrella of a parent known as The London and Suburban Traction Co Ltd, most of whose shares were owned by the Underground Group. The L.& S.T. also had a substantial shareholding in the North Metropolitan Electric Power Supply Co Ltd and owned all the ordinary shares in the Tramways (M.E.T.) Omnibus Co Ltd. To add to this tangled web of interlocking ownerships, the LGOC held all the preference shares in the Tramways (M.E.T.) company,

Above **Premier line ran an all-Leyland fleet of coaches, split almost exactly between Titan TD1 and Tiger TS3 chassis, with twenty-six seat bodies by either Duple or Lonmdon Lorries. This Titan, operating on its London – Windsor route A later became TD 179 in the LPTB fleet.**

Below left **Brush bodied 1722, one of the LCC M class four-wheelers which were drafted to Leyton corporation service, is seen here at Chingford Mount, where an Independent bus with the last style of Dodson body can be seen on the stand in the distance.** M.J. O'Connor

Below right **The influence of the LCC and the strong resemblance of their later E1 class cars, is evident in the design of Walthamstow Corporation's Hurst Nelson cars built in 1927 to work joint services into the county of London. Number 62, at the Liverpool Street terminus in Bishopsgate, displays the LCC-style notice advertising 'Cushion Seats & Pullman Comfort. Try It!!!' but there are few takers on this quiet Sunday.** B.J. Cross collection

while Metropolitan Electric had a considerable interest in the North Met Power Company and a substantial holding in its own parent, while London United also had a small shareholding in the parent company. All of this serves to illustrate the very complicated financial tangle of the Combine.

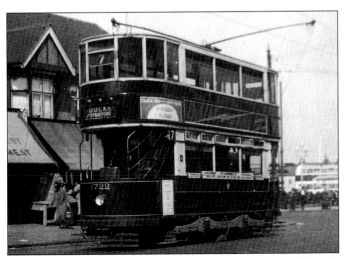

The 'non-Combine' bus companies varied considerably in size, the largest being the City Motor Omnibus Company, who owned thirty-nine buses, the next being Birch Bros with twenty-seven. A number had fleets of between five and a dozen, a handful owned two, while there were half-a-dozen companies, like F.C. Kirk (Empire), who owned only one. They all had two things in common. Most importantly, they had survived the effects of the route approval provisions of the 1924 Act. These had unexpectedly worked to the advantage of the 'Combine' because, by restricting entry into local operation, they had given the LGOC the opportunity to take over the weaker independents without the risk that another entrepreneur would move in to fill the gap. Also, they had nearly all been strong enough to modernise their fleets progressively.

The independents owned 276 vehicles, about six per cent of the total number in metropolitan service. Their fields of operation varied from running a few buses on one or more routes otherwise predominantly served by the LGOC or its associates, to running routes pioneered by them and operated more or less exclusively by them. Important examples of these exclusive routes, other than the 231 and 263 already mentioned, were the 511 (Chingford – Stratford) in east London, shared by no fewer than eight companies; the 526 (North Finchley – Wandsworth Bridge), primarily a Birch creation but by now with a substantial General contingent following the acquisition of the London Public Omnibus Company in December 1929; and, perhaps most famous of the lot, the 536 which straddled London from Archway in the north to Elmers End in the south and was operated, with buses in a common livery, under a joint agreement between City, Birch and United. The London General Omnibus Company was far and away the largest company. It directly owned and operated 4,250 buses and had effective control over another 427 which were owned by associated companies. Two of these, the Tramways (M.E.T.) Omnibus Company Ltd ('Metropolitan') and Overground Ltd, were fellow companies in the Underground Group, and the other two, Thomas Tilling Ltd and Tilling and British Automobile Traction

Ltd, were independent companies with whom General had working agreements. Between them they covered the whole of the London Traffic Area.

The London County Council owned 1,664 tramcars, making it the largest municipal operator in the country. The next largest London operator, with a fleet less than a fifth of the size, was M.E.T., with 316, followed by London United (210), West Ham Corporation (133), Walthamstow (62), East Ham (60), Croydon (55), South Metropolitan (52), Ilford (40), Bexley (33) and Erith (19).

After some years of poor operating results, all these operators began to enjoy an uplift towards the end of the 1920s and were poised to enter the 1930s in reasonably optimistic mood; but this was not to last long. By the autumn of 1930 the 'Depression' had begun to bite and industries began to close down, causing unemployment which was ultimately to reach massive proportions. The Underground Group announced net losses of traffic in 1931 of one per cent and in 1932 of two per cent. The LCC Tramways carried over three million fewer passengers in 1931-32 and suffered a financial loss.

Outside the Metropolitan Traffic Area services were still, for the time being, subject to licensing by local councils under the Town Police Clauses Acts of 1847 and 1889. The freedom of operators to work into some towns was severely limited by the attitude of the local Watch Committee but in other places licensing was virtually automatic and, on the whole, the situation was more free and easy than in London. This had led to an abundance of small independent proprietors working routes varying from the occasional market day service to relatively frequent town services in places like Watford, Slough and Gravesend. Irrespective of events in London, all this was poised to change as a result of two major legislative enactments. The first had been the success of the Main Line Railways in 1928 in obtaining statutory powers to operate road services, which they chose to exercise by purchasing interests in major bus companies, mainly by an agreement with the Tilling and British Automobile Traction Co Ltd. The vigour with which they did so wrought a

substantial change in the pattern of ownership and the size of bus companies. The other legislative change, yet to be enacted, was the Road Service Licensing provisions of the Road Traffic Act of 1930. The combined effect of these was to bring into being the domination of the bus scene by a few major groups and a kind of benevolent control of operations by the Traffic Commissioners.

Significantly for the future of London's transport, within an area roughly thirty-five miles from Charing Cross, the LGOC had taken a dominant position, either by direct ownership of local companies or by entering into operating agreements with already established companies. The boundaries of LGOC influence were broadly from Dartford through Sevenoaks, Westerham, East Grinstead, Crawley, Dorking, Guildford, Windsor, High Wycombe, Amersham, Tring, Luton, Hitchin, Hertford, Epping, Romford and Grays but the associated companies operating in these territories also ran to places well outside this sphere. In the south, East Surrey had been operating as General's agent for eight-and-a-half years and had become a subsidiary in 1929. Its area stretched from Sevenoaks across to Windsor broadly in the outer country ring but with services running as far afield as Uckfield and Handcross in the south. It also controlled Autocar Services of Tunbridge Wells, who operated two routes between Sevenoaks and Tonbridge. A similar agreement in the north had been made with National Omnibus and Transport whose area of responsibility ran from Bishops Stortford across to Aylesbury and Watford. As with East Surrey, National ran some services outside the main sphere of influence, notably to Royston. The gap around Amersham was covered by the Amersham & District Motor Bus and Haulage Co. Ltd, control of which General had acquired in August 1929. In addition to these arrangements, General also had 'area agreements' with Aldershot & District Traction Co Ltd, the Great Western Railway, the L.M.S. Railway, Maidstone & District Motor Services Ltd, Redcar Services Ltd and Thames Valley Traction Co Ltd, which established and protected its outer boundary.

The organisation of transport within this broad sphere of LGOC influence had been the subject of debate for many years. There was a fairly solid agreement that the 1924 Act was regressive and not an adequate instrument for developing passenger transport, although there were widely differing opinions as to what was needed in its place. At the start of 1930 the matter was in limbo, although it had been within an ace of being settled. Following a report of the London & Home Counties Traffic Advisory Committee in 1927, two Bills had been promoted in parliament, one each by the Underground Group and the London County Council, which would have set up a common fund and a system of common management but would have left the businesses in the hands of their current owners. The Bills had passed their third reading in the House of Commons and were awaiting the final stage in the Lords when the General Election of May 1929 brought a Labour government back to power and with it Herbert Morrison, who, as Minister of Transport had

rather different ideas. He therefore killed both Bills but did not announce what his alternative intentions were until December, when he revealed the embryo of his ideas for a publicly owned, non-political, commercially run body.

The need for some action to deal with the perceived problem of traffic and transport in London continued to be the subject of debate for much of 1930, each of the various factions taking every opportunity to air its own solution. It was not until 29th September that Herbert Morrison, in a speech at South Hackney, at last revealed his intentions in more detail. It must have come as a surprise to many and was certainly a shock to the LCC and its fellow municipalities, that his choice had not fallen on a joint municipal body, although he admitted that he had started with a bias in that direction. He believed that no adequate scheme of co-ordination was possible except by fusing all undertakings over a wide area into common ownership with a single management. If it was to be a public service, ownership needed to be public but for

success, quick action and efficiency, the highest quality of management and the advantages of the best quality of commercial enterprise were needed. He had in mind a small board of persons of proven business capacity and promised to make every effort to obtain the services of a chairman who could combine business acumen with wide knowledge and experience. The Board would have to command the confidence of both the investing and the using public and proper contact would have to be maintained between the Board and public opinion.

The new statutory body was to embrace no less than all the railway, bus and tramway undertakings of the Underground Electric Railways Company; the Metropolitan Railway Company; the local authority tramway undertakings; and other bus undertakings in the London area. Others would be added if it was found expedient to do so. Omitted from the plan were the suburban lines of the Main Line Railway companies, which it was accepted could not be unravelled; instead the Minister promised arrangements which would be fair to the amalgamated companies and would enable the suburban lines to play their part in a fully co-ordinated scheme of transport. This was the Achilles heel of the whole project and was to lead to the creation of the 'revenue pool' whose operation was to prove less than satisfactory.

Morrison saw as a benefit of the new authority that it would have no bias towards a particular form of transport and would be able to make decisions on the basis of public transport as a whole. Some were later to see the outcome as being biased against the tram but there was undoubtedly a major problem of entrenched positions which the 1924 Act, far from doing anything to unlock, had gone a long way to bolstering.

East Surrey number 259 was a Tilling-Stevens B10A2 fitted with a lightweight all-metal body by Short Bros of Rochester, one of three experimental buses acquired by the company in 1928/1929 and destined to remain unique. It was the first East Surrey bus to have roller blinds and spent most of its life at Swanley garage on route 407. R.S. Turnbull collection

When it came to defining the area, the Minister hoped it would not be too rigid. He particularly wanted to safeguard through facilities where these were demanded, a desire which was not to be wholly fulfilled in practice. Long distance services by road to and from 'the provinces' would be affected only where they competed with the Board's services by picking-up or setting-down within a prescribed distance of London.

It was not long before the proposals attracted the objections of the LCC who were mainly concerned about the lack of any municipal involvement in the proposed Board but also regarded the basis for acquisitions as being inequitable. They sought the support of other municipalities in their opposition but most of them were glad enough to hand over the burden to the new authority. Ilford Council, whose tramways had been running profitably, was not prepared to declare its attitude in the absence of precise information but believed that everybody would like to do what they could for the co-ordination of traffic in London: '..probably one day it will happen but this is not the occasion....'. This may well have been true but for the fact that Morrison had a powerful ally in Lord Ashfield, chairman of the Underground Group, who had been advocating common management for many years. These two vastly different people respected each other sufficiently to enable a compromise acceptable to 55 Broadway to be assembled. Not that Ashfield had an easy run with his shareholders. At a special meeting of Underground Group shareholders on 1st May 1931, faced with a good deal of opposition, he made a dramatic departure from his prepared speech to tell them that if they did not support the proposals, they would have to look for another chairman. He won the vote. With the dominant Underground Group behind the idea, this was indeed to be 'the occasion'.

The Bill was published on 13th March 1931, its broad provisions being in line with Herbert Morrison's proposals. The monopoly area of the Board was defined as the whole of the London Traffic Area with additions, particularly in the north and south, to embrace the sphere of influence of the LGOC and its subsidiaries. This would have covered a vast area stretching from Baldock in the north to Horsham in the south and from Maidenhead in the west to Wickford in the east. Furthermore, no restrictions, other than those imposed by the 1930 Act, would have applied to the Board working services outside that area.

Being a 'hybrid' the Bill went before a joint Select Committee of both Houses, which sat for the first time on 28th April. It faced eighty petitions and met on thirty-five days during which amendments were agreed which led to the withdrawal of opposition by provincial bus companies, the tramway owning municipalities and the manufacturers. The Independents (and the Metropolitan Railway) maintained their opposition but the committee released the Bill on 20th July to go through its remaining formal stages.

Many of the petitions had related to the financial provisions of the Bill but the changes which were to have the most important effect on the Board's operations were probably those wrought by agreement with the so-called provincial bus companies (Maidstone &

District, Southdown, Aldershot & District, Thames Valley and Eastern National). They were not happy about the effect on the 'Area Agreement' companies of the size of the Board's monopoly zone and its apparent freedom to spread outside the boundary. Under the agreement secured with the companies, the Board lost the right to run outside the statutorily defined London Passenger Transport Area, the size of that area was reduced, particularly in the east and west and monopoly powers were no longer to extend to the whole of it. The monopoly area (known as 'The Special Area') was reduced so that no part of it was outside the London Traffic Area, and, of course, those parts of the Traffic Area now outside the redefined London Passenger Transport Area were excluded.

This still gave the Board a slightly larger operating area than the Underground Group, as it extended out to Gravesend, Meopham and Wrotham in the south-east, continuing through Kemsing, Otford, Sevenoaks, Sevenoaks Weald, Edenbridge, East Grinstead, Turners Hill, Crawley, Horsham, Ewhurst, Shere, Guildford, Send, Old Woking, Chertsey, Virginia Water, Datchet, Slough, Burnham, Beaconsfield, Terriers (omitting High Wycombe), Holmer Green, Little Missenden, Wendover (excluding the main road between these points), Buckland, then immediately to the south of Ivinghoe, Dunstable and Luton, then Great Offley, Hitchin, south of Baldock, then Cottered, Buntingford, Braughing, Bishop's Stortford, Harlow, Thornwood Common, North Weald, Ongar, Brentwood, Warley, North Ockendon

and Grays. Provision was also made for unrestricted running beyond this boundary: from Weald Turning to Tonbridge; through Edenbridge; from East Grinstead to Forest Row; between Horsham and Strood Green; from Woking to Chertsey via Ottershaw; from Virginia Water to Sunningdale (Traffic Area boundary) and Ascot; Runnymede to Windsor; Slough to Maidenhead High Street; Loudwater to West Wycombe via High Wycombe; Little Missenden to Dunstable via Great Missenden, Wendover, Buckland and Ivinghoe; Great Warley to Shenfield and Hutton Station via Brentwood; and North Ockendon to Stifford. 'Restricted running', that is to say no passenger could be both picked up and set down on the section of route, was to be allowed from Tonbridge to Tunbridge Wells, from Hitchin to Letchworth and Baldock, from Buntingford to Royston and from Stifford to Grays and Tilbury via both Little Thurrock and Chadwell St Mary. In addition, the Board was forbidden from picking up and setting down the same passenger within the Borough of Luton.

Other operators were to be allowed to run into the area between Bat & Ball and Sevenoaks, Wonersh and Guildford, Old Woking and Woking, Addlestone and Weybridge, Eastworth and Chertsey, Virginia Water and Egham and Birtley Wood and Beaconsfield but would not be allowed both to pick up and set down the same person within the borough of Gravesend. There was also a general provision allowing both the Board and others to operate up to half a mile across the boundary to reach a convenient terminus.

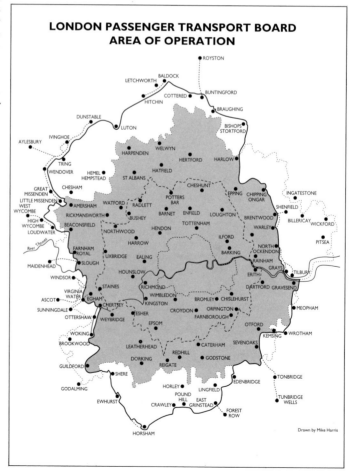

LONDON PASSENGER TRANSPORT BOARD AREA OF OPERATION

Drawn by Mike Harris

The London Transport areas as they were finally settled. The 'Special Area' where the Board was to have monopoly is the shaded portion; the statutory limit of operation is shown as a solid boundary line; and the dotted lines projecting beyond this show roads along which outrunning powers were granted. The area originally designated as the monopoly zone is that contained within the outermost boundary lines, whether dotted or solid.

The Special Area, within which no operator was to be able to run a bus service without the express consent of the Board, followed a more tortuous line where it differed from the main area. It excluded Meopham and Wrotham in the south-east and Loudwater, Terriers and Totteridge in the west but it was in the extreme south and north that it differed most markedly. The monopoly boundary took off from the LPT boundary just north of Marlpit Hill near Edenbridge and then ran in an irregular line westward through mainly open country north of Lingfield and Horne, through Outwood, south of Earlswood, north of Leigh, through Holmwood, Leith Hill, Westcott, north of Shere and Albury, to rejoin at Chilworth. In the north, the break was made east of Little Missenden and the boundary then ran through Chesham Bois, Latimer, west of Sarratt, through Kings Langley, Apsley, Leverstock Green, west of Redbourn, Flamstead, Kinsbourne Green, Ayot St Lawrence, Welwyn, Knebworth, Aston, Walkern, Ardeley, Great Munden, Puckeridge, west of Much Hadham, to a point north of Harlow.

The Labour government was defeated at the General Election in August and it looked at first as though the Bill would be abandoned by the new 'National' government. Instead, the new Minister, P.J. Pybus, issued a White Paper in July 1932 which maintained the basic principles of Morrison's Bill but with some important modifications. In response to representations which had been made against the new Board being in the hands of the government, the White Paper proposed that appointments to the Board should be made by a Board of Trustees; and the power to order new or improved services or facilities would rest with the Railway Rates Tribunal, rather than the Minister. Pybus took the unusual step of holding the Bill over to the new session, so that the time already spent would not be wasted. Indeed he made this a principal reason for his decision, arguing that the money spent should not be wasted in times of financial stringency, an argument which did not go down well with the Bill's detractors. Opposition continued until the very end, notably through a new association formed early in 1933 representing the trades and interests supplying the independent sector, who saw their potential customers reducing in number and foresaw the collapse of individual and small enterprises.

Although the Bill went through the House of Commons, achieving its third reading by a majority of 186, its final passage through the House of Lords, where there was a lot of support for its opponents, was by no means assured. The intervention in the debate of Lord Ashfield, who commanded enormous respect for his business acumen and visionary approach to transport problems, finally secured its passage with what was generally recognised as a masterly speech in support of the Bill. It was his first and last in the House. The Bill received the Royal Assent on 13th April 1933 and the Act came into force on 1st July 1933.

Above **The LGOC was also the principal provider of special services, including the Epsom Race Course route from Morden, which under the Bassom system was given a number 131. The leader of this long line of LTs and NSs at Morden is LT 459, a May 1931 vehicle with Strachan bodywork.** Lens of Sutton

CHAPTER TWO

LONDON GENERAL AT WORK

Above **The Combine dominant! STs, LTs and NSs of the LGOC are the only buses visible in this carefully framed official view of Trafalgar Square. Behind and above ST 190, on route 1A on the right, is the old Hampton Furniture store whose touch of retail domesticity was to be removed brutally from the square by a German bomb in an, as yet, undreamed of war.** LT Museum 22767

Seventy-three per cent of the Underground Group's business was carried on its bus services. Many, including Herbert Morrison, believed they were providing the profits which kept the railway activities afloat but there was no way of proving this because the Group always consolidated its published financial results. In a way it was already behaving rather like a regional transport authority, providing the most appropriate form of transport, irrespective of the profitability of the individual units, as long as the whole made a satisfactory profit. There were other respects in which the company presented a 'public service' face, rather than a purely commercial one.

The Group prided itself on being a good employer and was well known for the provision of amenities, like canteens, even though some of its competitors paid higher wages. The average wage of all its employees at the beginning of 1930 (47s 6d) had increased by 1s 3d in the year despite a fall in the cost of living. In the development of services in

new areas, General accepted that they would not immediately pay their way; some years later Frank Pick (then Managing Director) estimated that it took six years for a 'development' service of this type to move into profit. It was hardly surprising then, that Lord Ashfield was such a strong advocate of some form of common ownership for transport in London.

Ashfield and Pick could not have carried their shareholders with them, though, if what they were doing had not been seen as in their interests and for the wellbeing of the Group. Such considerations drove General to join the rush into 'suburban coach' services in 1929, despite being ill-prepared for it. The two Watford services which had started in 1929 were worked at first by twenty AEC Reliance private hire coaches with 'all-weather' bodywork, which were only available because the new routes started during the normally fallow winter season. It was not until new T class AEC 'Regal' coaches became available that the company was in a position to expand.

Having taken on 'Bucks Expresses' in direct competition between Watford and Charing Cross, the LGOC next directed their attack at Premier Line's successful Bush House to Windsor service by introducing their third route between Charing Cross, Slough and Windsor (calling at Premier's Bush House terminal on the way) on 20th April 1930. For this operation a new garage was opened in leased premises in Alpha Street, Slough to which six new Regal coaches were allocated. The new venture provoked an interesting response from the Great Western Railway who introduced cheap return fares from Windsor, Slough and intermediate stations to London at the single rate, from 7th July.

The threat posed to others by the Group's immense competitive strength was demonstrated on 6th June when East Surrey and Autocar were both commissioned by General to run similar routes, using vehicles supplied by the parent company, to Dorking via Epsom, Redhill via Croydon, Reigate via Sutton and Tunbridge Wells. Autocar's route took it into direct competition with Redcar of Tunbridge Wells and Safeway's Sevenoaks service but the East Surrey routes were all new, as was the alternative route to Windsor from Charing Cross, via Chiswick, Hounslow and Staines, which General itself introduced on 10th July, the coaches running from another new garage in London Road, Staines. This building was of unusual interest as it was a cheap temporary structure which had previously served in a similar capacity at Potters Bar while the new permanent building for the Overground company was being built.

The day before the Windsor route started, on 9th July 1930, the LGOC underlined the seriousness of its intentions by registering four new companies with their head offices at 55 Broadway: Green Line Coaches Ltd, Red Line Coaches Ltd, Yellow Line Coaches Ltd and Blue Line Coaches Ltd. The last three had a nominal capital of only £100 and had been registered only to secure the names against use by others. On the face of it there would appear to be no particular reason why a separate company was needed. Frank Pick claimed that it was solely for convenience of operation and to distinguish the services from the ordinary single-deck buses of LGOC, but this could more easily have been achieved by having a separate operating division with vehicles in Green Line livery. The more likely reason was to enable different employment conditions to be adopted and for the new company to be free of any area agreements which would have bound the parent.

It was Green Line that became responsible for most of the further development of coach services although, for technical licensing reasons or for operating convenience, many of the routes continued to be licensed to and operated by East Surrey, General, Autocar, Amersham & District and National, at least for a time.

The first route operated by Green Line on its own account was a half-hourly service between Guildford and Charing Cross, via Ripley and Kingston By-Pass which started on 17th July. This route had a slightly odd history. General's first application for a licence to Guildford Council, in February 1930, had been unsuccessful but by July the Watch Committee had decided to allow the Guildford to London bus service to be increased from one to two an hour and for coaches to be substituted for buses. This allowed the service to start but was a very puzzling decision because there was no hourly bus service to London. There was an interesting sequel to this muddle when during August the Guildford Watch Committee turned down applications for similar services from Ledbury Transport (Thackray's) and the Premier Omnibus Co.

The two pioneering Watford routes were also handed over to the new company on 17th July. They continued to operate from the Leavesden Road premises, using newly delivered T-type coaches. A week later Green Line moved east to do battle with Sunset Pullman Saloons Ltd between Charing Cross and Brentwood, on which line they also competed with Edward Hillman's route from Stratford.

In these early days, Green Line was not blessed with conveniently placed garages for all the routes it was starting and in the case of the Brentwood service the coaches were housed at Metcalf's Lincoln Works in Eastern Avenue, near Gidea Park, while the Guildford vehicles were parked in an open yard, owned by Rice and Harper's Filling Station in London Road, Guildford. At about this time garage codes were allocated to the Green Line garages: AL for Watford; BL for Slough; CL for Staines, DL for Guildford and EL for Reigate. It was reported at the time that new aluminium garage plates had been supplied for fitting to the coaches but, if they were, they must have been thrown away as they never appeared. There was a plan later in the year to alter the codes to a series with a G (for 'Green Line'?) prefix (for example, GW would have been Watford) but this came to nothing and the original codes soon fell into disuse.

Top **T 119**, unregistered and on Trade Plates, is paying a visit to the Underground Group's Headquarters at 55 Broadway, presumably for an official inspection of the 'GREEN LINE COACHES Ltd' fleetname, arranged in a circle in close imitation of the 'bullseye'. This style does not appear to have been adopted. Alan B. Cross

Centre **T 65** had a Hall Lewis body and was finished in the red livery of East Surrey subsidiary Autocar of Tunbridge Wells. It does not appear to be causing any congestion whilst occupying the kerbside at Oxford Circus. Alan B. Cross

Right **T 116** was one of the Regals from the first batch which carried the 'East Surrey' fleet name for a time and is seen working on the Dorking route which started from 6th June 1930.
W. Noel Jackson

Above **Rice & Harper's yard, London Road, Guildford, where the coaches for the first Green Line route were parked. Two of its eleven Regals can be seen receiving attention from fitters. The one nearer the camera is probably T 144**
LT Museum U7407

Left **The Skylark Motor Coach Co, another operator who chose green as a livery, found itself in head-to-head competition with Green Line on its Guildford route from 17th July 1930. This Duple bodied Gilford 168SD had gone into service a month earlier and later became GF 16 in the Green Line fleet and GF 127 in the LPTB fleet.**
Dennis Odd collection

Lewis's Cream Line Coaches was a comparative latecomer on the suburban coach scene and did not start its Brookmans Park to Charing Cross service until September 1930. Three Gilfords were acquired, two of them, including HX1264, with twenty seat Duple bodies. The area was just beginning to develop into a dormitory for London; the notice by the tree reads 'BROOKMANS PARK HOUSES & SITES FOR SALE' and the coach is standing in a roughly finished estate road alongside newly built houses. J.F. Higham

The first cross-London Green Line route was from Reigate to Welwyn Garden City. Weymann bodied T 246 has been dressed to operate a London 'short' on this route, after it had been extended to Hitchin. Alongside it in Reigate garage a year or so later, is T 320 a former East Surrey Private Hire coach with twenty-nine seat Hall Lewis bodywork, now carrying the Green Line fleetname as all Private Hire work was transferred to that company in January 1932.
Arthur Ingram

Further routes started up to the end of 1930, variously operated by General or its associates, to Sunningdale, Ascot, Tring, Welwyn Garden City, Harpenden, Godstone Green via Whyteleafe, Great Bookham via Epsom, Bishops Stortford via Finsbury Park and Loughton, Sevenoaks via Westerham, Chertsey via Richmond and Weybridge, Edenbridge, East Grinstead via Caterham-on-the-Hill, Crawley and Hertford.

The Tring route ran into the same opposition from Watford Council as had Red Rover and West Herts in 1928 and 1929; they would not allow it to ply locally in the town. In consequence when the route started on 8th September it ran non-stop between Bushey and Grovemill Lane and coaches running to the garage at Leavesden Road finished public service at Bushey. Watford council were particularly opposed to operators who were not based in the town, which is presumably why Bucks Expresses did not have the same problem with the service they started in October 1929.

Most of these services operated from existing garages owned by General or their associates but at Harpenden, Green Line coaches were stabled at the premises of Comfy Coaches in Luton Road, while at Addlestone an agreement was made for the use of space at the Weymann coachworks. At Welwyn, National somewhat surprisingly garaged the coaches at Jenner Parsons in Bridge Road rather than at its own Hatfield garage.

At the end of November, Green Line was granted twenty licences by Northfleet Urban District Council to operate a Gravesend to London service in conjunction with Maidstone & District. The agreement between the two companies which gave rise to the application would also have left the Maidstone Road beyond Farningham to be served exclusively

by M&D but the agreement was never initiated and Green Line never ran beyond Dartford in LGOC days. Included in this stillborn agreement was a proposal for a cross-country Green Line route from Dartford to Guildford via Farningham, Eynsford, Sevenoaks, Westerham, Oxted, Godstone, Redhill, Reigate, Dorking, Newlands Corner and Merrow and this revealed a new strand of the company's policy. Another such route planned at this time would have run from Guildford to St Albans via Woking, Windsor, Uxbridge, Rickmansworth and Watford and there may well have been others. However, although they received local licences, even these two did not materialise as the company did not have enough coaches in stock and the whole enterprise was then overtaken by the application of the Road Service Licensing provisions of the 1930 Road Traffic Act.

By October 1930 the Green Line name was in use almost universally, although many of the coaches were still owned and operated by East Surrey, Autocar and National. The ownership of the routes was transferred progressively from 13th September when coaches on the Reigate service operated by East Surrey began to appear with Green Line fleet names, followed in the next few days by those working to Dorking and Redhill, which were adorned with labels reading 'This is a Green Line Service'. Autocar vehicles on the Tunbridge Wells service followed next and so the arrangement gradually spread to the whole system. During the changeover, the complications of ownership led to some entertaining tangles such as East Surrey working vehicles owned by Autocar but labelled 'Green Line' and Green Lines appearing with labels saying 'Operated by East Surrey'. During October, the routes operated by General and the garage at Staines were formally trans-

ferred to the Green Line company, the identity being changed on the vehicles by means of paper labels bearing the 'Green Line' fleet name. At the end of 1930, after only a year of development, the network amounted already to twenty-four routes, which needed 160 coaches to fulfil the normal daily schedule with more being hired from associate companies at times of peak pressure.

This buoyancy was not at all popular with the traffic authorities who had long been chafing at the uncontrolled activities of coach operators. They perceived it as a prime cause of traffic congestion in central London but had so far done nothing about it. Perhaps in anticipation of some form of government action and, incidentally, following the example of one of their principal competitors (Skylark), Green Line prepared an elaborate plan under which all but five routes were to be linked with others to run right across London, the aim being to reduce the number of vehicles using kerbside terminals in town. The first two cross-London routes started on 10th December 1930: Reigate to Welwyn Garden City; and Great Bookham to Harpenden. Three more started on 14th January 1931, one of which was an entirely new route between Caterham and Hemel Hempstead via Coulsdon and Bushey, which like earlier services was not allowed to stop in Watford. The other linkings joined Crawley with Bushey and Godstone Green with Tring. The last cross-town operation to be introduced at this time was again not a combination of routes but an extension of two existing routes (from Ascot and Sunningdale) to a new destination at Dartford via Old Kent Road, Blackheath and Bexleyheath. None of the other proposals came into being and no further combinations were set up during the next two years.

Upminster Services Ltd was spared direct competition from Green Line on its Upminster route by the operation of the Traffic Commissioner's ban on new services. JD 21 was one of thirty Gilford 1680Ts owned by the company, all with twenty-six seat Wycombe bodywork. It was first licensed in 1930, and later became GF 12 in the Green Line series. The LGOC bus following on route G1 is ST 822, one of five which started out with Overground. *J.F. Higham*

Both sides of a single page leaflet for the Hertford service, December 1930.

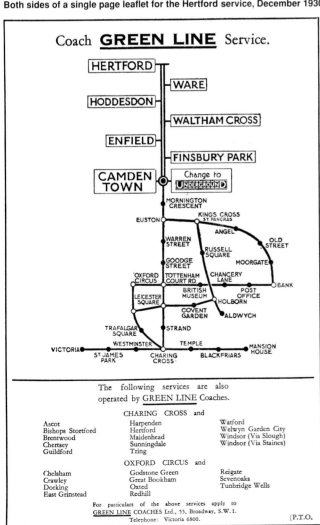

Coach GREEN LINE Service.

HERTFORD
HODDESDON
ENFIELD
CAMDEN TOWN

WARE
WALTHAM CROSS
FINSBURY PARK
Change to **Underground**

MORNINGTON CRESCENT
EUSTON — KINGS CROSS ST. PANCRAS — ANGEL — OLD STREET
WARREN STREET — RUSSELL SQUARE — MOORGATE
GOODGE STREET
OXFORD CIRCUS — TOTTENHAM COURT RD. — CHANCERY LANE — BANK
LEICESTER SQUARE — BRITISH MUSEUM — POST OFFICE — HOLBORN
COVENT GARDEN — ALDWYCH
TRAFALGAR SQUARE — STRAND — MANSION HOUSE
VICTORIA — WESTMINSTER — TEMPLE
ST JAMES PARK — CHARING CROSS — BLACKFRIARS

The following services are also operated by GREEN LINE Coaches.

CHARING CROSS and

Ascot	Harpenden	Watford
Bishops Stortford	Hertford	Welwyn Garden City
Brentwood	Maidenhead	Windsor (Via Slough)
Chertsey	Sunningdale	Windsor (Via Staines)
Guildford	Tring	

OXFORD CIRCUS and

Chelsham	Godstone Green	Reigate
Crawley	Great Bookham	Sevenoaks
Dorking	Oxted	Tunbridge Wells
East Grinstead	Redhill	

For particulars of the above services apply to
GREEN LINE COACHES Ltd., 55, Broadway, S.W.1.
Telephone: Victoria 6800. [P.T.O.

2550—5,000. 9-12-30. WATERLOW & SONS LIMITED, LONDON WALL, LONDON.

Coach GREEN LINE Service

HERTFORD & LONDON (Charing Cross Embankment)
via Ware, Hoddesdon, Waltham Cross, Enfield and Finsbury Park
Every 60 Minutes

To LONDON.	First Coaches.			Then at Minutes past each hour.	Last Coach.
	N S	N S			
	a.m.	a.m.	a.m.		p.m.
HERTFORD Waiting Room ... dep.	6 35	7 35	8 35	35	9 35
Ware Station ... ... "	6 40	7 40	8 40	40	9 40
Hoddesdon Clock ... ... "	6 48	7 48	8 48	48	9 48
Wormley (Queen's Head)... "	6 53	7 53	8 53	53	9 53
Waltham Cross (Falcon) ... "	7 1	8 1	9 1	1	10 1
Ponders End (Southbury Road) "	7 11	8 11	9 11	11	10 11
Enfield (Queen's Cinema) ... "	7 15	8 15	9 15	15	10 15
Wood Green (Wellington) ... "	7 28	8 28	9 28	28	10 28
Finsbury Park Underground Station "	7 38	8 38	9 38	38	10 38
Camden Town Underground Station ... "	7 53	8 53	9 53	53	10 53
LONDON (Charing Cross Embankment) arr.	8 8	9 8	10 8	8	11 8

To HERTFORD.	First Coaches.			Then at Minutes past each hour.	Last Coach.
	N S	N S			
	a.m.	a.m.	a.m.		p.m.
LONDON (Charing Cross Embankment) dep.	8 13	9 13	10 13	13	11 13
Camden Town Underground Station ... "	8 28	9 28	10 28	28	11 28
Finsbury Park Underground Station ... "	8 43	9 43	10 43	43	11 43
Wood Green (Wellington) ... "	8 53	9 53	10 53	53	11 53
Enfield (Queen's Cinema) ... "	9 6	10 6	11 6	6	12 6
Ponders End (Southbury Road) "	9 10	10 10	11 10	10	12 10
Waltham Cross (Falcon) ... "	9 20	10 20	11 20	20	12 20
Wormley (Queen's Head)... "	9 28	10 28	11 28	28	12 28
Hoddesdon Clock ... ... "	9 33	10 33	11 33	33	12 33
Ware Station ... ... "	9 41	10 41	11 41	41	12 41
HERTFORD Waiting Room ... arr.	9 46	10 46	11 46	46	12 46

Fare Stages.	Hertford and Ware.		Hoddesdon (Clock Tower).		Wormley (Queen's Head).		Cheshunt (The Old Pond).	
	Single.	Return.	Single.	Return.	Single.	Return.	Single.	Return.
WALTHAM CROSS (Queen Eleanor's Statue)	1/-	1/6	9d.	1/3	—	—	—	—
PALMERS GREEN (The Triangle)	1/3	2/-	1/3	1/9	1/-	1/6	—	—
FINSBURY PARK STATION	1/6	2/3	1/6	2/-	1/3	1/9	—	—
LONDON (Charing Cross Embankment)	*1/6	*2/6	*1/6	*2/3	*1/3	*2/-	*1/-	*1/6

CHILDREN'S FARES. Reduced fares for Children under 14 years of age. All children (except infants in arms) must be paid for.

* These Tickets entitle passengers to travel to and from Underground Stations in the central area as shown on map on other side, changing at Camden Town.

Passengers may hail, or alight from, GREEN LINE coaches anywhere en route

---

TICKETS ARE OBTAINABLE ON THE COACHES.
Light personal luggage allowed free. Lap dogs only carried at Conductor's discretion.
NOTE. The Company cannot be held responsible for failure to adhere to the scheduled times of the coaches nor can they guarantee the running of the services to be as stated, though every effort will be made to maintain them.

OPERATING AGENTS:
The National Omnibus & Transport Co., Ltd., High Street, Watford, Hertfordshire, to whom all enquiries and complaints regarding this service should be addressed. P.T.O.

The interior of the short-lived Poland Street coach station, with T 144 on the Guildford route, one of those which inaugurated the new premises. The passenger waiting room, Enquiry Office and other operational offices are on the right. LT Museum U7818

Green Line's other strategy for dealing with the problem of congestion at terminals, was to build itself a coach station in the heart of central London. This may seem to run counter to the idea of working across London as far as possible but at this time the company still had its eye on considerable expansion and was hoping to work to such far-flung destinations as Cambridge, Chelmsford, Bedford, Marlow, Oxford, Reading, Aldershot and Farnham among many others, so it presumably felt justified in making the investment. The former Higgins Brewery near Oxford Circus, a 7,300 sq ft site, was purchased and eventually became Poland Street coach station. As the plot was in Broad Street (later renamed Broadwick Street), lying opposite Poland Street between Ingestre Place and Lexington Street, this was a slight misnomer, presumably chosen for the greater publicity value of a street which joined Oxford Street. Also acquired and presumably intended for the expansion of the coach station was an adjacent site, twice as large, bounded by Broad Street, Hopkins Street, Ingestre Court and Ingestre Place, which was destined never to be used.

What was described at the time as 'a temporary section' of the station, with a capacity of twelve coaches, opened for business on Christmas Day 1930 but it was to have a short life. Who can tell what possessed the Group to acquire a site embedded in the congested streets of Soho, so saddling themselves with operational problems far worse than any they can have experienced, particularly on Victoria Embankment? It is probably safe to assume that it was a matter of expediency, as sites of such a size do not come onto the market every day and it was undoubtedly well placed from the point of view of serving the public, especially if the authorities clamped down on kerbside stops.

The routes which christened Poland Street were those to Windsor via Staines and to Guildford and these were followed by others on 4th, 11th and 14th January 1931. This left only four routes terminating in central London which did not use Poland Street; those to Brentwood, Bishop's Stortford, Watford and Windsor via Slough, all of them still using the Embankment terminus at Charing Cross.

Looming over all these activities were two official developments, one exercised under the 1924 Act by the London & Home Counties Traffic Advisory Committee and the other related to the new Road Traffic Act of 1930.

During 1930, the Traffic Advisory Committee had been studying the problems allegedly caused by coach traffic and had submitted recommendations to the Minister of Transport for ruthless restrictions. He in turn made Orders under the London Traffic Act of 1924 for these restrictions to come into force no sooner than 1st February 1931. They proposed that coaches should be prohibited at all times from entering a large area of the West End and excluded from an even larger area, encompassing part of the City, up to 7pm on Mondays to Fridays and 3pm on Saturdays. The area of total prohibition was within the ring bounded by Kingsway, New Oxford Street, Oxford Street, New and Old Bond Streets, Piccadilly, Grosvenor Place, Grosvenor Gardens, Victoria Street, Parliament Square, Bridge Street, Victoria Embankment, Norfolk Street and Aldwych (East). The larger area went out to Euston Road, Edgware Road, Park Lane, Buckingham Palace Road, Eccleston Bridge, Gillingham Street, Vauxhall Bridge Road, Albert Embankment, Lambeth Road, St Georges Circus, Borough Road, Borough High Street, Great Dover Street, Tower Bridge Road, Tower Bridge, Mansell Street, Royal Mint Street, Leman Street, Commercial Street, Old Street, City Road and Pentonville Road. The Regulations allowed for routes to be prescribed to enable coaches to reach garages and coach stations within the area but otherwise the ban was intended to be absolute. Anyone familiar with the Green Line network as it was to develop will recognise the origins of some of the strange gaps on the map and wayward routeings in central London, many of which survived for sixty years; but the immediate effect was an outcry from coach proprietors, particularly those catering for sightseeing traffic. As he could not make an Order which would exempt them, the Minister contented himself instead with giving lengthy general directions to the Traffic Commissioner under the 1930 Act which included a requirement that he should, when considering applications for Road Service Licences, have special regard to restricting coach operation within the specified area and that strict regulation and control was required within a six-mile radius of Charing Cross.

The other threat hanging over all coach operators was the new Road Traffic Act, which introduced a uniform machinery of regulation for all passenger services outside London. Among its many provisions was one requiring all routes to have a Road Service Licence issued by the appropriate Traffic Commissioner. The Traffic Commissioners were appointed at the end of 1930 and the Minister decreed that Road Service Licences would be mandatory after 1st April 1931, that applications would be entertained from 1st January and that any route started after 9th February could not continue beyond 31st March without a licence. If a route was already operating on 9th February, the operator could use its existence as an established facility to argue a case for being granted a licence but this was no guarantee of success.

There was a scramble to start new services before the deadline, in which Green Line participated fully. Apart from those already mentioned, the network was extended to include Hitchin, Bushey via Kilburn and Edgware, Hemel Hempstead, Amersham via Gerrards Cross, Chesham (curtailed at Amersham on instruction of the Southern Area Traffic Commissioner on 21st October), Dartford, Farningham, Sunbury Common via Richmond and Kingston, West Byfleet via Kingston By-Pass and Rickmansworth via Harrow. The last route to be introduced before the deadline illustrates the urgency of the scramble. Intended to run to Beaconsfield it had to be truncated to run only as far as Uxbridge, because not enough of the coaches needed for it had been delivered by 7th February when it started. Arrangements had to be made at short notice for the coaches to

be garaged at the AEC works in Southall. The only other case where special arrangements had to be made was for the Sunbury route to be garaged at a yard owned by J. Collis & Son in Hanworth Road.

The arrival of the deadline did not bring innovation to a stop. Somewhat quixotically, Green Line extended the Tring route to Aylesbury on 18th February and introduced a new route from Charing Cross to Barking, Becontree Heath and Upminster on 21st February. Both changes had to be abandoned after 31st March as required by the PSV (Transitory Provisions) Order 1931, while the Commissioner considered the licence applications. A planned and advertised service to Upminster via the Ilford route never materialised.

At the end of all this, Green Line submitted proposals to the Traffic Commissioners for twenty-six routes, nine of which were cross-London services, and including several new and improved services. New sections envisaged were: Great Bookham to Guildford via Effingham, Esher to Woking via Weybridge, Uxbridge to High Wycombe and to Amersham and Chesham, Tring to Aylesbury, St Albans to Dunstable, Harpenden to Luton, Stevenage to Baldock and Upminster via Barking. Only seven routes were granted licences in line with the applications. Eleven were refused outright, including, perversely, two of the cross-London routes, one route which did not enter the central area (Watford – Golders Green) and at least two which could be said to serve areas remote from railway facilities. Eight others were granted, with modifications which would have eliminated the London to Bushey service and the sections

between Westerham Hill and Sevenoaks, between Welwyn Garden City and Hitchin and between Epping and Bishop's Stortford. The only new section approved was to Dunstable but Woking was included as a modification to the Chertsey route diverting at Weybridge via Maybury, rather than as desired via Kingston By-Pass and Esher.

At the beginning of 1932 the Metropolitan Traffic Commissioner, Mr Gleeson E. Robinson, issued a policy statement for coach services within the thirty-five mile zone, which very much reflected the 'Directions' given by the Minister. Its principal theme was that coaches should not compete with railways but should be supplementary to them even if this meant sacrificing the door-to-door convenience of the motor coach, which he saw as becoming more and more impracticable if expansion were allowed to continue. He advocated feeder services to the Underground and suburban railways on the edge of the central area. There was some relaxation for firms operating in association with steamship companies between hotels and docks but he was otherwise quite firm in saying that all Road Service Licences granted by him so far, would not authorise operations in central London.

T 69 was one of five Regals transferred to the Amersham & District company to operate the new Amersham service in January 1931. By the time this photograph was taken at Oxford Circus, the subsequent extension to Chesham and the stop at Denham had been disallowed by the South Eastern Traffic Commissioner, hence the evident and cramped substitution of 'AMER' (SHAM) for 'CHE' and the gap between Gerrards + and Uxbridge on the side board. D.W.K. Jones

There were so many appeals against the Commissioner's individual decisions that the Minister decided to set up a Committee of Inquiry, chaired by Lord Amulree, to investigate, in particular, matters of principle and general policy arising from them and to hear representations from interested parties. By this time Green Line Coaches Ltd, alone, was operating twenty-five routes, with a fleet of over two hundred vehicles, on which 12,500,000 passengers had been carried in 1931. There was a great deal at stake for the coach industry.

The Inquiry opened at Middlesex Guildhall on 18th April. In his evidence for Green Line, Frank Pick quoted figures for the week ending 1st July 1931, a typical holiday week, when his coaches had carried 289,461 passengers, sixty-five per cent of whom were picked up or set down within five miles of Charing Cross and fifty per cent in the central area from which the Commissioner wished to exclude the coaches. The largest proportion, forty-four per cent, travelled between the peaks mainly for shopping and entertainment and another sixteen per cent were theatregoers who travelled to and from town in the evenings. Forty per cent travelled in the peak and Pick foresaw difficulty in accommodating them on other bus and rail services, which were already at full stretch, if the coaches were banned. He also argued that if this resulted in bus services being increased, there would be more congestion because buses stopped more often than coaches. Although General had entered the coach business to regain traffic lost to competitors, they had been surprised to discover that they had unwittingly tapped an entirely new source of business, which was still growing. Compared with the same period in 1931, during the first three months of 1932 Green Line had carried thirty-six per cent more passengers even though the volume of service had increased by only eight per cent. Far from showing the coach as a cause of congestion, this showed a remarkably high standard of efficiency.

Despite similar powerful evidence from other operators, traders and caterers, the first Amulree Report published on 18th June was hardly less uncompromising than Gleeson-Robinson's original decisions. It condemned the use of highways as coach terminals, pointing out that the streets were provided at public expense for general use. Coach terminals on the highway should not be allowed after March 1935 and the Committee told the industry that it was their responsibility to ensure that coach services from the built-up area of London started only from coach stations or yards on private property. The proposals for a restricted area were endorsed, except for a small modification to include Lambeth Bridge (which was about to open) so that coaches could avoid the congested junction on the Lambeth side of Vauxhall Bridge. The Committee further recommended that the restriction of picking-up points right up to the Metropolitan Area boundary should be considered. Applicants for services to central London would have to prove that they were necessary and not just desirable in the public interest.

The second part of the Inquiry was concerned with a detailed review of thirty-five of the appeals against the Traffic Commissioner's decisions and seven others where operators were appealing against grants of services to others. In its final Report, dated 2nd August, the Committee reviewed the appeals, upheld the Commissioner's decision in nineteen of them, recommended the granting of five and suggested modifications to the remainder some of which overturned decisions to withdraw some parts of routes. Rescued from oblivion, so far as Green Line were concerned, were the services to Farningham, Sevenoaks via Westerham, Caterham via Coulsdon, Great Bookham (but not onwards to Guildford), West Byfleet via Esher (but not Woking), Windsor via Staines, Rickmansworth (but not Chesham), Tring (but not Aylesbury), Hemel Hempstead, Hitchin (but not Baldock), Hertford, Bishop's Stortford and from Watford to Golders Green.

The Minister accepted the Committee's recommendations and decided that the new services should start on 19th September 1932.

There was widespread outrage among operators who held a mass protest meeting at Kings Cross Coach station on Saturday 20th August from which they sent a telegram to the King, hoping that there would be some further consideration by Parliament 'to preserve the livelihoods imperilled by the administration of the Road Traffic Act'. They also sought a deputation to the Minister. A month later, arising from a separate issue, the Motor Hirers and Coach Services Association applied in the High Court for a writ to test the validity of the Minister's way of handling appeals. They were granted a 'rule nisi' against the Traffic Commissioner and because of this the Minister suspended his decision to implement the Amulree recommendations and services were allowed to continue unchanged for the time being. Nevertheless, the biggest player in the field, Green Line Coaches Ltd, announced at the end of October that it accepted the decisions affecting its services and supported the committee's call for 'systematisation'.

Before all these momentous affairs got into their swing, Green Line at last got around to giving their routes individual identities, a surprisingly tardy decision, given Frank Pick's impeccable eye for order. In choosing the method, they again took a lead from a competitor. Premier Line had used route letters for its services right from the start and it was this style which was adopted by the Combine from 21st February 1931. Unlike later schemes, this one did not adopt a geographical sequence, the twenty-six routes being lettered from A to Z in a seemingly haphazard way, although some took the initial letter of their destination (like B for Brentwood). The Upminster route which started on the same day as the new lettering scheme was introduced, was called AV, there being no apparent reason for the choice of V for the second letter.

Duple bodied T 270 at New Scotland Yard on the newly lettered route A (Ascot to Dartford). Note the large display of timetables, an indication of the range of services available, yet the coach appears to be causing no difficulty by its presence, any more than are the parked cars further down the road.
Malcolm E. Papes collection

With the exception of one route to the new Whipsnade Zoo Park, which started on 24th March 1932 under the authority of a Road Service Licence, all route development ceased for the remainder of the company's existence. Enlargement of its activities did not cease, however, as the company now turned to a policy of acquisition of its main competitors. Whether it was the strength of the Group, the threat of Amulree or, most probably, the impending formation of the new LPTB, Green Line appeared to have little difficulty in taking over virtually all of its principal competitors between February 1932 and April 1933. The first to fall into its hands was the Skylark Motor Coach Company Ltd, which had been one of the first on the scene in December 1928 and had also pioneered cross-London operation. They were taken over by LGOC at a cost of £30,000 on 6th February 1932, when Green Line decided for some reason to split the cross-London routes to terminate at Poland Street and therefore added three routes to their portfolio: those to Hertford, Guildford and High Wycombe. Bucks Expresses (Watford) Ltd followed on 20th February at a cost of £5,000 and Green Line itself acquired Regent Motor Services on 2nd March (£5,500) giving Green Line control of two more routes: to Watford and Hertford. At the end of March the important route to Ongar, through Leyton and Chingford, came into Green Line's hands through the acquisition of Associated Coaches (Ongar) Ltd. In all these cases, to avoid the risks involved in transferring licences, the companies retained their separate identity, although their routes were allocated Green Line letters, were advertised by Green Line, and passengers were given the benefit, where appropriate, of ticket interavailability with Green Line services.

When the Paddington (Spring Street) to East Grinstead route of Blue Belle Motors was acquired by Green Line on 20th July 1932, it was absorbed into the Green Line network as route AU, because Blue Belle continued to exist as an independent company running coastal services. Payment was therefore in two parts, £5,688 for vehicles and £8,312 for goodwill. The treatment of Acme Pullman Services Ltd was also slightly different when it was taken over by LGOC on 22nd September. In this case the acquisition was complete and the company continued to trade independently but it was not given a route letter for its Newmarket service, which was advertised by Green Line as the 'ACME' route. The two remaining purchases were the Aylesbury service of Red Rover Saloon Coaches on 30th November for £15,500 and the Baldock route of Queen Line Coaches on 26th April 1933.

The shape and ownership of coach operations now took the form which would exist on formation of the LPTB, but before turning to the mainstream of LGOC's activities, it is worth mentioning some other developments relating to Green Line. Conditions for passengers at Watford (Leavesden Road) garage were improved early in 1931, when a new waiting room was built at a cost of £712, while part of route B started using the new Minories Lay-By at about the same time. This had been opened by the LGOC as a layover and meal relief point for bus services in June 1930 and was on a narrow strip of leased land alongside the District Railway. It was also used later as a refuelling point for the coaches. Apart from the other garages already mentioned, from the spring of 1932 the company also rented an open yard behind 21 Effra Road, Brixton to house Private Hire coaches, in place of temporary premises used during 1931 at 2 Effra Road, at Harmood Street Chalk Farm and at Leytonstone. New garages were also built at Church Road, off North Street Romford (July 1930), Leas Road, Guildford (1931/1932) and Horsham Road, Dorking (June 1932). Then, on 18th January 1933, Green Line opened its last garage as a private company, in St Leonards Road, Windsor opposite the hospital. It could house sixty vehicles and incorporated a small coach station with waiting room and enquiry office.

Above **Leaflet issued by the Underground Group bearing the name of Associated Coaches of Ongar, whose route, garage and ten vehicles were taken over for £20,000 in March 1932.**

This thirty-two seat Strachan Maudslay ML 3 was acquired by London General Country Services when they took over the local routes in Slough from the Great Western Railway in April 1932. It was transferred to Green Line along with another Maudslay and three Thornycrofts and is seen here at work on the newly acquired Skylark route, vying with other traffic in the congested streets outside Poland Street coach station.
R.S. Turnbull collection

Important though these events were, they were nevertheless concerned with only a small part of the transport business of London. Ordinary bus operations had continued to develop, although against a background of economic decline which caused business overall to slump. On the very first day of 1930 a change was made to the short local route 50 in Streatham which illustrates in microcosm the conditions in which these developments were taking place. The route, which had run for some years between Streatham Common and the charmingly named Lonesome (near Streatham Park Cemetery), was extended to serve new housing development in Rowan Road and Manor Road but, instead of continuing to the obvious local objective at Mitcham, General were obliged to terminate the service on Mitcham Common at 'The Horse and Groom' because the Beehive Bridge across the Southern Railway was not suitable for buses. This route also became an attraction for Independents and was chosen by Reliance, otherwise working in north and east London, as a suitable opportunity to expand in January 1931. General themselves progressively increased the service from a headway of five minutes to one of four and then three, raising the number of buses allocated from three to eleven in a matter of twelve months and further recognising its status by replacing the covered top NSs by STs in February.

It was not long before this activity attracted the notice of the Traffic Advisory Committee, who put a Restricted Streets Order on Greyhound Lane in September 1931, causing General to reduce the frequency of route 50 on 2nd September back to a bus every three-and-a-half minutes; two STs were taken off.

For an example of the grand approach, which could be used in appropriate cases by General because of its command of the network, it is necessary to look to north London. The areas around East Finchley, Hampstead Garden Suburb and Muswell Hill were growing fast and a big re-arrangement of local bus services in April 1930 brought buses for the first time to Lyttleton Road and Aylmer Road (route 608 Stonebridge Park to Hampstead Garden Suburb, extended to Hornsey Rise via Archway). Double-deckers were introduced at the same time to two sections hitherto restricted to the K class single-deckers on the 41A and 110: between Archway and Hornsey Rise (on route 608); and along Muswell Hill Road over which routes 43 and Sunday only 144B/C were diverted, away from East Finchley and Fortis Green. The 43 and 144 groups also lost their 'weekday' (Monday to Saturday) sections to Whetstone and Arkley, the 43 being diverted to terminate instead at the 'Swan and Pyramids' at North Finchley. The purpose or effect (depending on your point of view) of this change was to make way for the Potters Bar based subsidiary, Overground, to introduce an entirely new route 285A from Arkley to join its long established 284A from Hadley Highstone at Barnet and run alongside it to Victoria. The presence of suffix letters on both routes is a clue, under the Bassom system of numbering, to the fact that both had summer Sunday extensions, respectively to Hatfield 'Dray Horse' (284) and Borehamwood 'The Crown' (285). The scheme was completed by

Above **Route 32 was diverted to Raynes Park in the major changes of 28th May 1930, but this photograph must have been taken at least a year later as Merton's NS 860 has been fitted with a driver's windscreen.** Malcolm E. Papes collection

Route 608 reached Hornsey Rise in April 1930, replacing single-deck buses along St Johns Road. This NS, photographed on 31st May that year, was typical of the class as originally fitted with covered tops and pneumatic tyres but with the driver still unprotected in his cab. Alan B. Cross W. Noel Jackson Collection

The size of Overground's operation was enlarged in April 1930 with the introduction of route 285 as a companion to the long-established 284. In this rare picture taken in Buckingham Palace Road, Dodson bodied 4-ton number 3 is working on the summer Sunday extension of the 284 to Hatfield 'Dray Horse'. This bus was transferred to the LGOC in June 1930 in a programme under which all but two Dennisses were exchanged for ex-Public Leylands. W. Noel Jackson

the extension of the 27 from Highgate Station (as Archway was then known) to Muswell Hill via Fortis Green Road and a doubling of the service on route 143A (from London Bridge) through East Finchley to Hendon Central. All this put only four more LGOC buses on the road but ten single-deckers had been replaced by double-deckers and Overground had increased its stake in the network.

Apparently even these changes were insufficient to meet the growing demand because at the end of the year the Mayor of Hornsey was so incensed by the inadequacy of local services that he ran a Gilford single-decker between Archway and Muswell Hill as a protest against the Restricted Streets Orders which were preventing further improvements. Whether for this reason or not, dispensation was eventually granted for the operation of more buses and, in October 1932, Overground's 285 was diverted via Muswell Hill Road and Friern Barnet, instead of duplicating the trams on the main road (the 43 being cut back to Friern Barnet).

Other north London changes in April had the 29 pushing north of Hadley Woods (Cockfosters) to open up new territory out to Potters Bar (Station Road) and a substantial increase in the frequency of route 299 along the Great Cambridge Road to Edmonton. These were part of a set of changes which represented another strand of the LGOC's policy, the removal of unnecessarily competing bus services from roads served by its sister companies' trams. The 29 group as a whole suffered some stringent reductions in frequency, particularly south of Wood Green and the 129, which branched off the main group at Wood Green to run out to North Finchley over the MET tram route, was withdrawn altogether. Nearby, an old London Public route 212C, which ran infrequently between Charing Cross and Waltham Cross following the tram route most of the way, was withdrawn and no fewer than twenty-one buses were removed from the 69 group and the 369B by reducing the general level of service. The thirty-four buses which were released by these changes were redeployed for use in the development of new services. The Potters Bar service on the 29 was altered in August to run to the garage. Renumbered 629 it became yet another service to be added to the Overground portfolio.

This policy was taken a stage further in May, when a scheme devised in collaboration with the London County Council led to a substantial reduction in the number of buses along the main road from Clapham to South Wimbledon, whilst introducing buses to new areas around Banstead and improving services to Epsom and St Helier estate. As this was presumably the sort of joint planning which was intended under the abortive Common Fund proposals, it is worthy of detailed study.

Routes withdrawn from this section were: the 5 and 105 (between Clapham Common and their southern terminals at Raynes Park and Mitcham); the 51A (Oxford Circus – Putney Bridge via Wimbledon) – withdrawn altogether on Mondays to Saturdays; the 70 (between Clapham Common and Morden, except on summer Sundays); routes 80 and 180, which ceased to run north of Rose Hill to Charing Cross and went instead to Morden,

Route 180 lost its status as a trunk central London route in May 1930, when its northern terminal became Morden station. At its outer terminus, 'The Chequers', Walton-on-the-Hill, it met East Surrey route 35 from Leatherhead, a single-decker on which can be seen on the right. This photograph was taken in December 1930, by which time the NS had been fitted with a driver's windscreen. Lens of Sutton

while their weekend variant, 181 (Charing Cross – Epsom) was withdrawn altogether. Monday to Saturday route 32 lost its South Wimbledon to Wimbledon Common section and was diverted instead to Raynes Park but was given an increased service, as were routes 88 (Acton Green – Belmont) and 89 (Charing Cross – Wallington), all of which followed the same route out of London as the 51 and 80 group. The Sunday service to Raynes Park was supplied by route 51, which continued to run on this day but diverted away from Putney Bridge. In addition to the 70, the section from South Wimbledon to Morden also lost the 155 (which ceased to be a circular route) and the 165 (withdrawn between Raynes Park and Morden) and all these were compensated by the diversion and extension of the 93 from Wimbledon to Morden, with a substantial increase in its frequency as far as Putney Bridge. The considerable loss of service from Wimbledon Hill and the loss of direct services to the centre of London was not popular and led to strident comment in the local Press.

Alterations to local services included the withdrawal of single-deck 113 between Belmont and Banstead and the diversion in its place of the 164 which continued via Bolters Lane and College Road to Epsom, giving this section a daily service for the first time and introducing double-deckers to Banstead Village. This did have the unfortunate effect of withdrawing buses from Reigate Road, Ewell for all time, except that a local builder (Harwood's) did run a small one-man

bus for a time in 1931 between Longdown Lane and Ewell East station, restricted to season ticket holders and therefore avoiding the need for a licence. Epsom also benefited from the increased service to that town from Morden on the 70, which also compensated for the Ewell to Morden half of the circular 164. The changes to the 80 group and an increased service on the 164 brought extra buses to St Helier Avenue and strengthened links into Morden station. Altogether eighteen buses were taken off and a small move made towards further double-decking.

Further improvements came to the area in September when part of the 93 was extended to Cheam via North Cheam and a new 103 (Raynes Park – Wimbledon) brought buses, in the form of a K single-decker, to Ridgway and Cottenham Park Road. The 93 extension proved a little premature and was reduced to a peak hour only operation the following February.

Elsewhere in the south progress was slower but in September buses linked Grove Park and Mottingham for the first time through Chinbrook Road and Grove Park Road, when S-class single-deckers opened up new route 209 between Forest Hill and Eltham. Other expanding areas benefited from increased services rather than new routes, examples being the 109 (more buses between Penge and Chislehurst) and the new 193 between West Wickham and Croydon, which was really a 494 short-working but was given a separate Bassom system number because of a minuscule variation in Croydon.

The LGOC was still active in the taking over of Independent operators whenever the opportunity arose, although by now such opportunities were not abundant in the local bus field. Nevertheless, the business of E. Gray, who worked nine Leyland buses on routes 6 and 69, became ripe for takeover at the end of 1929 and was formally acquired by the LGOC on 21st February 1930. The licences on the 69, where General had already made substantial cuts, were allowed to lapse but five K type buses from Dalston garage were substituted for Gray's ailing Leylands on route 6 from 6th March. This was six days earlier than intended because the fleet was in such a state that the service was badly depleted and actually failed to run at all on 5th March.

On 2nd June 1930, the A & W Omnibus Co was acquired, together with three Guy BB and FBB thirty-two seat single-deckers, which worked on routes 140A (Pinner – Wealdstone) and 351 (Harrow Met. Station – Hatch End via Pinner Road and Paines Lane). The services were transferred into Harrow Weald garage and, within a week or so, the Guys were replaced by standard LGOC S-type single-deckers. At one time the Metropolitan Railway had hoped to secure an operating agreement with A & W with the idea of developing feeder services to its stations from newly built areas in Harrow and Wembley but the negotiations had fallen through when one of the directorships changed hands.

Harrow Weald garage was a brand new base intended to provide the capacity needed for the considerable expansion which was expected in the next few years, as more and more houses were built on the virgin lands of Middlesex. It had opened for business on 9th April 1930, with a mixed fleet of S-types, for routes 142A/B, 158 and 307A and covered top NSs for the 18 and 114A/B. The 114 group had transferred from the small South Harrow premises, which were closed on the same day, the others from Willesden (18) and Edgware.

The A&W Omnibus Co was taken over by the LGOC on 2nd June 1930. Among the assets was this thirty-two seat Guy FBB which ran for General for only two weeks after the takeover.
W. Noel Jackson

Changes in the Harrow area on 5th September 1930 eliminated route 307A, which was replaced by an extension of the 183 from Pinner to Northwood. Before Harrow Weald garage opened, the 307A had been operated by the K-class and its allocation of S-type, like S 637, therefore lasted only five months.
D.A. Ruddom collection

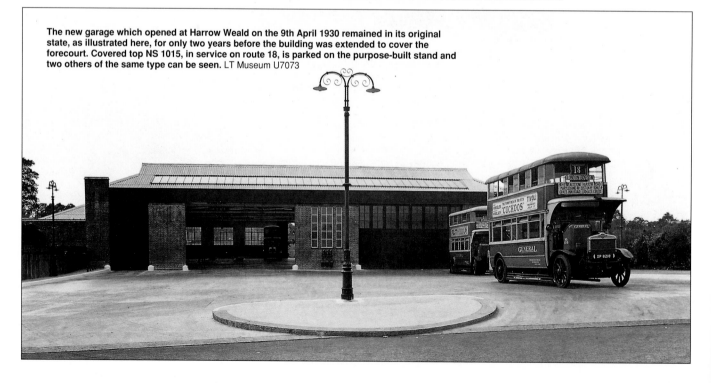

The new garage which opened at Harrow Weald on the 9th April 1930 remained in its original state, as illustrated here, for only two years before the building was extended to cover the forecourt. Covered top NS 1015, in service on route 18, is parked on the purpose-built stand and two others of the same type can be seen. LT Museum U7073

Other areas of Middlesex which got regular services for the first time in 1930 were: Preston Road in July (route 518 from London Bridge); Northolt Park and Northolt in September (114D from Harrow Weald); Headstone Lane, Harrow in September (new single-deck route 353 Pinner – North Harrow, also absorbing the former A & W 351); Iver Heath and George Green (new Dart operated 507 Uxbridge – Windsor); and Greenford Avenue in November (Dart operated 210A Hanwell Station – Greenford), which was also operated by Loumax. The 210A lasted only until January 1931, when improvements to Church Road, Hanwell allowed a northward extension of double-deck route 55 from Hanwell Broadway. Road improvements and tree pruning elsewhere on the route also made it possible to replace the open top NSs by covered top ones at the same time.

Essex was also developing at a fast pace, especially around Romford, Becontree and Dagenham and LGOC put on or extended many routes in the autumn of 1930, starting in November with a much sought-after extension of the 15A from East Ham to Becontree Heath via the By-Pass, Heathway and Wood Lane, the longer route being numbered 15B. Associated with this was a re-organisation of the complicated 23 group, which installed two new routes: 151 Marylebone – Becontree (Chittys Lane) and 293 Becontree Heath – Dagenham via Barking and included the withdrawal of mileage along Barking Road which had been taken over with the Invicta company in 1927. These changes still left much to be desired in the area and members of Dagenham Urban District Council went to see the Minister in an attempt to get more dispensations. Nevertheless, further improvements had to wait another year.

Romford was the centre of important changes in December, which coincided with the arrival of new ST class double-deckers at Romford (RD) garage where they replaced all the NSs. Although only a short section of

Route 15B reached its new Becontree Heath terminus on Guy Fawkes Day 1930 but this photograph must have been taken a year later as LT 829, which carried the first LT5/1 body, was not licensed until December 1931. The second bus in line is NS 842 on route 293, which started at the same time as 15B J.F. Higham

Eastern Avenue from Mawneys Road to North Street was newly opened to buses, there were substantial improvements to services on most roads radiating from the town. Central to the changes was the augmentation and double-decking of route G1, which was shortened at both ends to avoid unsuitable roads in Collier Row and the low bridge between Upminster and Cranham. The service to Collier Row was further enhanced by the extension of the G5 from Parkside to cover the lost part of the G1 and by a more frequent service on route 308 to Stapleford Abbots. The route to Mawneys Road was a new G2, which also took over the

Brentwood service from 187. The two routes combined gave a much enhanced frequency.

Sadly, November and December also saw the inception of many new schedules which cut or withdrew services where demand was falling because of the incipient economic slump. Five routes were cut on all days, Sunday morning cuts were made on thirty-six routes, Sunday afternoon cuts on four, all-day Sunday on four others and a six routes had slack hour cuts during the week. Four routes were withdrawn in whole or part, including the 606 (Ilford – Woodford Bridge) which eliminated daily buses from Manor Road.

NS 1851 passes through the stark newness of the Becontree estate near the end of its long haul on route 123D from Marylebone. The only other vehicle on this commodious road is an S-type double-decker which can just be seen turning the bend in the distance. D.A. Ruddom collection

In December 1930 there was an example of the considerable power wielded by the London & Home Counties Traffic Advisory Committee. Birch Bros had been trying to get an extension of route 231 from Hampstead Town Hall to a better terminal at South End Green and also to extend it at its other end to Harlesden but the former ran foul of the Restricted Street Order on South End Green and the latter was not approved. Birch had also pioneered bus operation along the new Watford and Barnet By-pass between Hendon Central and Mill Hill with a route which by April 1930 had settled down as the 214 which continued through Hale Lane and Edgware to Canons Park. The route was a great success but Birch's application to increase the service over its busiest section was refused. Insult was added to this injury when the LGOC was authorised to operate to Mill Hill on a long extension of part of route 12 from Oxford Circus, using Watford Way from its Finchley Road end. This became the 121 running all the way from Dulwich but from 15th January 1930 the Mill Hill end of service was localised as 121E from Hendon Central, thereby apparently removing the main justification for General's having been granted the licence rather than Birch. What is more, the NSs were replaced by brand new T type Regal single-deckers and these were used to shadow Birch's buses, 'pirate' fashion, in a remarkable inversion of commonly expected practice.

At the end of September, Birch approached the Minister of Transport about their various problems. It was seven months before he replied with a refusal to grant any of their requests but, in the meantime, the Advisory Committee had already ordered the two companies to sort matters out between themselves. This bore fruit surprisingly quickly as a co-ordination agreement, unique in the annals of the LGOC in being with an Independent which retained its independence. Under the agreement, which attracted the approval of the Minister and went into effect on 31st December 1930, Birch's London activities were limited to the level of mileage then being run, after allowing for the changes made by the agreement. General's contribution was to withdraw the 121E, and to reduce its share of route 526 (Wandsworth Bridge – North Finchley) by three buses. Birch in turn withdrew the Mill Hill to Canons Park section of the 214 and transferred three odd workings on routes 26E, 266, 284 and 227 to General. This left the LGOC free to go ahead with an extension of the 114B from Edgware to 'The Green Man', Mill Hill, originally scheduled for introduction on 3rd September 1930 but deferred while the negotiations had been taking place. The benefits to Birch included exclusive operation over the 214C and an increase of two runnings on the 526 (which operated initially displaying LGOC fare tables). The existence of the agreement softened the Minister's hard line on route 231 and he now issued the necessary amendments to the Regulations to allow its extension at both ends to run from Hampstead Heath to Harlesden daily. In its shortened form the 214C was suitable for double-deckers and the main daytime service was henceforth supplied by three of Birch's newly delivered Leyland Titans, with help from single-deckers in the peak. Through road-rail tickets to the

This peaceful scene at Hendon Central station belies the controversy surrounding the operation of route 214 during 1930 which had culminated in an agreement between the LGOC and Birch Bros giving the Independent sole rights on this route in exchange for mileage elsewhere. B 19 was one of Birch's 1928 intake, a Leyland PLSC3 with Birch thirty-two seat rear-entrance bodywork W. Noel Jackson

Underground were accepted by Birch on the 214 and, from April 1931, each accepted the tickets of the other on route 526 when passengers had to transfer as a result of a bus breaking down.

During its last two-and-a-half years, General continued to open up new areas, the speed of development being governed to a large extent by the pace at which roads in newly built areas were made suitable or were deemed to be suitable by the police or local authorities. The biggest areas of development in Essex were undoubtedly the already extensive Becontree and Dagenham estates, and the associated growth of the new Ford plant alongside the Thames. Ford Works got its own service from December 1931, when new route 224 linked the factory with 'The Chequers', initially with single-deck LTs but in May 1932 these were replaced by double-deckers. By July 1932 improved links to Fords were yet again needed, with new routes from Ilford (148B) and Upminster (172) and an extension of 175 from Dagenham. In January 1932, Oxlow Lane and Parsloes Avenue were newly served, respectively by the extension of 145 from 'The Five Elms' and by a diversion of 148 away from Wood Lane. In March, Barley Lane and Goodmayes Road were covered by a long extension of the 149 to 'The Five Elms', which also brought extra buses to Bennetts Castle Lane and Longbridge Road .

The LGOC had expanded its operations in the Romford area in sad circumstances earlier in 1931. One of the several successful local Independents was the Capitol Omnibus Co. who ran two services from Rainham Road (Maynard Chase) to Ongar and Epping via Stapleford Abbots and Passingford Bridge, for which four TSM buses (two each of B10A twenty-six seaters and B10A2 thirty-two seaters) were owned. Two of the buses were written off in a catastrophic fire on 12th July 1931 which also totally destroyed the garage and Capitol never ran again under its own

management. The LGOC drafted in four S-type single-deckers to work the Capitol schedules 'on hire', using the premises of Romford Ice & Cold Storage in Church Lane as a temporary garage. General then acted as manager of the business until the Traffic Commissioner could approve the transfer of licences, which he did in November. LGOC integrated the routes into its own schedules at Romford (RD) garage from 25th November.

In the north-east, the section of Church Street, Edmonton to the east of Great Cambridge Road was served from September 1931. At first route 204, on which twenty-seat DS class Dennises were used, was diverted to Edmonton station, leaving a section of the new Great Cambridge Road between Bury Street and Weir Hall unserved. This was restored in March 1932, when the 299D was extended to Bury Street and became 299. The short section of Lavender Hill west of Gordon Hill got buses in March 1932, when the 204 lost its Enfield to Edmonton end and became a circular route from Enfield via Baker Street and the Ridgeway. The Edmonton end was covered by an extension of short-working route 538B (Forty Hill – Enfield), which took the new number 539. Another fast developing area was around Chingford, which had been difficult for buses to reach, the main approach from the south being by a one-way route through New Road, Hale End Road (later renamed Larkshall Road) and Kings Road, with a return route via The Ridgeway and Old Church Road. The restrictions on Old Church Hill and Old Church Road were partially lifted in November 1931 so that route 602 (Muswell Hill Broadway – Chingford) could run both ways by this route (although the double-deck 38 and Independent route 511 were still not allowed to do so). The south-eastern approach was opened up in October 1932, when route 145 was extended through Whitehall Road from Woodford Wells.

The extension of the Piccadilly Line northwards from Finsbury Park to Arnos Grove on 19th September 1932 and onwards to Enfield West (Oakwood) on 13th March 1933 encouraged General to introduce feeder bus services. Route 603 (Muswell Hill to the Chase Side Tavern), on which Muswell Hill ran new single-deck LTs, started on 7th September 1932, and introduced buses to Powys Lane and Winchmore Hill Road. The opening of Enfield West brought route 307 onto the scene between Whetstone and Enfield Town and put buses into Longmore Avenue, East Barnet. It was operated by Overground from Potters Bar, using Dennis Lances released from the 629 which was also diverted to serve Enfield West, on an improved frequency, at the expense of losing the section parallel to the railway from Bramley Road to Turnpike Lane.

The LGOC was not slow either in reaping the benefits of expanding 'Metroland', which was gradually covering the green fields of Middlesex with mock Tudor and other forms of bricks and mortar. In April 1931 buses reached Eastcote, Ruislip, Ickenham and Swakeleys Road for the first time when Pinner and Uxbridge were linked by new route 181. Royal Highlander started operation on the same day. A different connection from Uxbridge to Ruislip was made in November 1931 by an extension of the 505, this time via Sweetcroft Lane (not Hercies Road, which was not yet available), Hillingdon and Long Lane. Both routes were operated by Dennis Darts from Uxbridge garage. Elsewhere in Harrow, Parkside Way, Headstone Drive, Christchurch Avenue and Kenton Lane got their buses in January 1933 when route 230 started, using five Darts from Harrow Weald.

The opening of the new Metropolitan Railway branch from Wembley Park to Stanmore provoked the diversion of the 114A to run via Whitchurch Lane and Marsh Lane, serving Canons Park station, instead of Edgware Road and Stanmore New Road (later renamed 'London Road') from 11th May 1932. Then, in October that year, there was a group of changes in which a new route 140, an amalgam of parts of routes 8 and 114, started running between Northolt and Colindale serving the new Stanmore branch station at Kingsbury. At the same time, by extending route 52 from Ladbroke Grove to Mill Hill Broadway, the LGOC brought buses to the top end of Ladbroke Grove, Stag Lane Kingsbury, Deans Lane, Selvage Lane and a further stretch of Watford By-Pass. Mill Hill's developing needs were also helped by the service on the 114B becoming daily but Deansbrook Lane (now the western end of Deansbrook Road) lost buses with the withdrawal of 104 between Edgware and Burnt Oak. Earlier, in December 1931, the nearby Cricklewood estate at Pennine Drive got a service (226), which also gave buses to The Vale, Golders Green.

The Royal Highlander licences for the 181 were acquired by the LGOC, along with the business in a takeover, made rather messy by a dispute between the owners, on 15th September 1932. Included in the deal were two routes in the Ealing area: 211 (Haven Green – Greenford 'Hare & Hounds') and 225 (Haven Green – Greenford, Rutland Road); and the associated Loumax route 206 (serving Eastcote Lane Housing Estate). Three Bean

fourteen-seaters, six Guy OND twenty-seaters and two Guy ONDF forward-control twenty-seaters were taken over but such was the condition of the vehicles that no service was running on the 225 and only one bus on the 181. The deficiency on the 181 could be covered by LGOC vehicles until the Guys could be overhauled but, because of width restrictions imposed by projecting trees in Gordon Road, the Beans on the 225 were of a special narrow design on which the body did not overhang the wheels, and General were obliged to withdraw the service temporarily while they were made good. It resumed on 2nd November but not for long.

Buses reached the Cricklewood housing estate straddling Pennine Drive on 31st October 1931 but from Golders Green station rather than Cricklewood itself. With a refreshing lack of pedantry the blind of DA 9 shows 'Claremont Road', rather than the lesser known Cotswold Gardens where the service actually terminated.
N. Hamshere

Royal Highlander were taken over by the LGOC on 16th September 1932 and their Guy buses on route 181A were transferred into Harrow Weald garage. General's existing operation using Darts from Uxbridge garage continued separately. DA 29, one of the second order, is at the 'Red Lion' Pinner. J.F.Higham

Left **Route 105 which started in June 1931, grew rapidly from a Dart-operated local Hounslow route to a substantial suburban service, reaching Teddington, after two extensions, in January 1932 when it was also given the larger, thirty-seat, S-type. S 873, in its final form with pneumatic tyres and enclosed driver's cab, is on the semi-rural stand alongside the 'Clarence Hotel', Teddington.** E.G.P. Masterman

Below **Thirteen years after the class had pioneered the forward control layout and six months after the withdrawal from regular service of the last of their larger S-type successors, K 869 was one of seven of the class still running at Hounslow garage until 21st June 1932. They were kept for route 90, which required buses with high chassis frames to clear the hump on Chertsey Bridge, until it was curtailed at Ashford Common.** J.F. Higham

Meanwhile General had been consolidating and expanding in the Ealing, Greenford and Park Royal area on its own account. Elegant modern factories and lines of semi-detached houses had been spreading along the new Western Avenue outwards from East Acton for some time although only the short section from East Acton to Gypsy Corner had a bus service (the 112). In May 1932 buses began to run all the way from Wood Lane to Greenford on a massive diversion of route 93 to Greenford 'Red Lion', serving the newly built Park Royal station on the way. This left Scrubs Lane to the trams and reduced the number of buses competing with Combine trams through Harlesden to Willesden.

The area to the south-west of Greenford had hitherto been served only as far as Rutland Road by Royal Highlander's 225. This was supplemented in March 1932 by ST type double-deckers on the 97, diverted there instead of to Sudbury Town, but both were replaced in November 1932 by yet another long extension of the 93 to Southall 'White Swan' past the Rutland Road terminus to serve Cornwall Avenue, Allenby Road and Carlyle Avenue for the first time. The other end of the 225 was covered by an increased 211.

In the west, Hounslow East station's relative isolation from buses came to an end in June 1931 when two Dennis Darts opened a new local route 105 which introduced buses to Kingsley Road, New Heston Road and Vicarage Farm Road. New territory south of Hounslow was added to the 105 along Hounslow Road to Hanworth in October and then, such was the speed of development, to Teddington via Uxbridge Road, Park Road and Hampton Road in January 1932. Nearby Yeading Lane, as far as 'The White Hart' at West End, was served by a diverted 95 and Stanwell Village by an extended 506 from March 1932; and the road from Ashford Common to Staines by an extended 90 from October 1932.

The 90 had reached Ashford Common in the previous June in a small group of changes which were of particular significance as their purpose was to make way for the withdrawal of the last remaining K class double-deckers which, because of their high chassis frame, were the only type of double-decker which could then cross the heavily humped Chertsey Bridge. It had been the intention to cover this end of the 90 with a new route from Kingston through Hampton and Sunbury but the approval for this was not immediately forthcoming. Instead it was replaced by a new Dart operated route 137 from Hounslow, replacing the 120 from Hounslow Heath to Feltham and incidentally serving virgin ground between Feltham and Sunbury. At its other end the 90 took advantage of the new Great Chertsey Road in an extension from Richmond Station to Kew Gardens Station via Lower Mortlake Road and Sandycombe Road, an older area not previously approachable by buses. In January 1933 the 137 was diverted to run along Harlington Road West, also virgin territory. The Kingston route eventually materialised, on Sunday 1st January 1933, as the Dart operated 198 but went to Staines, rather than Chertsey and in addition to introducing buses to Hampton Village, Harfield Road and Lower Hampton Road added School Road, Felthamhill Road and Stanwell Road Ashford to the growing bus map.

Another significant west London event was the opening of the new Hampton Court Bridge, replacing an old, narrow structure which was unsuitable for large vehicles. The rapidly expanding 105, whose capacity had by now been quadrupled by a doubling of its frequency and the allocation, first of S-class single-deckers on 30th December 1931, then of single-deck LTs from 30th November 1932, was again extended to run over the new bridge and pick up the route of the 171 onwards through Thames Ditton to Kingston. To do so it had to run via Bushy Park which had previously been used only by summer buses to Hampton Court. The 171 was also diverted to take the direct route into Kingston via the new bridge and Hampton Court Road. These changes took place on 21st June 1933, a week before the official opening of the bridge.

In the south, Sutton By-Pass and Collingwood Road got a diversion of the 157 in April 1931; Poynders Road, Cavendish Road and Streatham Place an extension of the 5 to Streatham Common in May 1932 (later continuing to Mitcham to absorb the 50 in October); and a new 152 came to Western Road and Christchurch Road, Mitcham and the unserved section of Kingston By-Pass between Malden and Tolworth in August 1932. Like Western Avenue, Kingston By-Pass and the areas surrounding it were attracting new industry and housing on a prodigious scale and the growth of demand also justified the allocation of two NS double-deckers to the normally single-deck 155 to run as 155C shorts between South Wimbledon and Malden from March 1932.

Over in the Croydon area on 5th August 1931, the 54 was diverted through Sussex Road and Selsdon Road, not to serve new territory but to avoid the bridge in Croham Road so that the open top S class double-deckers could be replaced by covered top NSs. This left Normanton Road to LGCS route 415 for the time being. Later in the year, on 16th December 1931, a service along Croham Road was restored when Thomas Tilling started new 254, as far as Croham Heights (Brent Road) using a couple of TSM Petrol Electric single-deckers. Introduction of the route had been delayed by the existence of Restricted Streets Orders on roads in Croydon and the estate owners, Costains, had been operating their own service for residents only which, by not plying for hire, did not have to comply with the Orders. Dispensation was eventually granted so that the 254 could be introduced. Approval was subsequently given for it to continue up the rest of Farley Road to Selsdon and this extension operated from March 1933.

Above **New route 609, which opened up territory between Beckenham and Hayes in April 1931, also had brand new AEC Renown single-deckers, like LT 1077 at North Street, Bromley.**
Charles F. Klapper Collection; Omnibus Society

London bade farewell to the double-deck S-type in December 1931, shortly before route 132 was given help between Eltham and Bexley by the extension of route 209. Typical of the class was S 196, a Sidcup bus seen at Lewisham.
W. Noel Jackson

The first service to penetrate the area of new housing lying between Beckenham and Hayes was the 609 which, from April 1931, linked Penge with Bromley North but via Hayes Lane and Westmoreland Road instead of the direct route taken by the 109. Other south-eastern areas newly served included: Crown Lane as far as Southborough 'Crooked Billet' (Tilling 136 extended December 1931); Perry Street and Halfway Street (609 extended from Bromley to Eltham via Chislehurst, absorbing 195, November 1932); Shooters Hill to Welling (joint Tilling/LGOC 20 extended); Westmount Road, Rochester Way, Welling Way to Welling (Tilling 109 extended); and Keston to Downe (the 146B, a Bassom-busting bifurcation of Tilling's 146A) all in May 1933.

From all this lively activity, it can be seen that north-west Kent was also developing rapidly but it would be wrong to assume that the bus services were able to keep pace with the spread of new populations here or anywhere else. Time and again companies were prevented from starting badly needed routes because essential roads were subject to Restricted Streets Orders; or the roads were not suitable; or because of some obstruction in or alongside the road, either natural such as a tree or manmade like a lamp-post. Addington was a good example. People certainly lived there but they had no bus service and if they wanted one they had the choice of walking the one-and-a-half hilly miles to Shirley or the one-and-three-quarter miles to Selsdon. Further into London, there was no bus service of any kind in the area bounded by Brixton Hill/Streatham Hill, Streatham Common, Norwood Road and Effra Road, an enormous area, undoubtedly populated but with various hazards which discouraged the Police from approving the routes offered to them from time to time. It would be tedious to catalogue them but similar examples could be quoted all over London. Finally, it has to be remembered that even in the 1930s, not everybody wanted buses in their backyard. For example, a planned extension of route 602 from Muswell Hill to Golders Green in 1932, which would have penetrated the heart of Hampstead Garden Suburb, via Bigwood Road, Meadway and Hoop Lane, was prevented by the opposition of Garden Suburb residents. The area remained unserved until the introduction of 'Dial-a-Bus' over forty years later.

Alongside all these new operations many of the established routes were also being improved, either by the allocation of new and larger buses or by scheduling more frequent services. One or two examples must serve to illustrate the point. In January 1932, the 209 was extended from Eltham to Bexley, effectively doubling the service jointly with the 132, while a further doubling was made as far as Blackfen in April 1933 when the 209A was extended from Eltham. Wherever possible double-deckers replaced single-deckers, even when on some occasions this meant reverting from nice modern vehicles to something rather older and less attractive. There were two such examples in this period: routes 95 (LT single-deck to covered top NS in December 1931) and 224 (single-deck to double-deck LT – May 1932). There were also two examples where larger single-deckers were substituted: route 105, from Dart, via S to single-deck LT, as already mentioned; and

the 195 on which thirty-five seat LTs replaced twenty-seater Darts in June 1932.

In company with the enlargement of its network the LGOC also devoted a full measure of effort to improving garages and other facilities. The arrangements made at Aldgate and for Green Line at Poland Street, Watford and Windsor have already been noted but these were only part of the story. At Kingston, where the front of the garage was already in use as a bus station, the amenities were upgraded at the beginning of 1930, with the opening of a passenger waiting room and refreshment bar. Included was a staff mess room and this was also part of a continuing programme of improvement which also covered the Minories lay-by and the garages at Cricklewood, Elmers End, Hanwell (HW) and Muswell Hill.

A development introduced by the LGOC in July 1931 illustrates the company's interest in trying out new ideas at all levels. A perennial problem for conductors on buses from London Bridge station in the morning peak was that most passengers travelled only the short distance across the bridge into the City and it was a race against time to collect all their fares before they alighted. To ease the problem the LGOC tried issuing tickets in advance from four Pullbar ticket issuing machines. Only penny tickets were issued and these were cancelled by being torn in half. The benefit gained must have been fairly slim and the machines were later replaced by kerbside conductors who issued tickets to the queues, a system which continued into the late 1940s. Both systems were supplemented by the crews themselves, whose own ideas were more basic: the driver proceeded at a funereal crawl until he received a signal from his conductor that all fares were in, at which point passengers were treated to a sudden increase in acceleration and a new found sense of urgency.

As a matter of policy, the company set about providing itself with purpose-built bus stands or stations wherever it saw a need or an opportunity. In most cases the policy was to provide the minimum of facilities needed to turn and stand buses and these were usually built where the availability of street stands was restricted or non-existent. They were provided as a matter of course wherever land was available alongside the new stations on the Piccadilly Line extension from Finsbury Park to Cockfosters. In other cases they were provided as part of a garage when other work was being carried out, two examples being Hanwell, which was enlarged, and Camberwell where the space underneath the new Divisional offices was designated a 'bus station'. Others were built on plots of land purchased or leased for the purpose, such as Park Road Edmonton, Gainsborough Road Hackney and at 'The Bell' Hotel, Upminster. At Edmonton, routes 39, 76 and 130A (Sunday route) were extended from the 'Angel' on 18th June 1930 and Park Road then became the normal terminal for the town. At Hackney, the opening of the stand in September 1930 led to the withdrawal of the 30 between Wick Road and 'The Queens Hotel' in Victoria Park Road. The 6 and 64 were extended along Gainsborough Road.

Another important programme was the progressive alteration of garages to increase headrooms to give adequate clearance for covered top pneumatic-tyred buses. Those dealt with between 1930 and 1933 were (in order of treatment) Hounslow, Old Kent Road, Twickenham, Cricklewood, Catford (Tilling), Croydon (Tilling), Streatham and those used by East Surrey at Chelsham, Leatherhead and Swanley.

The urgent need for extra garage capacity to cope with the swelling fleet encouraged LGOC to embark on an ambitious programme to enlarge existing garages and build new ones. The opening of the new garage at Harrow Weald in April 1930 has already been noted but even this new structure soon proved inadequate and authority was given in June 1932 for the building to be extended over the forecourt at a cost of £5,500, bringing the total cost of the garage to £20,963. More than twice this sum (£48,348) was expended on a spacious new garage for the Overground company at Potters Bar, which opened on 28th May 1930 on a site which had been in use since 1928 when a calamitous fire forced Overground to vacate its base in Harmood Street, Chalk Farm. The temporary building was moved to Staines for use by Green Line Coaches Ltd. Although steps were taken to transfer some operations from LGOC to Overground, the garage has remained forever isolated from mainstream operations and has never been able to realise anything like its full potential.

Much more in the heart of things was Upton Park garage, which was completely renewed and enlarged at the then colossal sum of £120,000. One of the first of the truly modern generation of garages, the new Upton Park was noted for having an entirely uninterrupted parking area, with accommodation for about 200 buses. One novel feature, which actually affected the appearance of its buses in a small way, was an overhead fuelling system. To enable this to work efficiently, all Upton Park buses had their fleet number painted on the back of the roof and this was to remain a unique feature of its fleet for a generation. The enlarged premises came into use on 7th October 1931 and replaced the former Atlas garage in Tilbury Road, East Ham (EH). Upton Park's total schedule required 155 buses. On the same day, another new garage which had been built at a cost of £40,000, opened on a site which had been out of use since 1920, somewhat off the beaten track at Clay Hall near Old Ford. Its old code Y was not revived; instead it was given CL, in accordance with a new policy which required codes to bear some relation to the name. Clay Hall's principal role then and for the rest of its existence was to operate the Old Ford routes, then the 8 group and 160, and it started with a schedule of forty-eight.

There were also major extensions and improvements to Barking and Muswell Hill garages to give increased capacity and preparations were well in hand for further expansion. Land had already been purchased for possible new garages in Fencepiece Road, Barkingside (18.75 acres) and Perivale Lane, Alperton (3.5 acres) and in 1930 a plot at Gillingham Street/Wilton Road Victoria was bought for £248,838. A further £30,000 was also spent on the acquisition of land for the extension of existing garages in Chelverton Road Putney, Well Street Hackney, West Green Road, alongside Plumstead garage and in Pound Lane and High Road, Willesden, all in addition to the projects on behalf of East Surrey, already described.

Expansion and fleet renewal were not taking place in a particularly favourable climate. Traffic was still in decline because of the Depression and General had to make a lot of fairly severe service cuts in the autumn of 1931 and spring of 1932. This was evidently not enough because in January 1932 all the Underground Group companies invited the Trade Unions to discuss a temporary reduction in wages of two-and-a-half per cent except that no wage would go below forty shillings. For a bus driver this would have reduced the basic wage from about £4 7s 6d to £4 6s 0d and a conductor from £4 0s 6d to £3 19s 6d. It was also proposed that the spare list should be reduced in length, so that fewer staff could be employed and ostensibly to reduce the number of staff who had to be laid off at the end of each summer season. After six months of negotiation, the proposals were rejected overwhelmingly by the staff at Branch meetings, although they did not then vote for strike action. The LGOC decided to go ahead with the cuts and at this stage another issue became embroiled in the blossoming dispute. The LGOC had made separate proposals for reductions in scheduled running times to take advantage of the improved performance of the new generation of buses and the move towards a fleet predominantly fitted with pneumatic tyres. In calling for a Delegate Conference to discuss the wage cuts, the Union linked them with the running time economies because the combined effect of all the proposals, by reducing opportunities for overtime and spreadover payments, was to increase the nominal wage cuts of 1s 6d and 1s 0d to average losses of earnings of 6s and 5s a week.

The dispute, which was threatening to develop into a major strike, had blown up during the absence of Lord Ashfield in Canada. On his return, he took charge of the negotiations with the T&GWU's powerful General Secretary Ernest Bevin and hammered out a compromise which left the standard rates of pay unchanged, in which respect the busmen did better than their railway colleagues. A number of technical changes were made to the scheduling agreement, including a reduction in the maximum spreadover by half-an-hour, which reduced earnings; but by far the greatest prize was the agreement to go ahead with the gradual introduction of faster schedules which was to be completed by 1st January 1933. Operation of the new schedules was to be monitored for three months each of winter and summer schedules and the T&GWU had the right to call for a review of monetary compensation at any time after 30th June 1933, a date whose wider significance was not then apparent.

The first new schedules were introduced with the Winter Programme on 5th October 1932, when twenty-one routes were affected. The average reduction on routes where six-cylinder engined vehicles were allocated was reckoned to be ten minutes in an hour but the actual amounts varied widely. Thirty-eight fewer buses were needed but straight economies were not made in all cases. For example, the extension of route 90 from Ashford Common to Staines was put in without having to use any more buses, while on route 120 it was possible to use the reduction to improve the headway from a non-clockface sixteen or thirty-two minute to a regular fifteen and thirty respectively. Another eleven routes followed in November and thirteen in January but the programme was not completed on time and the biggest programme came in February, when schedules for seventy-five routes were recast. Five more followed in March and the last two stragglers in April. The passage for these changes was not entirely smooth. On 17th January, the staff at Forest Gate garage, objecting to the increased average speed on route 40B from 9.2 to 9.9 mph, started an unofficial strike. They were joined by Upton Park the following morning, four more garages the next day and by 21st January a total of 150 routes from nineteen garages were affected. Support from the unlikely direction of tramwaymen at Hanwell and Stonebridge was forthcoming on 22nd January but, following a joint statement from Ernest Bevin and Lord Ashfield calling on staff to honour agreements freely entered into, the strike began to collapse on the 23rd and was over two days later.

Altogether, 217 buses were withdrawn because of the faster speeds and the number of crews reduced by 310 giving an annual saving of £267,000, £84,300 more than had been predicted in the negotiations with the staff. By the time these figures were published, the LGOC had ceased to exist and it was for the new Board to deal with the labour relations consequences.

The vehicle maintenance area of Upton Park garage in December 1931, two months after the rebuilt garage opened for business. The white tiled pits were the acme of modernity, with direct access from a low level working area equipped with an overhead crane for moving engines. Upton Park was the parent garage in its group, which explains the presence of NS 921, nearest the camera, in for docking from Forest Gate garage. *LT Museum*

The glass curtain wall of the newly built Daily Express building on the left, reflects a scene in Fleet Street, looking towards a Ludgate Hill as yet unscarred by wartime bombing, in which an LT on route 11E, contrasting sharply with the outmoded NSs, represents the new order in the bus world.

CHAPTER THREE

LONDON GENERAL IN THE COUNTRY AREA 1930-1933

Outside the Metropolitan Police District, the LGOC's interests were represented by a number of companies, with differing legal relationships. In Essex, Hertfordshire and Middlesex, services were run on their behalf by the National Omnibus and Transport Company using buses supplied by General from garages at Romford, Bishop's Stortford, Ware, Hatfield, Luton and Watford. In Buckinghamshire, General had a half share of the Amersham & District Motor Bus and Haulage Company, operating services in the Amersham and High Wycombe areas. It operated in an apparently independent fashion, but all major financial and strategic decisions had to be cleared with the LGOC Board. In the south, the East Surrey Traction Company was a wholly owned subsidiary and ran services in Surrey, Sussex and Kent from its own garages at Reigate, Crawley and East Grinstead and five others owned by General at Swanley, Dunton Green, Chelsham, Godstone and Leatherhead. Its fleet included a number of buses owned by LGOC but the greater part was directly owned by the company. East Surrey, in turn, owned the

small Autocar Services Ltd, based on Tunbridge Wells.

The LGOC also entered into 'Area Agreements' with the main line railways and the major federated companies, in line with normal practice at the time, to protect its outer boundary. In anticipation of possible closer relations with the railway companies comparable to what was happening elsewhere, in March 1930 General registered companies in the names of Northern General (presumably a possible joint venture with the LMSR), Eastern General (LNER) and Western General (GWR). The name 'Southern General' had already been appropriated by a company in Cornwall, so the fourth registration was in the name 'General Southern Services Ltd'. Nothing ever came of these as they were ultimately overtaken by the enactment of the London Passenger Transport Bill but negotiations for the formation of a Southern company, incorporating parts of East Surrey, Autocar and Redcar, reached an advanced stage.

There was nothing comparable to the phenomenal growth of suburban London yet

THE VALLEY CATERHAM. 6.

taking place, much of the business growth in these outer areas around 1930 being concentrated on the development of the coach network or by the acquisition of other companies but East Surrey did share to an extent in the suburban growth because its tentacles reached further into the sprawl than did National's in the north. Examples of this were: the extension of the 418 from West Ewell to Tolworth, to make connection with the London United trams, in April 1930; new route 31 to Chelsfield on 4th June 1930, which also gave Halstead its first service and replaced General's 147 south of Green Street Green (except on summer Sundays); and a new 422 between Eltham and Orpington through Albany Road and Chislehurst (October 1931). On the face of it, the 422 was a somewhat surprising curiosity, well outside East Surrey's normal sphere of operations but LGCS had plans to link it with the 31 to form a through route from Eltham to Sevenoaks, when suitable roads were available in Orpington. This never happened.

Bus services were also being put into some new areas. Chaldon was first served in April 1930, for example, when East Surrey route 30 was extended from Caterham-on-the-Hill to

Earlswood. Other areas to benefit in 1930 included Shoreham Village (401, February), Headley, Pebblecombe, (new 35, April) and Hurst Green (new 34, April). In the north, National was involved in supplying the needs of the new Whipsnade Park Zoo, which opened on Whit Monday 23rd May 1931 to enormous instant popularity. Routes 52A and 52B, N55 and N55A were extended to the zoo and a special service was laid on from Rickmansworth via Watford and Hemel Hempstead. In its second summer season, from 24th March 1932, the zoo was honoured with the first limited stop Green Line route, BH from Marylebone, which under the new Road Traffic Act required an express licence and had to carry First Aid equipment and a lifting jack.

The first major company purchase helped to strengthen the Combine's position at its weakest point in the south-west. By an agreement made between it, the LGOC and East Surrey, the Aldershot & District Traction Company bought the whole of the share capital of the Woking and District Motor Services (J.R. Fox & Sons) for £25,000, the sale being completed on 13th January 1931. The agreement gave the company's garage at

St John's, Woking to General and split the rest 74.4% to LGOC and 25.6% to Aldershot & District, General's share of the cost being £19,000. The split was based on the Area Agreement and General took the routes from West Byfleet Station to Windsor Castle via New Haw, Addlestone, Ottershaw, Chertsey and Staines (but later diverted to run direct from Addlestone to Chertsey, omitting Ottershaw) and those from Woking to: Ottershaw, Chertsey, Staines and Windsor (38); Send, Clandon, Merrow and Guildford (36); and via Send to Ripley (37). The Camberley and Knaphill routes went to the Aldershot company. The LGOC share was handed over to East Surrey, together with fifteen single-deck AJS, Daimler, Thornycroft and TSM buses whose capacities varied from twenty to thirty-two seats. The garage at St John's was rather remote from the routes it ran and East Surrey, after flirting with the idea of a building a new garage at Send, took the opportunity of renting premises in Walton Road vacated by Aldershot & District, when it moved to a new garage in the town. East Surrey moved into Walton Road on 31st May, when the summer schedules were introduced and the routes numbered.

Further expansion in this quarter was achieved on 10th April 1932, when the Great Western Railway ceased direct operation of buses in the Slough area. Again in accordance with the Area Agreement, the services were split between LGOC and the Thames Valley Traction Company Ltd. General took the group of routes from Slough to Beaconsfield (41, 41A, 42, 42A), handing them over to East Surrey to operate, while the Taplow service went to the Reading company. This was seen at the time as smoothing the way for the London Passenger Transport Board but is likely to have happened anyway as the GWR had been progressively transferring all its direct operations to associated Federation companies. Seven single-deck Guy, Maudslay and Morris buses and seven Guy, Maudslay and Thornycroft coaches were included in the deal. The coaches were transferred to Green Line Coaches Ltd.

In the heart of Amersham & District's territory was a small concern, the Chesham & District Bus Co Ltd, whose five Chevrolet, Dennis and Gilford buses operated routes to Pond Park Estate, Hemel Hempstead, Berkhamsted, Great Missenden, Tring and Beaconsfield. Recently formed to consolidate the businesses of the three men who became its directors, it was already struggling financially by early 1932 and was offered for sale. The LGOC was prepared to give Amersham & District the necessary financial backing and the company was purchased for £1,774 (plus the acceptance of liabilities of £1,476 12s 7d) on 8th December that year. The company continued its separate existence, although its licences were all in the name of A&D, until it was effectively wound up on 4th June 1933.

By now, it was clear that the LGOC was actively acquiring businesses to make for a smoother transition to the ownership of the new Board. Another gap was filled on 12th April 1933, when services in Boxmoor and Tring operated by the London Midland and Scottish Railway, were transferred, together with eight Leyland PLSC3 Lions, all thirty-two seaters and seven of them with Derby built LMS bodywork. In the same general area, on 9th May 1933, the services of C. Aston (Aston's Bus Service) of Watford and E & F Prentice (Chiltern Bus Service) were acquired. Both worked from Watford Junction to Aylesbury and Aston also ran from Watford to Abbots Langley via Garston. Chiltern's route from Aylesbury to Leighton Buzzard was sold to Eastern National. Both brought with them double-decker Leyland Titan TD1s, five in all, and single-deck Leyland Tigers (three). Otherwise, Aston's contribution comprised six Dennis E and F model single-deckers and an AEC Regal coach, while Prentice's other three vehicles were all Albions.

The very last takeover by the LGOC was as late in its career as 23rd June 1933, when the shares of another troubled business, the Watford Omnibus Co Ltd, were transferred to General and Arthur Hawkins became its chairman. The all single-deck fleet comprised ADC416s, AEC Regals, PLSC3 Leylands, Guys and a W&G. Five routes operating from Watford to Abbots Langley, Leavesden and Gammons Lane and between Harebreaks and Hamper Mill/Oxhey Hall Farm changed hands in the deal.

The Great Western Railway operated bus services on its own account in the Slough area which might have become part of a Western General company jointly owned with the LGOC. UV4088 seen here at Slough station on the route to Burnham Beeches (42B), had the uncommonly interesting combination of Thornycroft BC chassis and Vickers twenty-two seat body. It was acquired by LGCS with the rest of the GWR Slough area operations on 10th April 1932. R.S. Turnbull collection

One of East Surrey's 1931 delivery of small vehicles, a Commer with eighteen-seat Short Bros body, on route 401B at Dartford. J.F. Higham

One of the newest vehicles taken over from Woking and District was this Tilling-Stevens B10A2 with a Petty thirty-two seat rear entrance bus body, which was new in 1930. This photograph was taken at Egham Hythe in 1932, after East Surrey had been renamed LGCS. J.F. Higham

Other smaller acquisitions made earlier included: Sevenoaks and District on 11th November 1930 (one Bean on the 401E); Bus-de-Ville of Woking, who worked a Chevrolet and a Guy between Woking and Chertsey Church via Maybury, Old Byfleet and Addlestone, on 11th March 1931; and Blue Bird Omnibus Services of Essendon on 28th February 1933 (one Chevrolet LQ Hertford – Essendon).

In the meantime, the LGOC had been busy tidying up the organisation of its own services. The East Surrey board meeting on 14th December 1931 adopted a proposal to take over operational control of the services operated on behalf of LGOC by the National Omnibus and Transport Co Ltd, effectively extending the company's area to make a complete ring around London. The consideration payable to National was £2,500. Under its agreement with the LGOC, Thomas Tilling Ltd claimed a five per cent share of the coach business of National and this was agreed without argument by Pick. The name of the company was now inappropriate and a Company Meeting on 20th January 1932 resolved to change it to London General Country Services Ltd, which is what it became on 28th January. The new name began to appear on buses from 27th February and formal administration of the National services was transferred on 1st March. The Headquarters of the new company was established at Reigate but this was not completed until early May, until when a temporary northern Headquarters was set up at Watford (High Street) garage.

The London Passenger Transport Act was on the statute book by the time the business of C. Aston of Watford was taken over by LGCS on 9th May 1933. Included in the deal were two identical lowbridge Dodson bodied Leyland Titan TD1s purchased in 1930. UR6789, which is here still in full Aston livery but with legal lettering for LGCS pasted over the lower panel, became TD 170 in the LPTB fleet. J.F. Higham

A Metcalf bodied ADC416 of the Watford Omnibus Company before the takeover by LGCS on 28th June 1933. DR3734 did not survive to receive a London Transport number, being withdrawn in 1935.
Dennis Odd collection

The two aspects of National's operations in the north-eastern Home Counties before 1932 are still to be seen in this photograph taken at Bishop's Stortford in August 1933, after the formation of the LPTB. On the left an NS formerly operated by National on behalf of General is operating on LGCS route N11 to St Albans; on the right Eastern National 2384, an Associated Daimler, is working one of National's own routes to Chelmsford. D.W.K. Jones

The new LGCS livery carried by S 920 retained the red, white and black of East Surrey but with new fleetname in which the word 'General' was given startling prominence in gold with red pointing on a silver-grey background. The words 'Country Services' underneath were in gold on red. *K.W. Glazier collection*

The arrangement by which certain vehicles were owned by LGOC but operated by the other companies also came to an end and all such vehicles were transferred to the ownership of London General Country Services Ltd on 7th April 1932. Those already with East Surrey comprised twenty-six NS, seventy-one ST, twelve ADC416, one AEC Reliance, fourteen T, one Tilling Stevens, eight Thornycroft, two Daimler, one AJS, three Commers and four Morris Commercials. National handed over thirty-one NSs, nineteen STs, thirteen S-type single-deckers, six Guys, fifty-three ADC416, two ADC427 and fourteen AEC Reliances, nine of which were officially designated 'c.a.b.' ('chars-a-bancs').

The head office of Green Line Coaches Ltd moved from 55 Broadway to Reigate in April 1932 and on 11th May ownership of sixteen LGCS coaches was transferred to Green Line, followed in mid-October by the transfer of all Green Line coaches owned by General. The formal association of Green Line with LGCS was further cemented when the bus company adopted a similar green cloth to that used by Green Line for its summer 1933 issue of uniforms to staff. Although this may have presaged the livery change which eventually took place, at this time LGCS buses were still painted red.

One of the aims of the Underground Group in establishing the new organisation was to confine the activities of the parent LGOC company within the Metropolitan Police District and to concentrate operations outside it in the hands of LGCS. To this end, some exchange of services had already been taking place but they did not always have an easy ride. The replacement in June 1930 of the

weekday operation of route 147 by East Surrey 31 has already been noted. A similar change was made on 8th October 1930, when General introduced major improvements to its 59 group increasing frequencies between Thornton Heath and Camden Town and to Chipstead Valley. Among the changes was the withdrawal of the 59 on Mondays to Fridays between Coulsdon and Reigate and its replacement by a new LGCS route 459 between West Croydon and Reigate. Both the 147 and 59 changes were a reflection of the diminishing role of these long rambling stage carriage routes from London into the country now that so many coach services were being operated. Autocar and East Surrey had started their Tunbridge Wells, Redhill and Reigate coach routes in June.

The first straight exchange of services took place on 1st April 1931 and embraced routes 70D (Morden – Dorking), 99C (Erith – Dartford via Crayford) and Saturday only route 199A (Erith – Dartford via Crayford and Dartford By-Pass). Crayford garage also changed hands and General transferred the Crayford runnings on double-deck route 99A (Woolwich – Erith) into Plumstead garage. Five T-class AEC Regal buses were transferred to East Surrey for the 99C and five open-top NS for the 70B, rather than the S-type which General had been running. A plan to link the 99C with the 401 to create a new through service from Erith to Eynsford withered on the vine.

The rest of the basic service on the 70 (route 70B between Morden and Epsom), routes 80 (Morden – Lower Kingswood via Sutton), 180 Morden – Walton-on-the-Hill) and Sunday-only 228 (Morden – Lower

Kingswood via Epsom and Tadworth) were to have been transferred on 31st May 1932 but this fell through and half-a-century was to pass before something comparable was to happen to parts of these routes, in entirely different circumstances.

The final group of exchanges, which took place on 1st March 1933, were partly caught up with an appeal against a Traffic Commissioner's decision. In February 1931, General had introduced new schedules on routes 81 and 503, doubling frequencies between Langley, Slough and Windsor which had the effect of increasing the Slough to Windsor service from three to six buses an hour. The South Eastern Area Traffic Commissioner later ruled that the combined service over this section was excessive and issued an instruction that fifty-seven Monday to Friday journeys, eighty-three on Saturdays and twenty-five on Sundays should be withdrawn. The LGOC appealed against this decision but were unsuccessful. The new schedules introduced on 1st March 1933 to give effect to the decision included the withdrawal of routes 117D and 507 between Windsor and Slough and the transfer to LGCS of the Langley to Windsor section of the 81, the whole of the 503 (Langley Village – Windsor), the Windsor – Staines section of 117 and the whole of the 507 (Uxbridge 'Eight Bells' – Slough). LGCS combined the 81, 117 and 503 into new route 417 (Langley – Staines via Windsor). Also transferred was the 162B, by now running only between Windsor and Leatherhead, the operation to Slough having been withdrawn under the Commissioner's edict on 19th February. The LGOC garage in Langley Road, Slough was closed.

UC2265 was an unusual ADC416A fitted with a Short Bros lightweight double-deck body. One of three experimental vehicles delivered to East Surrey in 1928/1929, it was later fitted with an AEC Reliance engine. The Reigate and Redhill section of local route 21 was the longest established of East Surrey's services, dating back to 1911. J.F. Higham

GN4725 (later ST 1043) at Reigate on the new route 459 to Croydon, which replaced the Monday to Friday route 59 south of Coulsdon on 8th October 1930. Roy Marshall

Route 503, operated by Thames Valley on behalf of the LGOC until January 1929, got its third operator in four years on 1st March 1933 when services in the Slough area were taken over by LGCS. GX5337 (LT 1427), one of the pair of Renowns supplied to LGCS in August 1932 is parked on the stand at Castle Hill. J.F. Higham

There was less scope for transfers in the other direction and it is likely that General would not have wished to be too bold in this respect, because they benefited financially from the lower pay rates of the Reigate based company. Nevertheless, in the absence of any foreseeable opportunity to go ahead with the planned extension to Sevenoaks, the anomaly of the 422 could hardly be allowed to stand and this was handed over to General, together with the nearby 411 (Sidcup – Farnborough via Orpington and Green Street Green) on 1st March 1933. Operational responsibility passed to Sidcup garage which allocated open top NSs to the 411 and STs to the 422. Curiously, less than five months later, on 31st May, General introduced a new route 610 between Eltham and Chislehurst also using STs from Sidcup garage, which was virtually identical to the 422, the only minor difference being the use of Southend Crescent instead of Foots Cray Road, in Eltham.

The rounding off of the LGOC area within the Metropolitan Police District was not completed before the extinction of the company in July 1933. The surviving extrusions were mainly in the south, the only notable example in the north being the 84 to St Albans, although operations around Romford and out to Ongar could theoretically have fallen into this category. Other routes in the south which could have qualified in all or in part were the 115 and 620 to Guildford, 79 to Woking, 61 to Staines via Chertsey, 171 to Chertsey via Walton and 81 to Slough and Windsor. More marginal examples were the 132 to Dartford, 21 to Farningham, 75 to Caterham, the 65 to Leatherhead and, in the north, routes 142 and 158 to Watford Junction. There were also some sizeable intrusions by LGCS into Croydon, Kingston, Barnet and Enfield but these were on long routes coming in from distant country areas and were therefore presumably sacrosanct.

An LGCS route which operated substantially within the Metropolitan Police District was the 415 from Farleigh to West Croydon. PE2422, a 1925 Short bodied NS, still carries the 'East Surrey' name cast on its radiator alongside the LGCS transfer on the cab front. J.B. Gent collection

The continuing expansion of East Surrey's operations put an untenable strain on garage space and maintenance facilities and there was a great deal of investment in new and enlarged premises in these years. In November 1930 the LGOC Board authorised the enlargement of Swanley garage to house an additional twenty-four vehicles, bringing its capacity up to forty-two, at an estimated cost of £4,845 (completed in the summer of 1931). Expansion of Dunton Green to house twenty more buses, increasing its capacity to forty, at a cost of £7,768 and the extension of Chelsham to house sixteen more (to a total of twenty-four) at a cost of £4,408 were authorised in April and May 1931 respectively. The LGOC also spent a further £1,668 at Chelsham, Leatherhead and Swanley, to raise their roofs to give clearance for covered top double-deckers. On its own account, East Surrey enlarged Godstone, to bring its capacity up from twenty-four to forty and East Grinstead (twelve to sixteen) both in the spring of 1931. Land was also purchased for a bus station at West Croydon and for a garage at Chertsey but neither materialised during the tenure of the company.

By far the most ambitious project, however, was the new garage and company offices in Lesbourne Road, Reigate built at a cost of £30,000. They occupied a 1.2 acre site incorporating Bell Rope Field, the old paint shop and a cottage known as Glover's Lodge. A condition of the sale of the lodge was that the aspect onto Churchfields should not spoil the amenities and this was therefore designed in half-timbered style with gables and a section of tiled roof to disguise the main garage roof. The structure itself was by contrast very modern, with parking space for 170 buses in an uninterrupted covered space spanned by lattice girders 250 feet in length. The new premises opened for business in January 1932, from which date the overhaul of all East Surrey, Green Line and Autocar vehicles was carried out at Reigate. The basis of a Country Bus department administrative unit for the new Board had been established.

Above left **The interior of the new Reigate garage where some fairly heavy repair work is in progress on an ST and an ADC. Also in the picture are: a Reliance coach, an ADC 'All-weather' coach, a Dennis E, an ADC bus, a Reliance bus and a pneumatic tyred S double-decker.**
Arthur Ingram

Left **The workshops at Reigate where work is concentrated on bringing up to scratch vehicles taken over from Skylark, Associated Coaches of Ongar and Bucks Expresses.**
Snook & Son; R.S. Turnbull collection

CHAPTER FOUR   FLEET RENEWAL BY GENERAL

Top **The typical NS at the beginning of 1930, with covered top, solid tyres, open driver's cab and no headlamps. NS 1116 was one of Nunhead's large allocation and is seen on 24th June 1930 on route 63A at the much photographed Peckham Rye 'King's Arms' stop.** Alan B. Cross: W. Noel Jackson collection

Above **XX8833 was one of 116 Dennis 4-ton double-deckers taken over by General from the London Public Omnibus Company in December 1929. It had originated with the Cornwall Motor Omnibus Co in April 1925 and carried an S&B forty-eight seat body.** W. Noel Jackson

For twenty years, the LGOC had followed a policy of vehicle standardisation using mostly models produced by the Associated Equipment Company Ltd (AEC), another of the companies owned by the Underground Electric Railways Group. The oldest double-deckers still in service on 1st January 1930 were 798 forty-seat K-type mostly built between 1919 and 1921 and 776 of the slightly younger and larger fifty-four seat S-type, built between 1921 and 1923. More than half of the double-deck fleet comprised 2,199 of the revolutionary NS-type, a development of the S which had been designed from the outset to use pneumatic tyres and to have a covered top deck. The ultra-conservative attitude of the Public Carriage Office had ensured that progress towards a covered top, pneumatic tyred fleet had been slow and at the beginning of 1930 there were still sixty-one NS open-toppers and 1,781 with solid tyres. The rest of the double-deck fleet included: 119 Dennis four-ton forty-eight seat open toppers, all but three of which had been taken over with the business of the London Public Omnibus Co Ltd in December 1929; twenty-eight Leyland LB forty-eight seat open-toppers and fourteen six wheel Guy FCX covered top sixty-two seaters, also former Public vehicles; and eleven three-axle LS-type on Associated Daimler 802 chassis, representing what was to prove a short-term trend towards longer, higher capacity vehicles. These ADCs, most of

which seated seventy passengers, had proved to be a stepping stone to the first of a new generation of buses which was already in service, the three-axle AEC 'Renown' (LT 1), which had recently been joined by its smaller two-axle 'Regent' contemporary, ST 1. Perhaps the strangest vehicles owned by General were 100 Tilling-Stevens TS7 petrol-electric forty-eight seaters dating from 1923-4, totally at odds with the rest of the fleet but a natural choice for Thomas Tilling, who operated them on behalf of General and who had standardised on petrol-electrics for many years.

General's single-deck fleet was much smaller, the company's policy always having been to favour the largest vehicle physically and economically suitable for each route, which most often meant a double-decker. There were 316 single-deckers of which ninety-five, the largest class, were K-type, dating variously from 1921 to 1927, the older ones being converted double-deckers and the newer ones, built after 1926, having pneumatic tyres. Another fifty were S-type, new in 1923, all of which had been fitted with pneumatic tyres in 1928. The second largest

chassis type was the Dennis, all of them acquired from Public. There were seventy-one 2½-ton (DS class) and E-types (DE class), with seating capacities varying from twenty to thirty. More modern single-deckers were represented by a solitary thirty-four seat LS and forty-four T-class AEC 'Regal 662' model thirty-seaters. Finally, there were twelve Tilling-Stevens TS7 thirty-seat Petrol Electrics identified, like their double-deck equivalents, as the 'O'-class, which were in the livery of Thomas Tilling Ltd and operated by them on behalf of the LGOC.

Top **The Tilling-Stevens petrol electric was the standard bus in the fleet of Thomas Tilling, including the 166 owned by the LGOC. One of these was O 39, a TS7 dating from 1923, seen here in Bayswater Road approaching Marble Arch on route 112C, one of many services operated jointly with General.** J.F. Higham

Above left **Twenty-two of Plumstead's allocation of twenty-six buses on route 48 were, like K 587, operated under the 'Metropolitan' name. All buses on this route were fitted with 'Sprag' gear as protection against running away on the steep Blackheath Hill.** W. Noel Jackson

Above right **The Combine's first Regent, later numbered ST 1139, in East Surrey livery on route 414. The Short Bros bodywork was similar in style to the standard Leyland product, including the stepped upper deck front and was the only one on a Regent chassis bought by General to have an open staircase. Note the glass louvres above the full-drop opening widows.** Alan B. Cross

Only 348 NSs had both covered tops and pneumatic tyres at the beginning of 1930. The projection of the rear wheel beyond the sides of the body took the overall width beyond the 7ft 2in limit which applied before 1st July 1928, which was why the authorities would not approve their introduction. Even then, they could not be operated along tram routes until the limit was increased by another two inches to 7ft 6in. NS 347 is seen at Clapham Common on route 89, one of many which would have been caught by the latter ban. Capital Transport collection

Also owned by the LGOC and used for Private Hire were ten Associated Daimler 416A model twenty-eight seat coaches, twenty-four AEC 419 type twenty-six seaters and twenty AEC 'Reliance 660' model thirty-two seaters.

Other LGOC associated vehicles were disguised as the fleet of the Tramways (MET) Omnibus Co Ltd, whose buses were to be found scattered around in eleven of General's garages. The company was a relic of the days when the Metropolitan Electric Tramways Co was independent of the Combine but by 1930 the bus subsidiary, whose shares were owned by MET and LGOC, was operating effectively as part of LGOC. Nevertheless, for the time being at any rate, its fleet was separately identified in the books and retained a unique fleetname, 'METROPOLITAN'. In January 1930 its fleet comprised 162 K-type, fifty-eight S-type and ninety-five NS (with an interesting mixture of open and covered-top and solid and pneumatic tyres).

Also by now part of the Combine, as it was largely owned by the Tramways (MET) company, was Overground Ltd at Potters Bar. By agreement with its former owner, W.J. Dangerfield, it operated as though an independent entity and owned its own vehicles but its operations were part of the LGOC network. Its fleet comprised twenty-five

Dennis 4-ton double-deckers and thirty-two Leyland LBs, all forty-eight seaters dating from 1923-1927 and many of them former Public vehicles.

That left two companies genuinely independent of LGOC in terms of ownership but operating under mileage and service agreements with the larger company. The smaller of these was the London business of the Tilling and British Automobile Traction Co Ltd, working from premises in Rochester Mews, Camden Town. It owned thirty-three NSs, all identical covered-top, solid tyred examples and all finished in its handsome olive green livery with 'BRITISH' as a fleet-name. The other was Thomas Tilling Ltd, whose London business had been operating as part of the London Omnibus Pool since 1909. In addition to the 112 vehicles owned by the LGOC, Tilling itself owned 166 TS3A and fifty-four TS7 Tilling-Stevens petrol-electric forty-eight seat double-deckers. Despite the presence of 'Tilling' in the titles of both companies, they were independent of each other and traded separately, although Thomas Tilling Ltd had a major financial stake in Tilling and BAT.

Outside the Metropolitan area, LGOC also supplied vehicles to the East Surrey Traction Company and to the National Omnibus and Transport Company. Double-deck East Surrey

vehicles owned by General comprised twenty-three K-type, thirty-two S, twenty open-top and one covered-top NS, one ADC416, one LS and one ST. The ST (which eventually received the number 1139 in the 1935 Country Bus numbering), was the first short wheelbase AEC Regent and had been purchased by LGOC at the end of December 1929. It had been in service with ESTC as a demonstrator since July 1929 (apart from a short spell in the mauve livery of Autocar in August) and was therefore the first of the new generation to go into service with the Combine. Unlike the subsequent members of the class built for LGOC, ST 1139 had an open staircase Short Bros body of a design which closely resembled the standard Leyland product of the time and, when new, was fitted with board indicators rather than blinds, at the front. Single-deckers consisted of eleven ADC416, one Reliance and two AEC 202s. East Surrey also owned buses on its own account but all the buses operated by National on behalf of General were owned by the London company. They comprised nineteen S-type and thirty-one open-top NS double-deckers, while the single-deck fleet was made up of thirteen S-type, four Lancia, thirty-nine ADC416, six Guy, three Dennis, one Morris and fourteen AEC Reliances. There were also nine ADC private hire coaches.

East Surrey's own fleet contained forty-two double-deckers: thirteen K, six S, ten NS, twelve PS and one Tilling-Stevens B10A2; and thirty-one single-deckers: two AEC202, fourteen ADC416A, five ADC416D and one each of Renault, Guy OND, GMC, Bean and Commer. There were ten private hire coaches: six ADC419, three ADC426, one GMC. The PS was a type unique to East Surrey, being an adaptation of the S based on the heavier AEC502 chassis with 45 horsepower engine to work the company's more heavily graded routes but with a body similar to the NS.

From the foregoing it will be apparent that little had happened to the fleet since 1927. For all that it had been a major advance, the NS was nevertheless somewhat backward by the time the last major batch was delivered in June 1928. Its inelegant appearance and primitive interior finishings dated very quickly compared with the bodywork supplied for the new Leyland Titan range from 1927 onwards. The Associated Daimler LS class, produced in 1927 and 1928 perpetuated the basic appearance of the NS and did little to enhance General's reputation for advanced design. It was the arrival of George Rackham at AEC which had transformed the situation. He had been responsible for the remarkably successful range of new Leyland models and it was a major coup on the part of Lord Ashfield to secure his services, once again demonstrating his unerring talent for choosing the right people. Rackham was given the brief to design a whole new range of models for the company which were to transform both the fortunes of the manufacturing company and the fleets of LGOC and its associates.

The last new double-deck model produced by the Associated Daimler company before Rackham launched the new generation of AEC models was the three axle 802, designed for bodies up to thirty feet long. The single wheels on the rear axles enabled it to be fitted with pneumatic tyres without infringing the width restrictions then in force. The outdated appearance of the bodywork, radiator and bonnet are only too apparent on Tottenham's LS 7 at Victoria station. After having been spread around three garages on routes 16, 29, 33 and 69, all eleven double-deck 'London Sixes' were bought together on route 29 for a few months in 1930, before going finally to Cricklewood for route 16 in the autumn. *D.A. Ruddom collection*

LS 6 was unique in being the only single-decker in this small class. Like the double-deckers it had an Associated Daimler 802 chassis and was 29ft 8¼ long but the rear-entrance body seated only thirty-four. It spent its entire life working on route 104 (later 240) and was a familiar sight standing alongside the canopied building at the western end of Golders Green bus station. *J.F. Higham*

LT 1 as originally turned out by Chiswick in the summer of 1929 combined a thoroughly modernised body styling with a new, brighter colour scheme which introduced a large area of cream above the lower deck waist. Its origins as an experimental body for a shortened LS can be seen most obviously in the flat front panels on the upper deck, with their rounded corners. The exceptional number of opening windows may have been a response to the significant minority of passengers who objected to the enclosure of the upper deck. For the first time the bonnet number was applied by means of a transfer, but this was not immediately adopted on subsequent vehicles. The LTs and STs were the last buses to be equipped with a seat for the vehicle examiner, which can be seen immediately above the nearside sidelamp.
LT Museum U5733

Below **Simplicity of design was allied to high standards of finish and luxurious seating, to give the interior of LT 1 an air of quality hitherto unseen on an LGOC bus. Features not repeated on later vehicles included the pinch-clips at each end of the opening windows, the protrusions on the window frames enclosing the glazing bars and elegant armrests on the longitudinal seats.**
LT Museum U5740

The first to appear in LGOC service was the AEC Renown. Although it had supplanted the LS as the 'high capacity bus', the length of the older model had been a stumbling block with the police and the version of the Renown chosen by General was the short wheelbase 663 variety. This was suitable for a twenty-seven foot long body, a foot longer than allowed on two-axle vehicles but short enough to make it acceptable to the Public Carriage Office for more extensive London service than they were prepared to allow for the twenty-nine foot LS. Indeed the LGOC had been toying with the idea of shortening the LS and it was a body intended for such an experiment that was carried by LT 1 (registered UU6611) when it entered service on 6th August 1929. After burning its fingers with an attempt at an enclosed staircase on LS 1, which it had been forced to rebuild, the LGOC took no risk this time and retained the standard London type open staircase. Also retained was the shape of the front of the body between the upper and lower decks, as found on NS and LS class vehicles, which was flat across most of the width with curved corner panels. Another conservative aspect of the design was the upper deck, which extended only a short distance over the cab roof, leaving the cab to project out from the main bodywork in time-honoured fashion. Nevertheless, there were innovations, the most important probably being that the driver's cab was enclosed with a glass windscreen. In May 1929, the LGOC had finally persuaded the police to allow a trial with one hundred vehicles and LT 1 was the first of these.

Other new design features included the introduction of internally illuminated roller destination blinds, a much tidier arrangement of windows in six equal length bays on each deck and only two windows, instead of four, across the front of the upper deck. The destination blinds comprised single boxes sufficient only to display route number and destination, one each below the front and rear upper deck windows, supplemented by a route number box just below the rearmost short window on the nearside. There were no fewer than twenty openable half-drop windows, which might have been a response to the sizeable minority of passengers who objected on health grounds to the enclosure of the upper deck. For the passenger, the biggest contrast was in the interior design and finish which brought a degree of style and comfort hitherto associated more with a luxury coach than a mere Stage Carriage bus. All seats were deeply sprung (or 'super-sprung' as General had it), covered in moquette, were wider and gave more legroom than on earlier models. The standard of comfort offered such an advance on the preceding generation that it is difficult to conceive of there having been a gap of only two or three years between the designs. The luxury of the appointments inspired a famous cartoon showing a passenger on the lower deck asking the conductor 'What have you got upstairs, beds?'.

The interior panelling below the windows was finished in grey 'scratchproof' Rexine and matching grey polished wood was used for the window frames. Ceiling panels were white and, the final touch of outright modernity, the light fittings were concealed beneath non-flammable translucent 'Acetaloid' panels in the curvature of the roof, which contemporary reports describe as giving a soft glow throughout the bus. Traditional bell ropes were replaced by bell pushes, two in the lower saloon but only one on the upper deck, placed at the head of the stairs so that the conductor could not give a starting signal without seeing the platform.

Externally, the appearance was enhanced by the neatness of the windows, which were radiused at the top, and those at the front carefully lined up with the cab and radiator. The side windows also had radiused corners on the opening halves of their frames. The upper deck roof and driver's cab canopies were elegantly curved in harmony with the similar curvature of the new radiator design which AEC had introduced with these models. The unity of this arrangement went some way to overcome the somewhat maladroit box-shaped design of the driver's cab. There was also a new colour scheme, although this was to prove short-lived. The familiar LGOC red was confined to the panels below the waist, while the areas around the windows and between the decks was painted cream.

The Renown 663 chassis had a wheelbase of 16ft 6ins and was powered by the new AEC six-cylinder petrol engine, with 100mm bore and 130mm stroke, giving a capacity of 6.1 litres and developing 95bhp at 2,500rpm. Transmission was through a single plate clutch and four-speed sliding mesh gearbox to a rear axle of the semi-floating type and steering was of the Marles cam and roller type. An electric starter was fitted as standard equipment for the first time, although there was also a starting handle for use in emergency. As delivered to Chiswick on 24th June 1929, LT 1 had no front wheel brakes, an outdated design feature carried on from the LS class. It almost certainly entered service in this condition but was soon fitted with front brakes bringing it into line with the triple-servo arrangement usual on this model, which was adopted as standard for the rest of the class.

LT 1 mingles with an interesting array of contemporary commercial and private vehicles when in experimental service on route 16A in Edgware Road.
LT Museum 21832

General's original intention had been to order two hundred Renowns and authority for this was given by the Board on 25th July 1929 but this was cancelled on 5th December. LT 1 had been built under this authority but was presumably transferred to a second requisition for fifty approved on 9th November. The rest of this order, LTs 2-50, differed in several respects from LT 1, since they had purpose-designed bodies. When the LPTB introduced its chassis and body coding system in 1934, this batch was classified 1/2LT2, LT 1 having been 1LT1. To simplify some of the descriptions, these codes will be used from now on but it should be borne in mind that they were applied retrospectively after the fleet had undergone a number of changes, which is why they will sometimes appear irrational.

Externally, the most significant difference was in the design of the front upper deck, which on LT 1 was flat with corners curving sharply into the side panelling, a feature which betrayed its origin as an LS body since this would have been necessary to accommodate the route and destination boards of that design. On production vehicles, the panel containing the blind box was flat but on each side the panels echoed the window plan by being angled slightly rearwards to meet the side walls virtually square. A new feature, which was to be a hallmark of Chiswick's bodywork for all three models, was the prominent deep wooden moulding which ran along the sides below the lower deck windows. The design of the lower deck side panelling was also changed so that the straight side panels were carried down to a point just below the fuel filler cap and then continued in a sharper convex curve. Whereas most of these styling changes gave these buses a more modern looking finish, the decision to abandon the radiused corners on the opening sections of the

window frame had the opposite effect. Finally, the bright experimental livery was abandoned in favour of a more conventional arrangement in which the upper deck panels were painted red below the windows. Internally, spaciousness was sacrificed so as to squeeze in sixty seats (thirty-two upstairs; twenty-eight down) of a more utilitarian, square design.

Two of the batch, LTs 35 and 41, were fitted with eight-cylinder overhead camshaft engines, of similar design to the six-cylinder units but with a bore of 87mm, so producing the same output. Five of these engines were purchased by LGOC, the others being fitted to a T and two STs, but they were not a success and were soon replaced by standard units.

The production Renowns had the revised front upper deck styling first introduced on ST 1, with the outer panels angled in line with the windows to meet the side panels square. The side panels above the skirt were flat, instead of curved and the skirt itself more curved than on LT 1. The new !ivery was also soon modified to the layout shown on LT 12 on which the upper deck panels are painted red.
A.B. Cross: W. Noel Jackson collection

Left **The LT2 body had different front end styling from LT 1, including a rounded cab which remained unscreened at first. The colour scheme also reverted to a more traditional arrangement with the panels between the decks painted red. LT 74 was one of thirty-six allocated to Loughton in September 1930 and is here at the southern extremity of route 138, Victoria bus station. By now, some attempt was being made to include intermediate points on blinds, resulting in this very cramped display.**
Alan B. Cross

Below **The interior of the upper deck of LT 40, looking towards the rear. The seats on the nearside are more closely spaced to squeeze in another row of two, the remaining sections of the windows are not radiused and there is a new style pull-down window opener, but the translucent light fittings are retained for this batch.**
LT Museum U6272

Next to be seen in public was the first of an order for fifty of the single-deck model AEC Regal, numbered T 1-50 (1T1), the first of which entered service in December 1929. The wheelbase of seventeen feet made it suitable for bodies of either the twenty-six feet overall length required by the Public Carriage Office or the full twenty-seven feet allowed outside London. With one exception, the mechanical specification of the two-axle chassis followed the pattern of the Renown. The exception was T 43, which had one of the eight-cylinder engines as fitted to LTs 35 and 41. Because of the longer engine, the radiator had to be moved forward six inches, creating a slight 'snout' but this was compensated by reducing the body length at the rear by the same amount, causing one seat to be lost in the process.

The basic outline of the Chiswick-built bodywork had been foreshadowed on fourteen bodies mounted on AEC Reliance chassis supplied to the National Omnibus and Transport Co in June 1929 to replace S-type single-deckers operating on bus services in the Watford area. It bore a strong family resemblance to LT 1, with which it shared the same simplicity and elegance of design. In accordance with police requirements, the five bay, thirty-seat, bodywork had a rear open platform but the Ts were included in the 100 to which glass driver's windscreens were fitted experimentally. Unlike the double-decker, the canopy on the Ts did not curve downwards but was built straight to accommodate the centrally placed single aperture destination indicator box, which was wider than on the double-deckers and occupied about half its width. There was no rear box but a route number stencil was carried in the rear-facing window at the front of the platform.

In the event, only forty-nine entered service immediately because one of the chassis had been diverted for another purpose. The sudden development of suburban coach services had given rise to the need for a suitable vehicle with the ability to maintain high average speeds and offer a good standard of comfort to passengers. When T 38 appeared in March 1930, it was carrying a modified body with a hinged door across its rear entrance and only twenty-eight deeply cushioned and well spaced seats. The saloon floor was built higher than on the buses so that all seats could face forward without any being fouled by a wheel arch. Inside the rear entrance there were two steps leading to the saloon and, to meet Construction and Use Regulations, there was an emergency exit door in the rear bulkhead. Because of the higher floor level, the windows were set higher, noticeably increasing the depth of the side panels and giving the completed vehicle a much taller look than the buses. T 38 retained the six bay layout of the buses but used a different type of pillar which enabled a more rounded appearance to be given to the whole design, notably by means of a deeper curve to the skirt panel. There was also a more rounded canopy incorporating a narrow single-line destination indicator box, and a rounded cab, the first appearance of the design which was later to become standard on the main run of deliveries of all three new types. This vehicle did not appear until 25th March 1930 when it was allocated to Brixton (Waterworks Road) prior to its despatch to Watford (Leavesden Road) on 1st April to work on the Watford – Golders Green coach route. It was later classified 7T7. The fiftieth bus eventually appeared in July 1930, numbered T 156.

Facing page The front of the roof on the Regals differed from the double-deckers in being straight, to maintain harmony with the inset indicator box. They also had a modified version of the livery pioneered on LT 1, with cream around the windows and along the deep moulding below them and red on the main body panels.
LT Museum U6507

Above The basic design for the first Ts followed the principles established on LT 1 and the rear dome was similar to the rear end of ST 1. On two-man operated single-deckers the Metropolitan Police required open rear entrances, hence the arrangement on T 41 posed at Chiswick before delivery to Nunhead for service on route 621. Seats at the rear of the saloon were longitudinal, which is why the rearmost windows were fixed.
LT Museum U6059

Left The original translucent lighting panels fitted to the 1T1s were later replaced by the standard type of screw-in bulb assembly, as shown in this view of the interior of T 29 taken some years after it first entered service when otherwise the vehicle looked much as it did when new. The layout of the rear platform is of special interest, particularly the exposed position of the longitudinal seats facing the open entrance. LT Museum U23949

The trio of new models was completed by the announcement of the ST class in February 1930, although the prototype AEC Regent (ST 1139) had been in service with East Surrey and Autocar since July 1929 and the first LGOC vehicle also pre-dated the Regals, having been in existence for four months. This two-axle double-decker was based on the AEC Regent 661 chassis, with the same basic mechanical specification as the Renowns and Regals. The bodywork continued the high standard first introduced with LT 1 but went an important step further by incorporating an enclosed staircase. In deference no doubt to the obsession of the police with speed of boarding in London's congested streets, there was a capacious platform running the full width of the rear of the lower deck and the length of the passenger doorway. The staircase was designed in one straight flight rising from the front of the platform to a point about a quarter of the way along the upper deck. This layout was rather profligate of space but, given the restrictions imposed on axle and overall weight by Statutory Regulations, the carrying capacity was limited anyway, so this was a good selling point in enlisting the goodwill of the police in approving the design. The usual objection to the enclosure of the staircase was that in an accident in which the bus turned over onto its nearside, upper deck passengers would be trapped. This was overcome by incorporating a window in the rear upper deck bulkhead which was hinged to open fully in an emergency when a prominently placed plunger was operated.

Above **The rear nearside of ST 1 as originally built, with a wider rear wall containing two windows and narrower cut out for the rear platform than was acceptable under later regulations.** LT Museum

Left **The full-width platform introduced with the ST class was designed for rapid boarding and alighting, with an ample space for the conductor to retreat into the corner. The sliding window through which the conductor gave hand signals, and the flat section grab handle, covered in Rexine, around the platform and up the stairs, were also new.** LT Museum

Apart from ST 1, the ST abandoned the concealed lighting introduced on LT 1 but the tungsten lamps had glass covers, also later abandoned. The new type of pull-down window opener introduced to replace the pinch type tried on LT 1 was adopted as standard throughout 1930 and 1931. LT Museum U7231

As delivered ST 1 (UU6614) had seats for fifty passengers, of which thirty were upstairs all facing forward. Sixteen were in four double rows of two, each side of a central gangway between the stairs and the front bulkhead but the unique design of the staircase imposed an unusual arrangement further back. There were three seats for three on the nearside separated from the long stairwell by a gangway; and there was a bench seat for five across the back. Twenty could be seated downstairs, sixteen in four forward facing rows of doubles and four on a longitudinal bench facing the staircase wall on the nearside. Before it entered service, the foremost of the triple seats upstairs was replaced by a double, to improve circulation around the top of the stairs. The interior finishings were much the same as on LT 1 but the ST was also equipped with a staircase mirror so that the conductor could see the upper deck from the platform and another was sited on the staircase wall in the lower deck. This was to prove a hazard, according to LGOC officials, who claimed after some service experience that it had 'unlooked for results', one problem being that 'women in particular' were tempted to admire themselves and miss their footing, or so it was said.

General also made the curious statement that they were apt to confuse passengers as they were absent from other types, an assertion which could be used to avoid any innovation! Whatever the real problems, they were soon removed.

ST 1 was given an experimental licence on 31st October 1929 but it was not immediately cleared for service by the Police. Apart from being shown to the press at the beginning of February, it spent most of the next four months in the hands of the engineers, shuttling between Chiswick and Southall, on trial before it went into service on route 184 (London Bridge – Southall) at Hanwell (HW) in March 1930. The main reason for the delay may have been that it took time to convince the ever cautious Metropolitan Police of the safety and practicability of the enclosed staircase design. Perhaps another reason was that the LGOC appear to have cheated by fitting ST 1 with a glazed windscreen, which meant that the number authorised by the Public Carriage Office had been exceeded by one.

Meanwhile, LT 1 had gone into service at Cricklewood garage on 6th August 1929 and worked from there on route 16A, running alongside covered top NSs and a couple of LSs. In November, it went for a while to Plumstead where it worked on route 53 but it was back on route 16A by early January 1930. In January 1930, the first of the production run went into service at Cricklewood but this time on routes 121C/D and 526D by which time the pioneer had already been transferred to the 121. Others went to Nunhead to complete the

121 group and provide part of the stock on the 37 and to Hanwell for part of its allocation on the 218 and to complete the 526D. Deliveries were completed in February. In all cases the vehicles replaced were covered top NSs, which went elsewhere to displace S or K-type in the usual merry-go-round of re-allocations, which ultimately led to the withdrawal of elderly Ks. Not all changes moved in this seemingly orderly pursuit of gradual modernisation, however. In this programme, there was one example from many where the reverse was true: while route 218 was receiving shiny new Regents, its companion route 18E, worked by Willesden garage, lost its covered top NSs in favour of elderly open-top S-type. In other cases, this was sometimes tied to summer pleasure traffic, such as route 37, which frequently seems to have reverted to open-top from covered-top types.

January 1930 also saw the completion of delivery of the first forty-nine Regals. The first ten had gone to Romford (RD) in December 1929 for routes G1, G5 and 187, as part of a major restocking at that garage which also included ST double-deckers. The rest went to Cricklewood for route 104, Crayford (99C), Nunhead (621), Holloway (110) and Sutton (113). Except in the case of the 113, where single-deck S-types were displaced, all vehicles withdrawn were K-type single-deckers. An early addition to this list was Cricklewood, which took three, one each from Holloway, Nunhead and Sutton, to operate on the newly localised route 121E in competition with Birch Bros route 214.

Five new ST1/1s and about ten overhauled NSs line up at Chiswick awaiting delivery to their garages. The leader is ST 218, a typical example of the first production batch as originally built, without a glazed windscreen and with the new design of rounded cab front. Lens of Sutton

Despite the delay in getting ST 1 into service, General was sufficiently confident in the design to have placed an order for three hundred with Chiswick-built bodywork at the same time as they had ordered the fifty Renowns (STs 2-301 classified 1/1ST1/1). As LGOC had used up its allowance for fitting experimental glass windscreens and the Police were still unwilling to grant approval for their general use, these otherwise very modern vehicles took to the road with an open driver's cab. This prompted a change in the design of the cab front, which was curved in plan with two struts to support the canopy, presumably better to suit the open arrangement. An apron was provided for the driver to pull over the steering wheel in the event of rain and there was a metal valance projecting down from the canopy to give further protection to his face. Internally, this first production batch aban-

doned the translucent lighting panels in favour of individual lamps with moulded glass covers. The upper deck seating arrangement also followed that finally adopted on ST 1.

ST 1 and the first fourteen of the production batch, started their revenue earning careers on the 184 group from Hanwell garage on 28th February 1930 where they were joined by a further five on 1st March. The rest of the first hundred also went to Hanwell, seventy-two of them for the 184 (which needed 106 buses altogether, shared with Hammersmith) and the last nineteen to routes 218 (which they shared with the LTs delivered earlier) and 291. Hammersmith (R) took the next 105, again for the ravenous 184 group and then for routes 11E and 25A but these did not need so many buses and what actually happened was that twenty-three of those initially sent to Hammersmith were re-allocated shortly after-

wards to Shepherd's Bush for its share of the 11E. This allocation lasted only until November, when Shepherd's Bush exchanged its STs for covered top NSs from Hammersmith, where they had in turn replaced STs in September. The September changes were wrapped up with two things: the delivery of most of the remaining STs of the first three hundred to Seven Kings; and moves connected with the delivery of the next batch of LTs (of which more later), which gave rise to a need for additional STs at Cricklewood (121C) and Hanwell (218). Seven Kings took seventy-seven new Regents but needed ninety-three (plus spares) for routes 25, 26, 126 and 148 and therefore scavenged the rest from Hammersmith. Manœuvres of a similar kind were to occur throughout the period under review but full details of each are beyond the scope of this book.

There was one other new type of bus bought by LGOC at this time but it was not one of the AEC family. At the same time as the Regals had been authorised, the General Board had decided to order twenty twenty-seaters for one man operation of thinly trafficked outer suburban routes or for use where weight or size restrictions prevented the use of larger vehicles. They took a long time to come and when they did arrive, they were eighteen seaters. They were based on a normal control model newly introduced by Dennis Bros of Guildford, known as the 'Dart', which had a six-cylinder petrol engine capable of developing 60bhp through a single plate clutch and four-speed gearbox. Four-wheel vacuum brakes of the single servo type were fitted.

There were two distinct types but all had a miniaturised version of current Chiswick body designs, seating eighteen in two inward facing longitudinal seats and incorporating a centrally placed rear emergency door. The complete vehicle had an overall length of just under 20ft 11ins and an overall width of 7ft 2ins. Despite its compactness, like many vehicles of this type, it needed plenty of room to turn and had a turning circle of sixty feet, the same as a Regal and slightly greater than a Renown double-decker. On the earlier vehicles, the windscreen and side quarter glasses were carried right down to the top of the

rather flat topped bonnet, giving the front end a rather old-fashioned and ungainly look. This was given further emphasis by the original design of radiator shell which was straight sided and squatter than the final version. On the remainder the bottom edge of the windscreen was lifted to the same level as the side windows and a curved panel linked this neatly with a more 'shaped' bonnet. These also had the new, longer, more stylish radiator introduced by Dennis at this time, gently curved at top and bottom and with tapered sides.

The first Dart was licensed on 7th April 1930 and delivery of the first twenty (DAs 1-20) was spread over the next eight months, by which time a further twelve (DAs 21-32) had been ordered. DA 1 was allocated at first to Hounslow garage, probably for staff training as there were no candidates for small bus operation there at the time. By the beginning of June six Darts were in stock and four of them, including DA 1, were sent to Hanwell, the parent garage of Uxbridge, where they were to work. On 25th June they replaced K-type single-deckers on routes 505, a local route to Richings Park and 506, a longer route to Cowley, Wraysbury and Staines. These were joined by new route 507 to Slough and Windsor via George Green on 3rd September, just the sort of development route for which the class was so well suited but for which at this stage it was little used.

Another conversion from K-type took place in October when Slough garage got four to work the 162B and other similar exchanges took place in November at Sidcup (195) and Harrow Weald (replacing S-type on 353). Harrow Weald also got one on 8th November for another development route, the 210A and Romford two for the new G3 in the Romford area changes on 3rd December. The second order of Darts was used more for developing new services, the first being the 105 at Hounslow in June 1931, which eventually needed five. Two were sent to Mortlake on 31st August to operate route 207 between Barnes and Richmond Park Golf Club, an oddity taken over from H.A. Turner who had operated a Bean. Three others were allocated to Hendon for the 226 which started on 30th December 1931.

Chiswick bodywork for the Darts was in the same design mould as its larger contemporaries, which gave the complete vehicle a neat and workmanlike appearance but the match between the very low bonnet and high body was not entirely successful. DA 6 was one of six which replaced larger K-type single deckers on route 506, as well as the 505, in June 1930. N. Hamshere

Tilling 6017 (ST 841) in its original condition with route number stencils and board destination and route indicators, on route 36 at Marble Arch. The all red livery is relieved by two white bands and the prominent fleetname is in a new style using block lettering rather than script but the old fashioned indicators, high skirt, heavily domed roof and open staircase give it the look of a much older model, despite the undoubted modernity of the chassis. ACV Sales Ltd

In the meantime General's associate, Tilling, had been looking at the Regent as a possible candidate for its own fleet renewal and had tried out a Short Bros bodied covered top fifty-one seater (UU9161) on route 36 in the summer of 1929, alongside two Tilling-Stevens TS17A Petrol-electrics. This led to Tilling's historic decision to abandon the petrol-electric and to order 136 Regents, of which 124 were intended for London and twelve for Brighton. A further order for sixty-two Regents was placed in October 1930, along with one for twelve Regals, convincingly confirming Tilling's new allegiance to the AEC marque.

Compared with General's forward looking ideas, the new Tilling model was very much in the traditional mould, with bodywork closely following the authorised London layout, with open staircase. They seated two more than the LGOC version, twenty-five downstairs and twenty-seven on top. The lower deck had the usual arrangement of longitudinal seats over the rear wheel arches, with four rows of forward facing two-seaters and a single seat at the front facing inward to give good clearance around the protrusion of the gearbox. Upstairs, all seats faced forward.

The interior finish also differed markedly as facings were in polished mahogony, coated with cellulose as a protection against wear. The seats were covered in moquette of a registered Tilling design, edged in leather and the side panels and seat backs were given a covering of repp. Lamps were covered with specially designed fittings and the grab rails were in black and silver. Ventilation was provided by half-drop windows (two each side downstairs; three each side up) and by a patented system supplied by Ash and Co. which was claimed to give a complete change of air every four minutes.

Externally, the appearance of the vehicles was somewhat antique and spartan. The heavily domed roof and comparatively shallow windows gave to the whole a tall and narrow look, this being given a further twist by the use of three windows at the front of the upper deck and a deeper and much heavier looking canopy than on the General version. The skirt panels were also rather high off the ground, revealing the fuel tank and requiring a double lifeguard more reminiscent of buses from the earlier twenties than a modern double-decker. At first a full set of destination equipment using traditional boards was fitted but this was later altered to incorporate two small roller blinds for destination and an exceedingly small number, surmounting a board carrying intermediate points. The bodywork was built by Tillings at their Lewisham and Camberwell factories and by Christopher Dodson.

This rear view of Tilling 6016 (ST 840) on route 78A at the 'Grove Hotel' stand Dulwich, shows the revised arrangement of route number and destination using roller blinds which was introduced soon after the first Regents had gone into service. The arrangement at the front was identical. The rear bumper bar array was later removed.
Charles F. Klapper Collection: Omnibus Society

Tilling introduced a new fleet number series for the Regents, starting at 6001 and using matching registration numbers. The first twelve went to Brighton, so the first to go into service in London was 6013 which later was to become ST 837. It started work at Bromley garage on 27th June 1930 on route 36 to which the first thirty-three were allocated. Route 47 came next, after which the Catford runnings on the 36 were converted but the obvious course of next putting some onto the 136 was not possible as the route was not approved for covered top, because of overhanging trees and protruding lamp standards in roads like Baring Road and Burnt Ash Lane. It was left to the petrol-electrics for the time being and route 12 was given Regents instead. The next was the 146A, which had been an LGOC route but was transferred to Tilling operation on 5th November 1930 in an exchange of mileage with the 47 and therefore had the distinction of being the only route to be converted from S-type to Tilling ST.

Croydon began to get new Regents for route 59A at the beginning of July, with later deliveries in August and September going onto the 12A. Another constituent of the 12 group followed when Catford started running them on the 112A and 112E and with the completion of the 12A from Croydon in June 1931, all 139 buses on the 12 group of routes, provided by six garages and two companies, were either Regents or Renowns.

The arrival of the Regents enabled Tilling to clear out all its remaining normal control petrol-electrics, comprising twenty-two TS3s, including five former Cambrian Landray vehicles, and 166 TS3As.

Back at 55 Broadway, the LGOC had been looking to the needs of its newly burgeoning coach services. At its 11th February Board meeting, the purchase was authorised of what were described as one hundred 'bus coaches', which materialised as AEC Regals, numbered T 51-149 and 155, with bodies of a different and improved design compared with T 38. There were seven bays instead of six, the front one being shorter and the rearmost on the nearside longer than the others. London regulations limited their length to 26ft, which reduced the rear overhang so that there was not enough room for a sliding door; instead the rear entrance had a recessed swing door and the emergency exit, instead of being at the rear, was placed in the front offside bay. This arrangement reduced the seating capacity to twenty-seven. Chiswick built fifty bodies, the others being shared equally between Hall Lewis & Co of Park Royal and Short Bros of Rochester, all in the standard LGOC colours of red, white and black. A repeat order for fifty of the same design (Ts 157-206) was placed in October, these being shared between Hall Lewis and Shorts.

T 155 (GF525) was actually the first of the batch but was delivered without a number and

was allocated to the Private Hire fleet until April 1930, when it was given its number and became one of eleven sent to Slough for the new Windsor service which started on the 20th of that month. These were followed by a further eleven in May and June. Another eleven went to Watford in May, where they replaced the former Private Hire Reliances and the last five to carry the 'General' fleet name went to Staines for the Sunningdale service in July. Seventeen of those licensed in June had the 'East Surrey' fleet name and went to Reigate and Leatherhead for the Redhill, Reigate and Dorking services, while another nine carried the 'Autocar' insignia and went to Tunbridge Wells. From July onwards the coaches began to appear with the 'Green Line' name and subsequent deliveries went in this form to start new services from Romford, Guildford, Watford, Hitchin, Reigate (second batch), Harpenden, Bishop's Stortford, Staines, Addlestone and Romford (second batch) garages.

The first batch of Regal coaches had two-step rear entrances with a folding door across the top step. The deep cushions on the passenger seats can be seen on the seat visible through the open doorway. The first to be licensed was T 155 which, in common with the rest, was finished in the red and black livery of the LGOC, including lining out of side and rear panels, and had its intended route signwritten on the louvres above the saloon windows. LT Museum U6407

T 117 as later modified, with an additional aperture inserted above the destination blind to display 'GREEN LINE' and an external rear view mirror. In this photograph taken outside the newly built garage at Dorking, it is also painted in the green and black livery of Green Line Coaches Ltd and has been fitted with side route boards.
Arthur Ingram

UC2204 is one of the ADC416As which were transferred to National in 1930 after being given new bus bodies similar in many respects to the bus Regals. It is seen at Borehamwood on route 304 after formation of LGCS. D.W.K. Jones

The LGOC, East Surrey and Autocar vehicles were transferred to Green Line from October 1930 but just as this programme was being completed in January 1931, seven were transferred to and repainted in the colours of Amersham & District (T 69, 71, 89, 96, 104) for the new Amersham service. The rest were repainted into the new coach livery of green and black.

The five missing numbers (Ts 150-154) were a batch of coaches, also on AEC Regal 662 chassis but built to the full nationally permitted length of 27ft as they were intended for Private Hire. The bodywork was supplied by the Weybridge firm of Hoyals and was very similar to that fitted to the ADC coaches and to Reliances R 6-25, modified to suit the different chassis. It was therefore quite different in appearance from the Green Line Regals. The thirty-two seat all-weather bodies had four long bays flanked by two shorter ones of unequal length at the rear and one short one at the front. The arrangement at the back was dictated by the presence of a passenger door in the larger section on the nearside, while the front bay contained the emergency exit door on the offside and a passenger door on the nearside. The long windows combined with a shallower roof profile to give an impression of greater length. The cab was also square, but had a slight inward slope in plan which gave it a less severe look than the earlier LGOC model. The completed vehicles were allocated to Brixton garage and were transferred, with the rest of the Private Hire fleet, to Green Line in 1931.

Immediately before the delivery of the five Regals, the LGOC had obtained five brand new AEC Reliance coaches also for the Private Hire fleet. This anachronistic order was associated with a programme of rebodying and standardisation which was then going on in the coach fleet. The new chassis were fitted with coach bodies removed from older ADC416A chassis which were in turn given new bus bodies and transferred to National. Another five 416As had their bodies exchanged with newer bus Reliances and also went to National. Finally, the thirty-three 1927 AEC 419s (AW 9-41) were supplied with new Short Bros bodies, similar to those on the Reliances and the five previously operated by National were transferred to the LGOC in exchange for five more Reliances. The process was completed in January and February 1931 when another four 416A coach bodies were switched with Reliance bus bodies, giving National a coach fleet of nine Reliances and fifty-three ADC416A buses.

At its April 1930 Board meeting, the LGOC had given authority for work to proceed on a further batch of one hundred Renowns (LTs 51-150) and another two hundred STs (nominally 302-501 but in practice the batches overlapped each other). Orders were placed with Short Bros of Rochester and Strachan for each to supply fifty ST bodies, otherwise the bodywork was to be supplied by Chiswick. The LTs began to arrive during August and were in most respects identical to the production batch already in service. The important difference was that, like the STs, they had no windscreens and were fitted with the rounded cab front. The first two went to the south-east London garage at Plumstead, where they were joined over the next couple of months by another thirty-seven for operation on the cross-London trunk routes 48, 53A and 153 and local route 99C. The balance of Plumstead's requirements was filled by second-hand vehicles from the LT 2-50 batch transferred from Cricklewood and Hanwell where they were replaced by STs.

Loughton followed in September and its allotment of thirty-six, for the 100 group and route 138, made it the first all LT garage. The remaining twenty-five, whose delivery was completed in October, went to Leyton for the 138's companion route 38, which they shared with covered top NSs as a temporary measure until more LTs became available. In other cases where different garages shared the operation of a route, mixed operation was likely to continue for a long time, as was the case on route 53A where Old Kent Road operated S-type open-toppers, later replaced by covered top NSs. This was because the LGOC's policy was to unify vehicle types in garages rather than on routes so that the full benefit of standardisation could be realised as quickly as possible.

More or less simultaneously with the arrival of its Renowns, Leyton began to receive a batch of STs, with which it restocked routes 10 and 35, although the 10 lost them again a couple of months later when they were transferred to join new deliveries in completing the modernisation of the 38. The remainder of this second order went to Norwood, Chalk Farm and Elmers End for the 68 group of routes (including the 168 and 169), to Nunhead for these and the 82B, to Forest Gate and Seven Kings for routes 125 and 186, to Romford for the 66 and Harrow Weald for the 183B. In all cases the buses replaced were NSs, which were redeployed to allow Ks to be withdrawn.

The first Short and Strachan bodied vehicles began to run in November 1930 and their delivery, which continued until March 1931, overlapped with those from a further batch of three hundred (nominally STs 518-817 and eventually classified ST2) which had been authorised in August. (The missing nineteen numbers were allocated to a batch intended for National and are covered later in the chapter.) Although similar in appearance to the ST1s, these buses were the first to be affected by new regulations requiring an increased cutaway between the rear platform wall and the nearside, to allow space for passengers to escape should a bus overturn onto its nearside. As the rear window was now narrower, the split design of the ST1s was replaced by a single-piece frame. Although this design change was not required on older vehi-

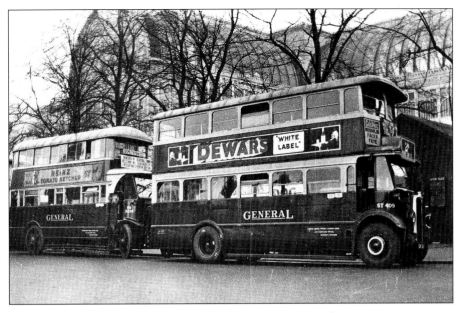

Only ten bodies were built of the ST2/1 type with indicators set into the cab roof and only one went into service immediately. When new in November 1930 ST 409 had a standard body and was allocated to Leyton garage but by the time this photograph was taken it had been fitted with an ST2/1 body, to which the route board has been added, and transferred to Hendon. The southern terminus of Saturday route 2B was in the shadow of Paxton's elegant Crystal Palace which provides a delightful period backdrop for the ST and 'clerestory' NS 2236 on route 108B, which reached this point from 3rd September 1930. The Omnibus Society

cles, the earlier STs were all eventually rebuilt to this modified design. Internally, there was an additional forward facing double seat on the nearside downstairs and a shorter longitudinal seat for only two behind it. The seat design was also new, with a rounded back giving a softer and perhaps more luxurious appearance. Otherwise the original design of the ST2 was identical to the first five hundred vehicles.

Ten bodies built under this order had a further design modification in which the destination indicator was carried in a box set into the cab roof, an arrangement which was to be more common on the LT class. On these buses, which were later classified ST2/1, the panel below the front upper deck windows was left blank at first (perhaps with the intention of using the space for advertising?) but was soon to be used for an additional display, as will be seen later. They were built at the end of the construction run in September 1931, as part of the float of fifteen bodies and, apart from one, did not appear until chance brought them out during the overhaul programme. The exception was the last, which was one of two experimental bodies on which the staircase was moved back to the side of the platform, increasing the capacity to fifty-one. The first to be built had been a modified ST2 which appeared on ST 538 in December 1931, the same month that ST 550 emerged from overhaul carrying the modified ST2/1 body; these were classified ST6 and ST6/1 respectively.

A visit to the Public Carriage Office was a regular event in the life of any London bus and this was a typical line-up, comprising an NS, two STs (ST 470 leading), an S and one of Reliance's new Dennis Lances. Charles F. Klapper collection: Omnibus Society

The second production batch of LTs had the new rounded lower deck front and reverted to an unprotected open cab, in the absence of approval for the general use of glass windscreens. In this close-up of LT 115, the apron for use in wet weather can be seen rolled up (rather untidily) on top of the cab front and the protective valance is prominent below the canopy. The unusual double garage plate displaying 'CHISWICK' indicates that the bus was temporarily assigned to the Training School when this photograph was taken in 1930.
LT Museum U8032

Strachan and Short Bros again shared the body contract with Chiswick, supplying twenty-five and seventeen respectively. The chassis were of an improved specification which had been introduced by AEC in the autumn of 1930, with a new D124 gearbox incorporating a constant-mesh third gear and worm and nut steering instead of the Marles type. The improved steering may already have been included on STs 302-501 and LTs 51-150 but in any case, during 1931, it was fitted retrospectively to all earlier vehicles (including the Regals), together with the other specification improvements.

One hundred and sixty-two of this batch were formally owned by the Tramways (MET) Omnibus Co and carried the fleetname METROPOLITAN. By a new agreement ratified in May 1931, these were licensed to the LGOC although remaining in Metropolitan ownership. The first went into service in December 1930, on route 30 at Leyton garage. The 30 was an established Metropolitan route but there was now some exchange of mileage which added routes 35 and 106 to the Metropolitan portfolio at Leyton, for which further STs were allocated. Some of the Regents displaced from the 35 went back to the 10 once again and onto Leyton's allocation for the 40, 100, 148 and 604. Later MET deliveries went to Willesden (route 8) and to a new garage for this company, Middle Row, where the 7 group (including the 166) and the 118 had also become MET routes. In passing it is worth noting that the routes which lost their MET buses were the 54, 179 and 494 (Elmers End), 69/369 (Camberwell), 90 (Hounslow) and 93E (Sutton). The MET vehicles replaced were mainly K type but four S type also went.

The Board minutes of the Tramways (MET) company show that the purchase of two further batches of STs was authorised: on 1st October 1931 for seventy-nine second-hand from General to replace a like number of S-type; and on 7th July 1932 for eighteen, again second-hand, to replace 'Dennises'. By this time, however, the company owned no S-types, had never operated Dennises (although this was probably a mishearing of 'NSs' by the meeting secretary) and there is no record of any of these additional STs appearing in MET livery. What is more, the number of buses carrying the company's fleetname had been in decline since 30th July 1931, when the remaining fifty-four Ss had run for the last time, after which overhauled buses appeared with the GENERAL fleetname until the last NS ran on 20th July 1932. It can only be assumed that the ninety-seven STs were officially owned by the company, although this does not show in the Chiswick stock record books.

This rear view of ST 768 illustrates the emergency escape arrangements, notably the wider platform cutaway, required by new Regulations, introduced with the ST2 body and the single platform window associated with it. Also illustrated, in the open position, is the emergency window first introduced on the CC and ST bodies.
LT Museum U8543

Five other vehicles from this order also appeared in the livery of an associated company, Overground Ltd, who ran them on route 285 from February 1931. STs 822-826 were part of a batch of fifteen (822-836) which are said to have been ordered for the Potters Bar company. However, the minutes of the Overground Board show that these buses were hired from LGOC at a rental of £20 a month, to cover deficiencies in its ageing Leyland fleet and this is consistent with their return to General. ST 824 was returned for repainting on 26th February and went into LGOC service in March, and the remainder went for repainting on 26th October for service in November 1931. Two others from this batch (833/834) were allocated to East Surrey and will be dealt with later, along with the nineteen vehicles which went to National and the vehicles bought on behalf of those companies.

The rest of the STs in General livery went into service between March and July 1931 at Norwood and Hendon (2 group), Turnham Green (route 55), Kingston (65) and Hammersmith (25A and 52). Among the last to go into service (in May 1931 at Norwood) was ST 2 which had been in use as a training vehicle, originally carrying a K type body. The last LGOC ST into service was ST 777 at Hendon but this was far from the end of the story, as the class was constantly redeployed to different garages and routes in subsequent years.

The withdrawal of K type double-deckers continued until the end of May by which time only the fifteen needed at Hounslow to work route 90 were still kept in service. It was now the turn of the S class, which had already started to disappear in February but only on route 2 were they replaced directly by STs; in all other cases NSs were displaced and redeployed.

Although most STs were in all essentials identical, there were some non-standard vehicles among them. ST 211, which first saw service at Leyton in October 1930, had the only metal-framed body on an ST and the only one supplied by Metro-Cammell. Although easily distinguishable from its peers by its smoother looks and a differently shaped roof, it was built to the same basic design as the Chiswick product. It was in effect the prototype for a batch of similar bodies on Dennis chassis, which was to be supplied later for Overground.

The Tramways (MET) Company's Regents were camera shy but ST 830 was caught at Liverpool Street when working from Middle Row on route 7. George Robbins collection

Centre **Like NS 1485 seen on the stand at Old Ford 'Lady Franklin', most of the Tramways (MET) Company's NSs had covered tops and solid tyres. The fleetname began to disappear in July 1931 and had gone altogether within a year.**
Malcolm E. Papes collection

Right **Overground ST 529 and one of the Dennis Lances, parked alongside the garden in front of Potters Bar garage, demonstrate the change of livery which took place in about 1932. The Regent has the later version which was all red, including the roof, with white only around the window frames, while the earlier version on the Lance has a similar division between the colours as was practised by the LGOC, complete with a silver roof.** D.W.K. Jones

STs 462, 464 and 466 were London's first oil-engined buses when they went into service on route 183 from Harrow Weald garage in December 1930 as part of an experiment which was also to include three coach Regals and nine LTs in the following year. They were fitted with the newly introduced experimental AEC-Acro A155 engine which was a six-cylinder unit having a capacity of 8.1 litres which gave the same power as the 6.1 litre petrol unit, 95bhp at 2,400rpm. The extra weight of the engine, dynamos and 24-volt battery system, would have taken the completed vehicle over the 9½-ton maximum laden weight then permitted on two-axle double-deckers, so five seats had to be sacrificed, reducing the capacity to forty-four. The engine was 4½ inches longer than the standard unit and the bonnet projected ahead of the cab front in the short 'snout' which was to become a familiar recognition feature on later conversions of the LT class. This was not compensated by any alteration to the body length on these buses, as the Public Carriage Office gave the necessary dispensation. Standard petrol units were fitted when the three buses had their first overhaul a year later, at which time the seating capacity was restored to the standard forty-nine. The class took no further part in these experiments.

The oil engines had not been a success in service. George Rackham had decided at the design stage that they should be ungoverned, a feature which was to remain unique to this design and which left them vulnerable to catastrophic speeding of the engine if they were

One of London's first oilers, ST 466 on route 183B. The only external evidence of the difference was the longer bonnet, for which special dispensation was given by the Public Carriage Office. *D.A. Ruddom collection*

driven too enthusiastically or if the throttle stuck in the open position. They were therefore prone to frequent bearing and crankshaft failures and it was not long before Rackham authorised an approach to Ricardo & Co of Shoreham-by-Sea to help develop a more reliable engine. This eventually emerged in September 1931 as the A161 8.8 litre engine in which the cylinder bore was increased to 115mm and a power output of 130bhp was available at 2,400rpm. (There was an A164 variant but this was not used by LGOC.) In this form the engine gave a satisfactory combination of economy and reliability and produced excellent performance, so AEC set about designing a production model which differed

from the A161 in a number of important respects. Most significantly, the AEC designed governor and separate Bosch fuel pump were replaced in the new version by a CAV-Bosch fuel pump which was integral with the CAV governor. Among other changes, the two seven-inch engine mounted dynamos of the A161 were deleted in favour of a single eight-inch unit mounted under the saloon floor. The new engine was designated A165 and became AEC's standard oiler for the next four years. The engines from the three STs were altered to the A161 specification and fitted to three LTs, which is the class most closely associated with the further development of this programme.

The final version of the standard ST dispensed with lampshades and left the light bulbs exposed, starting a fashion which was to endure for nearly forty years. A new style of seat with rounded back and a metal grab handle was also introduced with the ST2. *LT Museum U8552*

The arrival of the last of LGOC's own STs, is an appropriate point to consider the matter of destination equipment, which was about to be subjected to a number of changes. The very limited displays introduced with the new models in 1929 had provoked a hostile response from the public, who were accustomed to the highly detailed displays shown on all sides of older vehicles. LGOC's first attempt to mollify opinion was to supply a route number stencil plate at the top of the rear bulkhead window but this was not acceptable to the Public Carriage Office who decreed in the spring of 1931 that the full standard of display should be fitted to future vehicles and that those already in service should be modified when they were presented for recertification after their next overhaul. The full extent of the improved arrangement was: a larger, deeper box at the front capable of displaying the route number, destination and three lines of intermediate points; a side display, the same size as the original front box, to show intermediate points; and a strip box across the back above the platform window (in place of the registration number) to show route number and destination. The registration plate was transferred to a position above the rear bulkhead window. The removal of the rear box display and fitting of a larger side box was carried out on some vehicles before the other changes were made and some buses appeared with the rear blind when new.

On bodies where the indicator was in the cab roof, there was a different modification which involved the partial reversion to a board to display intermediate points. This was attached to the panel above the canopy and on these buses the roller blind display remained the same as before, with a large route number above the ultimate destination. This cheap solution had the drawback that the board was not lit at night and it was not long before the company was obliged to do something to put matters right. The slightly Heath Robinson solution was to fix what looked rather like a desk lamp to the centre window pillar, to flood-light the board. This design was to be more familiar on the LT class. These arrangements, although apparently acceptable to the Police so far as existing buses were concerned, did not meet the letter of the decree and there were to be two further improvements incorporated in later batches of the LT class which are described later.

The original improved arrangement of rear blinds on LTs and STs (top) was further improved by the addition of a strip indicator showing route number and destination above the rear platform window. A consequential alteration was the removal of the registration plate to a position on the platform previously occupied by a stencil route number. The original single aperture display in the front panel (centre left) was first moved to a position in the cab roof (centre right), where it appeared to achieve little improvement other than to bring the display further forward. This was later again improved by the addition of a route board indicator on the panel above (right) and, later still, a lamp was fitted in the centre pillar to throw light onto the board at night. The final version (far right) restored the full three piece display.
LT Museum

ST 274 in action crossing Tower Bridge shows the final version of the destination equipment carried by the LTs and STs not fitted with the cab roof display. A larger box projects from the front panel and contains route number, destination and three lines of intermediate points. The side blind has also been altered to carry route information, leaving the number and destination to be indicated at the back.
John Aldridge

The LGOC were by now becoming closely interested in the epicyclic gearbox and, perhaps less enthusiastically, the fluid (or, as they seemed to prefer, 'liquid') flywheel. They therefore decided to order a trial batch of three of the new Daimler CH6 model which had both features combined with a 5.7 litre sleeve-valve petrol engine. The Daimlers were given standard ST type bodies, modified to suit the different chassis characteristics and numbered DST 1-3. They were completed in February 1931 and sent to Harrow Weald, which seemed to be the favoured garage for experiments at that time, where they ran on route 18. The Daimler engines were of the same type as had been fitted to the LS class vehicles, where they had proved less than successful and had been replaced by AEC engines at their first overhaul. When a new Daimler poppet valve engine was offered later in 1931, therefore, one was fitted experimentally to DST 3 but it was apparently not enough of an improvement to justify similar treatment of the other two. On the other hand, Chiswick was sufficiently impressed by the transmission to have it fitted to three other buses from the current building programmes, ST 746, LT 439 and LT 448. The ST was ready in June 1931 and went to Harrow Weald to join the Daimlers on route 18 but the two Renowns went to Plumstead. The outcome of the experiment on the ST is not

London's first new buses fitted with epicyclic gearboxes and fluid flywheels were three Daimler CH6s, which were allocated to Harrow Weald and ran on route 18. They had bodywork identical to the STs and, when delivered, had open drivers' cabs. Charles F. Klapper Collection: Omnibus Society

The second tranche of Regal coaches differed from the first hundred in having front entrances and an emergency exit door in the rear wall. They were also fitted from new with indicators incorporating the panel displaying the 'GREEN LINE' fleetname but this was underneath the destination blind instead of above as on the modified coaches. T 266, on Victoria Embankment near Horse Guards Avenue, was one of the fifty fitted with Duple thirty-seat bodywork. Charles F. Klapper Collection: Omnibus Society

known but at some stage it was converted to standard transmission. All three Daimlers remained at Harrow Weald until they were withdrawn by London Transport in 1935. Further experiments with this form of transmission were to be on the LT class, largely concentrated at Plumstead, and will be covered later.

Coincidentally with the order for the last three hundred STs, LGOC placed a further order for a hundred 'bus/coaches', which the authorisation curiously described as 'one-man operated'. This may have been because they were fitted with front entrances, an arrangement then normally only approved for one-man buses. A neater styling was achieved by the adoption of seven equal length bays, an emergency exit placed centrally at the rear and by transferring the illuminated 'GREEN LINE' panel at the front from above the destination indicator to below it. The neater layout was able to accommodate thirty seats. The new vehicles were needed urgently for new services before the deadline of the Road Traffic Act was reached and the bodywork for Ts 207-306 was therefore contracted entirely to outside suppliers. Ransome, Sims and Jefferies of Ipswich and Weymann of Addlestone each supplied twenty-five and Duple Motor Bodies of Hendon the remaining fifty.

Mechanically, the Regals had the improved specification brakes and gearbox already noted on the later STs with the added refinement, on all but three of the batch, of the new, more powerful, AEC A162 petrol engine. This was a 110mm-bore unit with a swept volume of 7.4 litres, which developed 120bhp at 2,200rpm. These coaches were also fitted with a higher geared rear axle ratio (5.2:1), and were capable of a top speed of 60mph. The complete vehicle was later classified 1/7T7/1. The whole batch, which completed the LGOC's programme of coach purchasing, was licensed between December 1930 and February 1931, the first at Slough, then at Romford, Reigate (and also allocated to other East Surrey garages), Ware (National), Watford, Hitchin, Addlestone, Sunbury, Tunbridge Wells and Southall (AEC).

The three exceptions were Ts 216, 274 and 305, classified 2/7T7/1, which were the three fitted with AEC-Acro oil engines of the same type used in the three STs already described. These coaches also retained the 6.25:1 axle ratio associated with the 100mm bore petrol engine. The new engines were no less troublesome on the Regals than they were on the STs and, later, the LTs and they were reworked to the Ricardo specification early in 1932. They remained in this condition until withdrawal or, in the case of T 216, until rebodied as an 11T11. They were all allocated to the High Wycombe route, which meant that they were housed at the AEC works in Southall when they were first licensed in February 1931.

The needs of the single-deck bus fleet were not being neglected either. At the same time as the original three hundred Regents and fifty Renowns had been authorised, the LGOC Board had decided to buy fifty long wheelbase 664 model Renowns for use as single-deckers (LTs 1001-1050, classified 1LTL1). Their gestation was elephantine, however, and the first, LT 1001, did not go into service until January 1931. The body design was similar in general appearance to the 1T1s but longer and with a rounded cab front. It also had a doorless front entrance, a feature which was to become standard on single-deckers operating in the Metropolitan Police District for the next thirty years. The idea had first been tried as a conversion on T 27 but if this was intended as an experiment before building the LTs, then not much time was allowed for thinking, as T 27 was altered only in December 1930. It was destined to remain unique in its class until May 1933 when a programme was started of rebuilding the Regals still owned by LGOC to front entrance thirty-seaters. The programme was not completed until March 1935, when T 8 appeared in the new guise. The five which had passed to East Surrey in April 1931 were never altered.

Apart from the rounded cab and greater length, the bodywork supplied by Chiswick for the LTLs was essentially the same as fitted to the fifty Regal buses. Eight from the second batch, LT 1082 among them, were sent to Nunhead to operate on the busy circular route 621. E.G.P. Masterman

The first version of the rear end of the LTLs lacked a destination blind box and instead perpetuated an arrangement of boards with the destination display slotted into the bottom of the window on the emergency door, as illustrated here on LT 1077 at Bromley North. There is evidence of a different arrangement with the destination board on the roof but this was not adopted generally.
Charles F. Klapper Collection: Omnibus Society

The last seventy-six single-deck LTs were given modern rear destination blinds, similar to the arrangement at the front. LT 1136, photographed at Finsbury Park on 19th August 1931 when only two months old, was among ten of the class allocated to Tottenham garage for route 263A. There was a short-lived fashion for rear bumper bars at this time but these were subsequently removed.
Alan B. Cross: W. Noel Jackson collection

Wider pillar spacing was used on the Renowns than on the Ts, except that the seventh bay, over the rear overhang, was shorter than the rest. There was no rear destination indicator box but a bracket for a destination board was carried at the bottom of the rear emergency door window. This was changed by the conductor from inside the saloon by opening the door, sometimes perilously while the bus was moving. Some earlier LTLs had this bracket on the roof, above the emergency door. LT 1001 differed from the main production run in having a differently shaped rear dome. Internally, there were thirty-five seats arranged as two longitudinals over the rear wheels, seating six on the offside and five nearside and the rest as spaciously laid out transverse two-seaters. The moquette and colour scheme were the standard grey and the seats were the straight backed type.

LT 1001 went to Edgware to work on route 104, where it could show its paces in some fairly arduous territory. Its qualities were tested even more when it was transferred to Muswell Hill in March to work on the hilly, busy and tortuous 111 between Finsbury Park and Muswell Hill, where it must have outpaced the poor old Ks phenomenally. The rest of the batch went into service in April at Muswell Hill (111) and Holloway (110).

In the meantime a further fifty had been ordered in January and then the final hundred in March. The three orders constituted a continuous delivery of vehicles throughout 1931, although the last seventy-six bodies had a rear destination indicator box and also the later type of round backed seat, causing them to be classified LTL1/1. Six of the LTL1/1 bodies were for the float and did not appear in service until January 1933. Only 199 single-deck LTs were built, as one chassis was diverted for use as an experimental double-deck Green Line coach.

Holloway received more for routes 41A and 297B and the rest went to Dalston (108D), Nunhead (621), Sutton (87, 113 and 155B), Elmers End (609), Hounslow (95), Edgware and Cricklewood (104), Leyton and Tottenham (263A), Enfield (201, 538, 551, 602), Sidcup (209), Edgware (141) and Barking (224). The Barking ones were there for only nineteen days as route 224 was transferred to Upton Park on 31st December, when it was also increased in frequency and got an additional allocation of LTLs. The earlier deliveries all replaced, directly or indirectly, the K type single-deckers, the last six of which were withdrawn in June. Later vehicles replaced the S class which was reduced to a mere eighteen examples by the end of 1931, working at Hounslow (105), Enfield (306) and Uxbridge (501, 503). At Enfield and West Green, however, it was the former Public Dennises which were routed, leaving only a couple of small twenty-seaters working (as two-man buses) on the 204.

The last six K type single-deckers were withdrawn in June 1930. K 1054, on route 297A at King's Cross, was originally a double-decker, one of 115 which were so converted. W. Noel Jackson

Single-deck LTs replaced most of the S type single-deckers during 1931, including those like S 433 on route 155B at Morden station. Alan B. Cross: W. Noel Jackson collection

The interior of LT 1041 looking forward towards the front entrance. The unusual arrangement of longitudinal seats at the back, rather than near the entrance, was dictated by the need to clear the rear wheel arch. LT Museum U8560

LT 189 was one of ninety with Park Royal bodywork built to the standard Chiswick design, which was similar to the most recent STs. When new in February 1931 it had an open driver's cab but was soon fitted with a windscreen once Police approval was given in March 1931. It is seen here at the southern terminus of route 134 at Addiscombe.
The Omnibus Society

So far as double-deckers were concerned, the 1931 vehicle replacement programme was also dominated by the LT class, of which over 700 were to enter service in the twelve months. The first order authorised by the LGOC Board was for another one hundred chassis with Chiswick-built bodywork but this was soon augmented by another for two hundred and fifty with bodywork built by outside suppliers. These orders went to Park Royal Vehicles Ltd (ninety), Short Bros (eighty) and Strachans (eighty).

The first of the new Renowns was registered in January 1931 and had the modified chassis specification already noted on the ST class with the addition of the new 110mm bore A145 7.4 litre petrol engine which AEC had produced with the Renown in mind. For the larger engine the rear axle ratio was altered to 6.75:1 from the 8.66:1 of the earlier double-deckers. Although very similar in appearance to the first 150, the bodywork differed in being of the enclosed staircase type with a layout and interior finish similar to the production STs, which limited the capacity to fifty-six, rather than the sixty of the open-staircase model. Compared to the ST, there was an additional row of transverse seats upstairs while downstairs the nearside longitudinal seat was lengthened to seat five instead of four and a rear nearside longitudinal seat for two was introduced. All seats were of the older, straight-backed design, which gave these buses a more old fashioned appearance than their contemporary Regents. The interior light fittings were also very much simplified to the arrangement which became standard for all future London Transport designs during the reign of the tungsten lamp. The light bulbs were simply screwed into the socket and left exposed, although on these early examples they were still set into a shallow cone-shaped protrusion from the ceiling.

The earlier deliveries had open fronts to the driver's cab but, at long last, in March 1931 the Police finally relented and allowed the provision of glass windscreens as standard.

From then onwards all new vehicles were fully screened and a programme was immediately started to fit them to all earlier Ts, STs and LTs and to most NSs. All 350 also had the old, smaller indicator boxes at the front when new, although they did carry side and rear boxes. Modification of these to the new standard was authorised by the Board in July 1931 and the work was carried out on overhaul.

One vehicle in this batch, LT 345, was built with an inward curving upper-deck and a domed rear roof profile which softened the severe, though handsome, appearance of the bodywork. It was the only LT4 body but this design, with a less pronounced tumblehome, formed the basis of the bodywork adopted for the next 450 Renowns. The first 350 had the modified route and destination indicator box built into the cab canopy (classified LT5) but the last hundred (LT5/1) had yet a further improvement to the blind display. On these,

the route number was carried on a box which projected from the front of the roof, the destination on a strip blind across the cab roof and the intermediate points in a box on the 'tween-decks panel, of the same type and size as had been fitted to the older STs and LTs. The route number had to be changed by leaning out of an upper deck window and turning the handle which hung below the box. Although the arrangement was obviously a compromise and potentially a design disaster, some thought the actual result one of the most handsome of the designs of this period. Internally, this batch had the curved back seats as fitted to the ST2 type. The LT5s were nominally numbered in the series LT 501-850 and the LT5/1s LT 851-950 but the numbers actually overlapped considerably both with the batch below LT 500 and between these two batches, with LT5 type bodies appearing from new on vehicles numbered above LT 850.

Strachan bodied LT 361, outside Elmers End garage after transfer from its first home at Tottenham, was one of the first to be fitted with a driver's windscreen. Later it was fitted with the larger indicator display which it is carrying in this picture. The route number, which should be at the bottom of the display, has been wound out. J.B. Gent collection

70

LT 345 had an experimental body with an inward curve to the upper deck sides and a domed rear roof. A less pronounced curvature was adopted for the LT5s which followed. LT Museum U 8527

The interior of the upper deck of the unique LT 345, looking towards the front. The heavy inward slant of the window pillars, running into the curve of the side ceiling panels, gives a distinct impression of an abnormally sharply domed roof, but the design does not quite come off and it is not surprising that the production version had a less pronounced slope. LT Museum U8534

The chassis specification of the majority of these eight hundred vehicles was the same but there were a number of variants. Perhaps the most significant was the fitting of AEC-Acro oil engines to LTs 191-199, which were licensed at Harrow Weald in March 1931, alongside the three STs with similar specification. The engines were converted in 1932 to the more successful AEC-Ricardo specification (A161 type), and the similarly modified engines from the STs were fitted to LTs 590, 948 and 949. Twenty of the new A161 type were supplied in the summer of 1931. The first had been fitted to LT 643 in time for it to go up to Manchester in September 1931 to be displayed alongside rival units from Leyland and Gardner at a meeting of the Municipal Transport and Tramways Association, called for the purpose of discussing oil engines. The other nineteen were fitted to LTs 750-768 which entered service, again at Harrow Weald, between November 1931 and February 1932.

Another important development incorporated in twenty-four of this batch was the fluid flywheel and epicyclic gearbox. The first two, LTs 439 and 448, had been supplied early in 1931 and were licensed at Plumstead on 2nd and 3rd July respectively. Two others did not appear at this time and were apparently held as floats but the balance of twenty (LTs 549-552, 566-571 and 583-592) were delivered in the summer of 1931. The bodies were of the LT3 (LTs 439/448) or LT5 type but as they were fitted with additional door traps to give access to the gearbox, they were classified LT3/2 or LT5/2. As the transmission had to stay with the bodies, when these vehicles were overhauled it was transferred from chassis to chassis and the fleet numbers varied over the years up to 1940, after which they settled on LTs 271, 401, 451, 469, 470, 571, 573, 580, 582, 588, 591-593, 649, 651, 652, 658, 659, 662, 786, 798, 827, 909 and 914. They spent the whole of their operating lives at Plumstead garage.

The first of the 1931 delivery of LTs went into service during January on the 73 and 173 at Mortlake and the 5, 133 and 134 from Merton. These long straightish routes were obviously considered the ideal stalking ground for the Renowns as next on the list came the 23 and 123 from Barking. Others went to Nunhead (63, 82, 112 and 168D), Elmers End (12A) and Tottenham (73 and 76). At about this time Nunhead began to get new LTs in place of their original allocation of the open staircase type and Plumstead also lost half of its similar vehicles with the arrival of the twenty-two preselectors. Their destination was Leyton, where, with the help of some new ones, they were used to complete the allocation of route 38 and to replace the STs on the 10, 148 and 604. Nunhead took enough Renowns to cover routes 63 and 168D, leaving only part of the 37 still served by covered top NSs.

Towards the end of the Nunhead batch, in June 1931, the first of the LT5 bodied vehicles began to appear and these also featured in the deliveries to Muswell Hill (43), Hammersmith (11E), Shepherd's Bush (11E), Dalston (11E), Chalk Farm (77/177 group) and Harrow Weald (18, 114, 142 and 158). In November Upton Park began to receive what proved to be the largest single allocation of Renowns so far, the total of 157 (in addition to its seven single-deckers) taking until February 1932 to complete. During this run, the LT5/1 bodies began to appear and were to figure prominently on Upton Park's routes.

At the end of 1931 Harrow Weald's STs were replaced by a mixture of oil- and petrol-engined Renowns. On route 183B, the home of the original nine oilers, petrol LT 773 would have co-habited at Golders Green with other recent deliveries all the way up from the south-east on Plumstead's route 48, as well as earlier examples on the 526D and single-deckers on the 104. LT 773's LT5 body has had the intermediate point board added above the canopy but, as yet, it lacks any form of illumination.
N.Hamshere

An LT5/1, with full three piece indicator display, on route 126 in mixed traffic in Piccadilly, including two horse drawn vans.
Arthur Ingram

One vehicle from the 1931 orders which stands out as having the most obvious and immediate impact on London bus design was LT 741, which carried a prototype body for the 1932 deliveries. In this design the upper deck was at last carried forward over the driver's cab and the straight staircase was abandoned in favour of a more conventional curved arrangement, rising from the centre of the rear wall. This enabled the seating capacity to be increased to sixty (thirty-four up; twenty-six down) in an orthodox arrangement of mostly forward-facing pairs, with a longitudinal seat for five over each wheelarch downstairs. Two features which were to characterise Chiswick designs for the next eight years also made their appearance for the first time on LT 741: the penultimate row of two single 'armchair' seats at the back of the upper deck; and a new design of upper deck emergency exit window.

The handle was outside the body and could be reached by hitting a red knob to displace a triangular shaped section in the centre of the window. The fallen section was held in place by a chain, which prevented glass getting broken.

The seats were of a new lightweight type using a frame of plywood shaped to curve and recline, and cushions filled with foam rubber. There were top grab-rails on the seats and on

the lower deck these effectively replaced the vertical stanchions, which LGOC claimed it was possible to omit because of a strengthened design of lower deck roof. It would probably be nearer the truth to say that all of these 'improvements' were designed first and foremost to save weight.

Externally, the shape and detail were much more rectangular than the earlier types, with a square cab, upright front and straighter sides. The windows were also squared off, with no top corner radii. Surprisingly, this body was built with the original small type of front indicator box, presumably because it had been designed before the decision to improve these displays. In this form, the effect from the front was one of great severity with the projecting roof, lacking embellishment or relief of any kind, appearing to frown angrily at the onlooker. This was soon rectified and LT 741 was fitted with a full set of blinds, as fitted to the LT5/1 bodies. Another similar body was fitted to the last of this order, LT 950, presumably as a pre-production prototype. On this vehicle, the interior was predominantly blue, including a new style of moquette, adding a good deal of cheerfulness to what had been a series of sombre interior finishes. Possibly (but not certainly) because of this, the finished vehicle attracted the soubriquet 'Bluebird'.

There was one other double-deck LT built in 1931: LT 1137, quite different from all the others and destined to remain unique in being the only long wheelbase double-decker built for London. The chassis was one of those ordered as a single-decker, hence its number in the middle of that range and it was built as a prototype double-deck coach for Green Line service. In appearance, the basic body structure was very similar to the LT5/1 but had a strikingly different front end design in which the upper deck front windows and panels were raked and swept forward to join the canopy roof in a concave curve. Another novel feature was the front entrance, allied to a rear staircase, an arrangement which forced all upper deck passengers to walk the length of the lower saloon twice and could hardly have been an inducement to travel upstairs. Why a front entrance was chosen is not clear but the decision to adopt a rear staircase was obviously intended to avoid obstructing the view of lower deck passengers, which could equally well have been achieved with a rear entrance. At first no door was fitted as the position into which it would slide was occupied by the fuel filler neck. This was later moved back and an externally sliding door fitted.

It had one bay fewer than the buses, making the windows unusually long, and an abbreviated rear overhang, the whole vehicle at about 27ft 6ins being only six-or-so inches longer than the standard bus. Fifty seats of 'coach' type were fitted and other coach features included a roof of the 'sunsaloon' type in which the centre portion could be opened and folded back, and glass louvres over all windows. LT 1137 (coded 1/1LTL2) was painted in Green Line livery and went into service from Reigate garage on route E between Bushey and Redhill in September 1931.

Top **The offside of LT 1137, dressed for route J after the 1933 restructuring of services. The position of the staircase at the back is clearly visible rising across the rear lower deck window; and the high backs of the longitudinal seats over the rear wheels occupy much of the next two windows. The diagonal stripes on the cantrail are ventilators for the lower deck, while upper deck ventilation is through the three scoops which are visible alongside the raised centre section.** LT Museum U15300

Centre **The upper deck of LT 1137, looking towards the front. The inward curve of the side panels and roof combine with the high backed seats to create a rather claustrophobic appearance and a poor forward view for passengers. The arrangement for opening the folding centre section of the roof, comprising a pair of rods along which the roof attachments run, is clearly visible. The clock in the front dome and the heater fan on the bulkhead are noteworthy but the bare plug-in lamps are a surprisingly less than luxurious feature.** LT·Museum

Right **The attempt to make the front end of the Green Line Renown distinctive was not altogether successful but it was certainly eye-catching, if not exactly attractive. The bulk of Hungerford Bridge can be seen looming out of the mist in this view of LT 1137 en route to Bushey on route E.** J.F. Higham

Included in the 1931 programme was a unique batch of twenty-five buses ordered for the Overground company. The chassis were Dennis Lances and were mounted with forty-nine seat metal framed bodies built by Metro-Cammell, similar to the one fitted to ST 211. Overground numbered them D1-25 but they were always known as the DL class by LGOC and they eventually became DL 1-25 under LPTB management.

Their mechanical specification comprised a six-cylinder 6.1 litre petrol engine, rated at 100 bhp, dry multiplate clutch, four-speed 'crash' gearbox and fully floating rear axle. Brakes were vacuum servo-assisted and steering was of the Marles cam-and-lever type. At 16ft 6ins the wheelbase was longer than the ST and this could be detected in the large gap which was left between the nearside front wing and the bulkhead. The rearmost bay was shorter than on the Regents, resulting in a slightly narrower doorway. When delivered they had the original arrangement of small destination indicators, although these had now been superseded on standard types by more elaborate displays. This was corrected as part of the LGOC's modification programme. The first went onto route 629 on 11th October 1931 and the rest to route 285A, with a few on the 284A.

Delivery of the Lances continued until 9th February 1932, although all but DL 25 were in service by December 1931. They replaced the borrowed STs and about twenty-seven of the Leyland LBs, leaving twenty-six LBs still in service. Modernisation of the Overground fleet was completed between October and December 1932 when twenty-seven LGOC STs were repainted and transferred to Potters Bar.

Before completing the story of the Renowns and their successors, it is necessary to return briefly to the Dennis Dart. On 9th August 1932, the LGOC Board authorised the purchase of a further eight of the type at a cost of £785 per vehicle. These had an improved body layout with three rows of transverse seats in the rear section and two inward facing three-seaters at the front. Numbered DA 33-40, they entered service between 31st December 1932 and February 1933, replacing earlier Darts which were used to start new routes 198 at Kingston (1st January 1933) and 230 at Harrow Weald (4th January).

Two further Darts were sanctioned by the LGOC Board on 1st November 1932 but these were of a special design for operation on route 211, where clearances were tight. They were only 6ft 6ins wide and had seats arranged longitudinally for only seventeen passengers, with nine on the offside and eight nearside. DA 41 and 42 were licensed at Hanwell on 12th May 1933 and replaced two of the three Beans.

Top **At least three Overground Dennis Lances can be seen in this view looking down Buckingham Palace Road towards Victoria station, the leader being D 8 (later DL 8) on route 285A and the rearmost being on route 629.** E.G.P. Masterman

Centre **Overground D 1 and D 17 on the stand outside the 'Two Brewers' Hadley Highstone, the northern extremity of route 284A.** J.F. Higham

Right **ST 544 was one of twenty-seven Regents which were repainted in Overground's darker red livery in the autumn of 1932 and used to replace Leyland LBs. It was renumbered 16.**
Charles F. Klapper Collection: Omnibus Society

On 30th June 1931, the LGOC Board had given authority for the construction of 250 LT-type double-deckers and these were to form the bulk of the 1932 deliveries of the class (LTs 951-999 and 1204-1404). The final order for double-deck Renowns was authorised in April 1932, when the Board decided to take twenty-two with compression-ignition (oil) engines (LTs 1405-1426). The bodies on all these vehicles followed the pattern set by LT 741 as modified in LT 950 and all were built at Chiswick. The basic chassis type of the first 170 was similar to their 2LT predecessors, comprising 110mm bore petrol engine, the D124 gearbox with constant mesh third speed, and triple-servo brakes, but they were classified 5LT. There seems to have been no reason for this distinction, although with the exception of LT 1232, which took the 1931 type body intended for LT 950, they always remained with the Bluebird style of body. However, in addition to LT 950, there were three other earlier chassis which were to carry Bluebird bodies in later years, apparently without difficulty: LT 910 between 1934 and 1937 and LTs 725 and 810 after 1946. There were no fewer than five variations from this basic model in the remaining 102, a sign of the fast changing times into which these buses were born.

Thirty (LTs 1325-1354; 6LT6/1) were built with fluid flywheels, Daimler preselective gearboxes and Lockheed vacuum-hydraulic brakes, whilst retaining petrol engines. This unique combination ensured that these vehicles remained intact and stayed as a group at Plumstead throughout their operational lives, although the equipment on LTs 1325-1329 was later transferred to LTs 964 and 1235-1238. The next twenty, numerically at least (LTs 1355-1374) were the first London vehicles to unite oil engines with Daimler preselective gearboxes, the basic combination which was to be the standard in London for the next twenty-two years. They may well have been the first of their kind anywhere and were certainly among the first. Their specification also included Lockheed vacuum-hydraulic brakes, another feature which was to become standard on London buses up to 1939. They were also the first to carry the later design of gear selection lever, the ball type with a flattened knob, which came into general use the following year. Another group of thirty (LTs 1375-1404) were fitted with A165 8.8 litre oil engines but were otherwise of the same specification as the standard petrol vehicles and were classified 7LT6/2.

The twenty-two oilers authorised in April 1932 materialised as LTs 1405-1426 but even within this relatively small number there were two different types. Prototype Bluebird LT 741 had been fitted experimentally with a Gardner 6LW engine in September 1932 and this proved to be a forerunner of a similar specification for the last ten (LTs 1417-1426), which were among the first buses anywhere to have this highly successful and widely adopted engine. The 6LW engine was longer than the AEC 8.8 unit and the bonnet had to be correspondingly longer, causing the radiator to project nine inches further forward than on the petrol-engined version, giving it a pronounced and not very elegant snout. This arrangement, which enabled the front bulkhead and gearbox to remain in the same position, increased the

Above **The last ten Renowns were a pioneering batch which had the new Gardner 6LW oil engine. The longer bonnet, which is clearly visible extending beyond the headlamps of LT 1425 at King's Cross, meant that the rear overhang had to be shorter than on others of the same type.**
A.D. Packer

Left **A busy scene in Cheapside showing several types of LT on routes 184 and 185 and a couple of NSs in the distance. Many of the commercial vehicles in this scene are horse drawn and the congested conditions which they help create make runs like the one being made by the Bluebird in the front of the picture to Wembley Stadium potentially irregular.**

CHEAPSIDE, LONDON. (864)

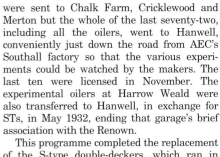

front axle loading of these buses to the extent that it was found necessary to fit low geared steering. To keep the completed vehicles within the 27ft 6in length limit for six-wheelers in London, the rear overhang was 3½ins shorter than on the standard Bluebird bodies and these buses were classified 9LT7. The other twelve had the AEC-Acro A165 engine and were similar to LTs 1375-1404. All twenty-two differed from all other LTs in having one large fuel tank instead of two and a different position for the batteries. For this reason LTs 1405-1417 were classified 10LT8.

The Bluebirds began to roll in February 1932, the first going to complete Upton Park's requirements, then to replace STs at Forest Gate on route 125 and at Seven Kings on route 25. With these allocations, the two main trunk roads out from London to the east through Ilford and Barking were dominated by the LT class, putting to shame the municipal trams with which they competed. Delivery of the preselectors to Plumstead took place in June and a couple of standard vehicles were added to enable the release of the remaining open staircase vehicles. Other small allocations

were sent to Chalk Farm, Cricklewood and Merton but the whole of the last seventy-two, including all the oilers, went to Hanwell, conveniently just down the road from AEC's Southall factory so that the various experiments could be watched by the makers. The last ten were licensed in November. The experimental oilers at Harrow Weald were also transferred to Hanwell, in exchange for STs, in May 1932, ending that garage's brief association with the Renown.

This programme completed the replacement of the S-type double-deckers, which ran in regular service for the last time on 22nd December 1931. By then a start had been made on withdrawing the older Dennises and the last of these ran on 15th January 1932. The last of the Ks had also been withdrawn on 22nd June 1932, when route 90 ceased to use Chertsey Bridge. For the most part, these older models were not replaced directly by new buses but by NSs, many of which were themselves dislodged by STs whose work was taken over by new Renowns. For example the surplus of STs created by the arrival of new LTs at Forest Gate and Seven Kings enabled NSs to be replaced on routes 8 (Clay Hall), 15 and 118 (Middle Row), 43E and 67A (Camberwell), 54 (Elmers End), 58 and 159A (Old Kent Road), 74D (Hammersmith), 83E and 84 (Hendon). Not all the NSs were redeployed, however, because once the Dennises had gone it was time for this huge class to give way and by the end of the LT deliveries, 330 had already been withdrawn.

That was the end of the LGOC's brief commitment to three-axle buses. At the beginning of 1932 the Regulations had been changed to increase the maximum permitted length of two-axle double-deckers from 25ft to 26ft and the maximum laden weight from nine tons to ten. In response AEC had now produced a version of the Regent with a wheelbase of 16ft 3ins, which when combined with the design ideas from the Bluebird, allowed sixty seats to be squeezed into a two-axle bus. This was the basis of the STL of which LGOC ordered fifty (STL 1-50) in August 1932.

The bodywork supplied by Chiswick for the new Regents followed the principles of the Bluebird but lacked the majestic style of the longer vehicle. The upper deck of the STL was almost as long as the Bluebird and projected beyond the driver's cab to finish in line with the radiator. This gave room for thirty-four seats, the same number as on the LTs and laid out in the same manner. The lower deck, although shorter than on the LT, also had the same capacity but this was achieved by capitalising on the smaller wheelarches and having five rows of transverse seats, with two inward facing three seaters. The seats were of the same lightweight design as used on the Bluebirds but the moquette reverted to the grey lozenge design used on earlier STs and LTs and the attractive blue colour scheme was abandoned in favour of the more traditional grey.

The route number box in the roof, which had done so much to give some distinction to the LTs, was omitted and instead the number was carried in a small box on the offside of the intermediate point display, both being above the destination blind. A similar three piece arrangement was carried on the back, the first of its kind. There was also a single aperture box for the display of intermediate points on the nearside over the platform, complemented by a new design of route number stencil, oblong shaped, fitted to the bottom of the rear-most lower deck window. There was one other difference; the moulded waist panel, a familiar feature on the Bluebird and earlier Chiswick designed bodies of this period, was replaced by flush panels.

The mechanical specification of the STLs was based on the 1931 modifications to the ST, except that Lockheed hydraulic brakes of the type used on some Bluebirds were fitted as standard. Petrol engines were specified because the contemporary design of oil engine would have lengthened the bonnet beyond the legal length limit. Inevitably in such fast moving times, there were experimental variations. STLs 1-10 and 41-50 had a new design of fully-floating rear axle which had just been introduced by AEC and could be distinguished from their semi-floating peers by their thicker diameter rear hubs. Two other experimental vehicles were STL 47, which had a Simms coil ignition system instead of the conventional magneto; and STL 50 which had a Daimler built Wilson preselector gearbox allied to a conventional clutch, rather than a fluid flywheel. The older design of pedestal gear changer was fitted on a bracket from the engine, rather than the later ball type fitted to some of the LTs and subsequently adopted as standard by AEC.

STL 1 was completed on 8th November and plated by the Police in December but the honour of being the first to enter service went to three others, STLs 16, 20 and 32, which appeared on route 8 on 3rd January 1933. All fifty went to Clayhall garage in east London for the 8 and 160, the last (STL 47) starting work there in May. STL 50 probably never ran at Clayhall as it was transferred on 10th April, only four days after arriving there, to Plumstead where it was more at home with the pre-selector LTs.

The STL1s had not been the first LGOC-owned long-wheelbase Regents to see service in London, however. An order for eighty had

Although similar in design to the Bluebirds, the greater overhang at the front of the upper deck and the absence of the roof box combined to make the STLs rather less attractive buses. STL 32 was photographed at Kingsbury on route 8B when still quite new in May 1933. J.F. Higham

A full display of route number, intermediate points and destination was re-introduced to the rear on the STL1 body, which was otherwise very similar to the Bluebird LT. Although ordered by LGOC, STL 178 was delivered to the LPTB who put it into service at Elmers End garage on 31st July 1933. Sharing Beck Lane, which seems to have been regarded as an extension of the garage, are two LTs, one double-deck and one single-deck. The Omnibus Society

been placed in the summer of 1932 to replace a like number of 'O'-type Tilling-Stevens TS7 forward-control open-toppers and the first of these began work in November. They were allotted fleet numbers STL 51-130, which they had painted on their dumbirons, although STL 51 was at first labelled 'ST 837'. On the face of it this seems to be an error but it could have emanated from an earlier intention, as the LGOC Board minute approving the purchase of the first STLs referred to them as 'long-wheelbase ST' and this had been the policy with the LT class in which no distinction, other than the official type code, was made between short and long vehicles. The twenty-two numbers STL 131-152 were reserved for a planned repeat order to replace the last of the TSMs but this was never placed because the formation of the LPTB intervened.

The AEC Regent chassis were of the same type as the General version but had a number of differences, reflecting Tilling practice. The A140 engine was downrated to produce a swept volume of 5.5 litres, Luvax shock absorbers were fitted and the self-starter was omitted. The last seven had fully floating rear axles.

Their bodies were built by Tilling, mostly at Lewisham, but nine were built in the company's Hove works and six may have been assembled at Peckham. Although they were paid for and owned by the LGOC, Tilling had a free hand in their design and the vehicles which appeared were nothing like the Chiswick product. They were instead a development of the earlier ST design, to the extent that the lower deck was virtually identical, although much improved in appearance by an extra section of skirt panelling. The upper deck was carried forward over the driver's cab and the staircase was enclosed. The outline was more curved than the LGOC version giving the whole a softer appearance but the three window layout at the front was perpetuated, and at the back the upstairs emergency window and the platform window were both small and made to look more cramped by being divided into two. The destination indicator layout followed the arrangement started by the STs, but the intermediate point display was now on a cramped roller blind. Almost identical vehicles supplied to the Brighton operation in 1934 had a much deeper intermediate point box on which a very large route number was carried and it is a pity that something similar was not adopted for London.

Internally the Tilling STLs were better looking, more luxurious and indeed more modern looking than the spartan LGOC version. The fifty-six seats, arranged in classic style with thirty upstairs and twenty-six down, had an advanced design of lightweight tubular steel frame with deep cushions covered in moquette. Interior finishings were similar to the Tilling STs. The complete vehicle weighed 6tons 1cwt, three hundred-weight heavier than the General model.

STL 51 went into service on route 36 from Catford garage on 29th October 1932 and a further eleven started work there in November and December. Bromley and Croydon each received their first STLs in December for the 36 and 59A respectively and the very last went onto the road on 30th June 1933, the last day of the LGOC.

The compact platform area of STL 1 almost eliminated intrusion of the top of the staircase into the lower saloon. LT Museum

Although a development of the ST, the Tilling version of the STL was much improved in appearance by the extended upper deck front, the enclosed rear end and by having a deeper skirt panel. Even so, the retention of the three window layout at the front, the small side windows and the confined design of the indicator boxes all conspired to give the complete vehicle a cramped look. STL 104, here seen parked at the Camden Gardens terminus of route 59A, entered service at Croydon in March 1933. D.W.K. Jones

Earlier in 1932, Tilling had taken delivery of twelve AEC Regals (Ts 307-318) to replace the single-deck petrol-electrics working on route 109. Their Tilling built twenty-eight seat bodies resembled a single-deck version of the ST, except that they had the deeper skirt like the STLs. A distinctive feature at the front, which always identified this type of body, was an exceptionally wide destination indicator box, shallower than the General version but with a separate route number display. All twelve went into service at Bromley garage between 28th August and 1st October 1932.

Meanwhile Rackham had been developing a revolutionary new chassis design, the side-engined Q and one single-decker was prepared for experimental service with the LGOC. Mechanically, the specification of the Q was similar to double-deckers of the time, with an engine of 110mm bore and 130mm stroke giving a swept volume of 7.4 litres, modified to allow it to be mounted outside the frame on the right hand side of the chassis, immediately behind the front wheel. Transmission was through a conventional clutch and crash gearbox. The rear axle was placed near the rear of the chassis, giving a wheelbase of 18ft 6ins, a foot more than was by then standard on conventional single-deckers. This reduced the weight on the rear axles sufficiently to allow the use of single wheels which, in turn, made it possible to have an almost straight transmission line.

Numbered Q 1, the completed vehicle had a thirty-eight seat centre-entrance body built at Chiswick to a design which must have looked like something from a futuristic novel to an audience accustomed to, at best, the Ts and LTs. The smooth panelled, fully-fronted, six bay design with gently curved front and rear profiles and top and bottom radii on the window frames was very forward looking. The interior finishings, with rounded window cappings, were also years ahead of their time. The only jarring feature was the use of square backed timber framed seats then in favour at Chiswick. These were arranged in seven rows of forward facing pairs behind the stepwell, a longitudinal seat for five over the engine, a single inward facer in front of the door and two forward facing double seats at the front.

Compared with other contemporary Chiswick single-deck designs, the rear emergency door was less obtrusive and the whole rear end effect a great deal tidier because the door was much wider, with a window large enough to avoid the need for flanking windows as seen on Ts and LTs. The balance of the front view was upset by the position of the headlamps which were immediately below the windscreen and the modernity was undermined by a metal frame bumper bar, which carried the registration plate.

The chassis (762001) was received at Chiswick on 5th May 1932 and its completed body was mounted on 12th May. It would then have spent some time in trial running before being presented to the Public Carriage Office for approval. This could well have been a slow and difficult process. It was hardly more than a year since glass windscreens had been approved yet Q 1 had a fully enclosed cab complete with door. It also had the distinction of being the first 27ft 6in long two axle single-decker to be presented for operation in London. It was probably at this time that the pair of seats on the offside at the front were removed and the offside longitudinal seat lengthened by one, reducing the capacity to thirty-seven. At this time Q 1 was owned jointly by AEC and LGOC but General purchased it outright on 1st January 1933.

Q 1 finally went into service on 5th September 1932 at Hammersmith garage, who ran it on route 11E. A month later it moved to Nunhead for route 621, where it remained until being transferred to the Country Bus department in February 1934.

The LGOC's last fling in the double-deck field was to authorise the construction of one hundred STLs, fifty with 'crash' gearboxes and fifty with Wilson transmission. The bodywork was also split into two batches of fifty, the first (STLs 153-202) to be similar to the first fifty and the second (STLs 203-252) to be of a new, fifty-six seat design. The gap of 102 numbers was reserved for a batch of Tilling vehicles, although only eighty were actually built. None of the fifty-six seaters had arrived by the time General's stewardship came to an end but twenty-five of the first batch were in service by 30th June. These were much the same as the 1STL1s but had the coil ignition as tried on STL 47, automatic brake adjusters on the front as well as the rear wheels and a different lubricating system, so were classified 2STL1.

The first six started work on 20th June 1933 at Hendon garage and the rest went to Middle Row and Camberwell, where the last went into service on 30th June. The following day, the LPTB took over and the rest of the batch was deployed under the new management. The Board's very first new buses were the three STLs which completed Camberwell's allocation on 14th July. Fifteen of the remainder went to Elmers End.

That completes the history of fleet renewal so far as it affected the LGOC's London operations but the company was also engaged in this period in replenishing the fleets of its associates and subsidiaries working in the Home Counties. In the cases of National and East Surrey, this was largely achieved within the range of standard products, except that there were some interesting variations which remained unique to the outer area operators. Amersham & District, on the other hand, despite having to have its investment decisions ratified by 55 Broadway, carried on quite independently, apart from the Regals for Green Line work already mentioned.

East Surrey took delivery of twenty-two AEC Regal 662s with rear entrance bodywork by Hall Lewis, sixteen thirty-seaters identical to the 1T1s and six twenty-eight seat private hire coaches. Ten of the buses and all the coaches were owned by East Surrey, the rest by LGOC. The buses were numbered 260-275 in the East Surrey series but, in 1935, they became Ts 372-379 and 383-390. They were licenced for service in March and April 1930, replacing five older AEC 202s. The coaches, which were licenced in April and May, were unnumbered but later took the numbers T 309-314 in the Green Line series and eventually T 393-398 in the LPTB series. Their five-and-a-quarter bay bodies were twenty-seven feet long with folding roofs, half canopy cabs, full drop opening windows and the high waist line favoured by General at this time. There were two swing passenger doors on the nearside, one in the second bay and the other behind the rear wheel. There was no emergency door; a single, curved window occupied the back instead. They were coded 8T8/2 by London Transport.

The Reigate company also shared in the delights of the AEC Regent. Forty-two were taken into stock between April and July 1930, numbered 213-254 (STs 1091-1132), thirty of them owned by LGOC. They had bodywork by Ransomes Sims and Jefferies of Ipswich and were of special note in being to the same design as ST 1 with a square cab. They replaced Ks. Eighteen identical vehicles were supplied to Autocar in June and July and four of these (Autocar 130, 136-138) were transferred to East Surrey in November. Only these four were acquired by London Transport and became STs 1085-1088. All sixty were coded 2/1ST9.

Ransome Sims and Jefferies of Ipswich built their forty-eight STs to designs based on drawings of ST 1 and therefore re-introduced the square cab to the type. Unlike the prototype, however, they were fitted with swing doors on their cabs, although only up to waist level, and the side lamps were carried in the traditional positions on each side of the canopy. KR3892 (ST 1086) was one of four transferred from Autocar to East Surrey in November 1930 and is now in the parent company's red livery working from Dunton Green garage on route 402 at Bromley North.
Charles F. Klapper Collection: Omnibus Society

One of the fourteen STs which stayed with Autocar, KR3895, on the Uckfield route in Sevenoaks. These buses did not pass to the LPTB but went instead to Maidstone & District in July 1933. J.F. Higham

The National Omnibus and Transport Co also took delivery of Regents between April and June 1930 to replace LGOC-owned S-type double-deckers. They should have been STs 502-516 but were instead selected from the LGOC's own series between 107 and 163. When STs 502-516 eventually arrived they were in LGOC livery and were put into service as part of the renewal programme then taking place. All fifteen Nationals had Short Bros bodywork but 136, 140, 141, 157, 162 and 163 were of the lowbridge pattern for use on route N6 (later 336) while STs 107, 111, 116, 129, 132, 135, 143, 152 and 159 were of the standard LGOC design (but, unlike the East Surrey ones, with rounded cab) for use on the N1 (321). The lowbridge bodies were standard Short Bros products with two sunken gangways, one on each side of the upper deck. The upper deck seats were arranged in eight rows of three on the 'island' and the total capacity was forty-eight. These were coded 2/1ST9/1, while the highbridge examples were 2/1ST9s. Like their East Surrey contemporaries, these fifteen vehicles never had their destination indicators modified and were to run their whole lives with the original small display. Four more STs went to National in February and March 1931 to replace its four remaining S-type at Ware. These were STs 818-821, again taken from the main LGOC run.

Two others went to East Surrey in March, this time from the batch allegedly ordered for Overground, STs 833 and 834, co-inciding with the start of another batch of thirty whose delivery stretched over into July. These were later numbered ST 1040-1069 but ST 1051 did not survive to carry the number assiduously allocated by Chiswick in 1935, as it was destroyed in a catastrophic fire on Reigate Hill in 1933. Short Bros supplied the bodies, which were to the LGOC standard with rounded cab and were later coded 2/1ST9. They were used to replace PS-type double-deckers but twelve of these had to be retained for the time being for route 410 which was not suitable for covered top buses, owing to the low bridge at Oxted.

In April 1931, five LGOC Regals, Ts 15, 21, 25, 26 and 35, were transferred to East Surrey, along with responsibility for route 99C. These had the distinction, having escaped from Chiswick's clutches at the crucial time, of avoiding conversion to front entrance and remained in rear entrance form throughout their lives. Their arrival coincided with that of three new Regal buses (T 380-382), which went into service in June and July. Ironically, these had front entrance thirty-seat bodywork by Weymanns of Addlestone, the first to be supplied by the manufacturer destined to be so closely associated with Country Buses over the next twenty-four years. They were effectively a twenty-seven foot long version of the T1 but differed in a number of details from the Chiswick design. Perhaps most notable was the front destination indicator, which projected in a handsome curve above the roof, a feature imposed by the shallower roof profile adopted by Weymann. These vehicles were included in the miscellaneous code 1/4T6.

East Surrey's choice of small buses for its 1931 programme did not follow LGOC practice, although quite a number of the vehicles were owned by General. Not for them the Dennis Dart, although one had been tried early in 1931. Instead they opted for the Morris Viceroy and the Commer Invader. Eight twenty-seat Viceroys were taken into stock between May and July 1931, two coaches and two buses owned by East Surrey, the other four buses owned by LGOC. Six eighteen-seat Invaders, all LGOC-owned, were delivered in June and July, although the first four were allocated to Green Line Private Hire work for the summer and were not released for bus work until August (one) and September. All six were sold to East Surrey in September. The Morrises replaced the four surviving K single-deckers and, with the help of the Commers, the four Beans acquired from the Darenth Bus Service (Hever) in July 1930, and the twenty-seater Guy and eighteen-seat Chevrolet formerly owned by Bus-de-Ville.

Although East Surrey became London General Country Services in January 1932, the East Surrey and National buses owned by LGOC were not formally sold to LGCS until 7th April 1932. In the meantime, the LGOC had authorised the purchase of twenty-three Regent double-deckers and two long wheelbase Renown single-deckers for the new company, all of which were licensed in August.

The two single-deckers had bodies virtually identical to the LTL1/1s of the parent company, except that they were equipped with the new type of lightweight seat as installed in the Bluebirds. They eventually received the numbers LT 1427 and 1428 and were coded 2LTL3. The double-deckers were altogether more interesting. Their chassis were standard ST-type AEC Regents but the bodies were a shortened version of the Bluebird, which looked just as handsome in this four bay arrangement as in the longer design. No advantage was taken of the scope for increasing the capacity, possibly to avoid taking them into a higher cost licensing bracket and they had only forty-eight seats. Compared with the standard model, additional seats were put into the lower deck, which seated twenty-two, but upstairs there was more than ample legroom between its sparsely laid out twenty-six seats. They eventually became STs 1032-1039 and 1070-1084 and were coded 3ST4. They seem to have been intended to operate routes handed over to LGCS by General and were allocated registrations from an LGOC block (GX5314-5346). The first ten (STs 1070-1079) were probably intended for the 70B, 80 and 180 and were duly licensed, with their GX registrations. When the transfer did not materialise, eight were switched to Watford for route N1 (321). Eight of the remainder were licensed by Reigate in March 1933, therefore taking Surrey registrations (STs 1032-1039: APC162-166/168-170) and were sent to Windsor. The remaining five were then sent to Ware to operate on the 310 and consequently acquired Hertfordshire registrations (STs 1080-1084: JH4646-4650).

The three new Regal buses licensed by East Surrey in June and July 1931 had Weymann thirty-seat bodies which, unlike those taken over from LGOC, had front entrances. PL6458 (T 382) is working in the Surrey Hills on route 22, after the formation of LGCS.
Charles F. Klapper Collection: Omnibus Society

The 1932 intake of Regents for LGCS had a shortened version of the 'Bluebird' body which re-introduced full route indicator displays to the company's buses and were the first to have sidelamps at waist level. The eight licensed for work at Windsor were registered in Surrey, hence APC162 (ST 1032) on the Castle Hill stand in Windsor. D.W.K. Jones

JH4648 (ST 1082), seen here at Enfield in the summer of 1933, was one of the five Bluebird STs which were sent to Ware for route 310. These were the first (and last) modern LGCS buses to have a full blind display but, as on the LGOC LTs, there was no separate rear route number blind. The rather clumsy arrangement of the destination blind box straddling the cantrail may be compared with the much neater design, contained between the cantrail and the upper deck windows, introduced only four months later on the STL shown on page 80. D.W.K. Jones

Amersham & District's only double-deckers were two forty-eight seat lowbridge AEC Regents, delivered in April and May 1930 (STs 1089/1090), which supplied A&D's share of route N6 (336). ST 1089 had bodywork by Short Bros, which was identical to the six supplied to National by the LGOC except for having an offside fuel tank. ST 1090 had a body by A&D's favourite manufacturer, Strachan, which differed in appearance, particularly at the rear of the upper deck, but had the same interior layout.

For single-deckers, the Amersham company had tended to prefer Dennises and three of that marque were taken during 1930, one EV (numbered 28) with thirty-two seat rear-entrance bus bodywork and two eighteen seat GLs (32/33), all bodied by Strachan. Two Gilford's were also added to the fleet in 1930, one a thirty-two seat front entrance bus and the other a thirty-seat rear entrance coach, both with Strachan bodies. Strachan bodywork was again chosen for the 1931 purchases, four AEC Regal coaches which eventually became Ts 359, 361, 362 and 364. They were followed in May 1932 by two similar coaches (Ts 365, 366). The LGOC provided finance for five of these. Other vehicles in the 1932 programme were again Dennises, one eighteen-seat GL and a thirty-two seat rear entrance Lancet, which became DT 3 in the LPTB fleet. Amersham & District's very last vehicle purchase was authorised by its Board as late as 26th April 1933, only a month before the LGOC took full control and at a time when the inevitability of the new Board must have been abundantly clear. This last vehicle was an AS6 model Gilford with twenty-seat bodywork, inevitably by Strachan, which became GF 194.

Top **Castle Hill, Windsor, was the southern extremity of Amersham & District's operation, which number 30 (KX5055: ST 1090) has reached on the route from High Wycombe. The two lowbridge Regents normally operated the company's share of route N6, on which National worked its virtually identical lowbridge STs. This one had a Strachan body, the company's favoured manufacturer, but its companion had an identical body supplied by Short Bros of Rochester, to a design resembling the contemporary Leyland 'piano front'. The upper deck seats were arranged in rows of three on an 'island' between the gangways.** Alan B. Cross

Centre **Amersham & District's favourite combination for single-deckers was a Dennis chassis mounted with Strachan bodywork, like thirty-two seat Dennis E number 25 which was bought in 1929.** D.A. Ruddom collection

Right **Amersham & District's preferred manufacturer, Strachan, supplied the thirty-two seat coach bodywork for the four coaches bought in 1931 but LGOC influence may be detected in the choice of the AEC Regal 662 chassis. No.35, seen here on the Amersham to Windsor service, became T 362 in the London Transport fleet.** The Omnibus Society

The only distinguished aspect of LT 1000's career was that it was the first new generation six-wheeler to carry an enclosed staircase body. The exceptionally long bonnet, designed for an eight-cylinder engine which was never fitted, can be seen projecting well ahead of the front axle, an arrangement which is not enhanced by the graceless radiator design, nor by the LS-like brackets between the front bulkhead and the canopy. *Alan B. Cross*

The history of LGOC's bus developments in this period cannot be closed without reference to a strange little digression indulged by the company in 1930 and 1931. At its meeting on 17th January 1929, the General Board authorised the construction of sixteen experimental buses by AEC and the Union Construction Co, the company formed to assemble bodywork for the Feltham trams, A class trolleybuses and some Underground rolling stock. AEC's share was modest: two long-wheelbase 664-type Renown chassis, onto which maximum capacity bodies were to be mounted; and two Regent chassis, one which became ST 1 and the other (which eventually became ST 169) for the Training School. The others were to be complete vehicles, six three-axle double-

deckers (the CC-type) and six two-axle single-deckers (CB), nominally built by UCC but actually assembled at Chiswick Works. In the event, the two Renowns were cancelled, presumably because they were unlikely to be smiled upon by the Metropolitan Police and the number of complete vehicles built at Chiswick was reduced to seven.

Design work had already been going on for some time but it was nevertheless eighteen months before the first was to appear. This was a CC, rather oddly numbered in the Renown series, although taking the then high number LT 1000. The other three were numbered LT 1051, 1202 and 1203. LT 1000 appeared in July 1930 (before the second batch of open-staircase LTs) bearing a lengthened version of the body designed for ST 1 and thereby became the first LGOC six-wheeler to have an enclosed staircase body. The chassis specification included a six-cylinder petrol engine manufactured by Meadows of Wolverhampton but the bonnet was designed to accommodate an eight-cylinder unit and was five feet in length. In the event, as already described, the experiments with the larger engine took place on standard AEC products and none of the CCs was so equipped. The long bonnet had the effect of pushing back the front bulkhead and reducing the capacity to fifty-four. The transmission was through a single

plate clutch and separately mounted four speed gearbox to a fully floating rear axle, the latter being an advance on the design of the Renowns.

The bodywork, although generally similar to the LT3s, had several important differences. The most obvious was the treatment of the front end, where the upper deck and the driver's cab canopy were carried further forward, to compensate for the bulkhead being further back. The short front window was therefore noticeably longer than on the standard ST and LT bodies. Three more similar bodies were built but were not used on CC chassis; instead, in March 1931, they were adapted for use on Renown chassis, with a longer cab front and an extra bonnet panel to close the gap between the bonnet and the bulkhead. The last two CCs (LTs 1202 and 1203) were fitted instead with modified LT5 bodies.

All four eventually went to Nunhead to operate on route 121 but LT 1051, although completed in October 1930, did not actually go into service until September 1931 and LT 1202 and 1203 did not appear until October and November 1931. By this time the project was already a dead duck, General's faith having been demonstrably invested in the AEC models by this time. These oddities were to survive until 30th April 1939, spending their last four months at Streatham.

Only three single-deckers were built and these too were given unlikely fleet numbers: T 1000-1002. Like the double-deckers these had Meadows engines but the bonnets were of normal length and no adjustment had to be made to the bulkhead. Another difference was the choice of a three-speed gearbox. T 1000 was completed in May 1931 and had a body similar to the earlier single-deck LTs, with thirty square-backed seats and no rear destination indicator. Ts 1001 and 1002, which were ready in November and December, had the later specification with round-backed seats and a rear destination box. All three went to Kingston and always ran on route 79.

LT 1051 was fitted with a Gardner 5LW oil engine in February 1932, apparently in the mistaken belief that the bonnet would not accommodate a 6LW unit. In this form it was hardly likely to be successful but LT 1051 went to join the other experimental oilers at Harrow Weald and later Hanwell. In September 1932 it was given an AEC petrol engine, as were the other three and the Ts in 1933.

The single-deck version of the Chiswick built chassis was less grotesque looking than its double-deck counterpart, as the standard 1T1 body could be married with it more happily. T 1001, seen here at Byfleet, entered service at Weybridge garage in November 1931. All three of the type were destined to spend their entire operational lives on route 79 and its successor 219. J.F. Higham

The old exhibition grounds at Earls Court were used as a bus scrapyard by George Cohen & Sons. In this January 1931 view, four K type bodies can be seen in various stages of demolition and, in the foreground, a radiator, a steering wheel and the cab dash of K 584. LT Museum U7850

CHAPTER FIVE

THE LAST YEARS OF THE INDEPENDENTS

There were fifty-four Independents operating buses wholly in the London Traffic Area at the beginning of 1930. There were also three who operated just inside or into the fringes of the Area thus qualifying them for eventual inclusion in the Second Schedule of the London Passenger Transport Act: The Colne Service (F. Steer) of London Colney which deployed a mixture of Dodges and Gilfords on routes 358/A, Filkins and Ainsworth Ltd of Harefield who ran small Crossleys on the 354 and 357A/B/C and St Albans and District, who worked into the Area on routes 304A and 355A using a variety of single-deckers which also operated on other services in the St Albans area.

Outside the London Traffic Area but very much part of the greater London bus network, were the companies working in and around Romford. Romford & District Motor Services ran a fleet of Chevrolets and one Dennis on services to Harold Wood, Noak Hill and Emerson Park. A.E. Blane, who worked services from Romford to Rainham and Collier Row to Upminster under the 'Imperial' banner, also favoured the Chevrolet and he also had one Dennis.

Except in the Romford area, there was little scope for service development because of the restrictive nature of the London Traffic Act and most inner London operators were settled into the operations which were to see out the Independent era. This did not stifle their enterprise, however, and all but six companies were engaged in fleet renewal during these years. No fewer than 144 new or substantially modernised double-deckers were purchased between 1930 and 1933 but single-deckers were less common and only twenty-three were bought, many of them for suburban expansion rather than fleet replacement. Of the double-deckers, the most popular model, by a very wide margin, was the Leyland Titan, of which there were 107 (three-quarters of the total), including fifteen of the later TD2 model.

There were nine other Leylands all for City and unique to that company in one way or another, three Titanics and six City rebuilds, bringing the proportion of new buses supplied from Lancashire up to eighty-one per cent. Dennis was the next most popular manufacturer but its earlier dominance had waned by this time in the face of the severe competition of the highly successful Titans and the belated

arrival on the scene of its Lance, only eight of which were taken by various operators. There were also five of the earlier H model family. The recently introduced AEC Regent made little headway in this market, only ten going into service and nobody bought the Renown. Other marques represented were Daimler (two CF6s and one CH6) and one each from Maudslay and Sunbeam. A summary of the vehicles delivered to Independents between 1930 and 1933 is shown in Appendix Four.

Above **The company which started it all, Chocolate Express, always remained small but efficient. B 6 (XU7498), a Leyland LB5 with standard Dodson forty-eight seat London style bodywork, was the company's fourth vehicle, purchased in September 1924 and survived to become LPTB's L 56. It was working an 11B 'short' from Buckingham Palace Road to Liverpool Street and is parked in front of an Overground Dennis Lance.** E.G.P. Masterman

The bodywork chosen by the Independents was dominated by the products of the firm of Christopher Dodson Ltd, which was dedicated to their needs and refused to supply the Combine companies. The covered top design introduced in 1929 continued in production with little change until a striking new and more modern product appeared at the Commercial Motor Exhibition in the autumn of 1931. The 1929 model had an open staircase of the approved London design, and a five bay structure with a stepped back upper deck and projecting driver's cab. Most characteristic was the three window layout at the front of the upper deck, with the side windows angled in plan towards the rear, in line with the 'tweendecks panels. The five bay arrangement gave way to six bays in the summer of 1930 and there were many minor variations specified by different operators. The 1931 design was to some eyes less harmonious but nonetheless more modern, with the upper deck carried forward over the driver's cab. Between the cab and upper deck was a vertical panel into which roller blind destination and route indicators were incorporated. The upper deck front windows were set back slightly, leaving a narrow ledge, and then raked sharply backwards to the roof. The Show bus, which was mounted on a Maudslay ML7C2 chassis, had a 'Plein Azur' sunshine roof and was the property of the Gordon Omnibus Company.

Another important supplier of bodywork was Birch, although much of its output was for its own use and the number produced was in any case considerably smaller than by Dodson. The basic outline of the Birch body was similar to the Dodson product but shallower windows were used and on some the cab roof was more slender, with a pronounced downward slope. Birch's final design, of which sadly only three were built, was streets ahead of anything else then running in London in its modern and clean looking finish. The frontal appearance was greatly enhanced, by comparison with both the Dodson product and General's contemporary designs, by combining an uninterrupted profile with a gentle rearward slope from waist to roof. All three had route number boxes in the front roof canopy which, combined with their modern overall styling, made them look like something from the later thirties.

Dennis lost ground in the London market when the Titan appeared because its Dennis H was an outdated design. Red Line bought this Dodson bodied one in 1929 but sold it to Birch in 1931 in exchange for a new AEC Regent. The King's Cross stands were a favourite background for photographers, who were often asked by crews to allow them to pose.
Dennis Odd Collection

Centre Single-deckers were not generally favoured by the Independents as their earning potential was limited but a development route like the 50, along Greyhound Lane Streatham, was a good place to try them. Peræque operated this 1928 Dodson bodied thirty-two seat Leyland PLSC3 in competition with LGOC double-deckers and Renown single-deckers. J.F. Higham

Right Adelaide started their London activities with this Dennis 4-ton with forty-eight seat Dodson body in November 1924 and retained it as a spare when a new Leyland Titan was purchased in January 1931. The 3A and the 27 group were the routes normally operated and on this occasion XW2210 is outside the Wellington Hospital on Highgate Hill on a summer working to Hampton Court. D.W.K. Jones

Above **Glen's GJ8489, which later became TD 2 in the LPTB fleet, was a 1930 Leyland Titan TD1 with the standard Dodson double-deck body of that year whose distinguishing characteristic was the three window arrangement at the front. The scene of this photograph is Bishops Bridge Road at its junction with Porchester Road, the only building surviving today from those shown being the Royal Oak on the far corner.**

Below **The most popular 'first generation' Independent bus was the Dennis 4-ton, of which there were 232 in its heyday. By 1930, the number had sunk to 69 and included Ambassador's four-year old YR3672, whose original solid tyres had been replaced by pneumatics. The forty-eight seat bodywork, painted in a smart red and white livery, was by Dodson. The company operated on route 212 on Sundays only, which explains the extreme emptiness of the area outside the National Gallery when this photograph was taken on 4th June 1933, just twelve weeks before the company was acquired by the LPTB.**
H.C. Casserley

Duple was the only other coachbuilder to supply bodies for Titans after 1930, all its products going to one operator, Premier, who took the sizeable total of twelve. Other manufacturers for double-deckers included Park Royal, who supplied five very late open top bodies for Chas H. Pickup and Ransomes Sims and Jefferies of Ipswich, who built five bodies for and to the design of City. Single-deck bodywork was built by a proportionately wider range of firms, six being chosen to body the twenty-three vehicles: Birch, Dodson, Duple, Metcalfe, Thurgood and United Automobile.

New buses were licensed by seven companies during January 1930, all but one of them being TD1s with Dodson fifty-two seat open staircase bodywork. One of the vehicles which was nominally replaced was uncommonly interesting in being a 1924-vintage Straker Squire owned by Supreme (MF5720), the last operational remnant of an original 130 of this chassis which had operated in London. Happily, it was allowed to survive another year as a spare until the arrival of a second Titan displaced the 1925 Dennis 4-ton bus which became the new spare.

The Premier Omnibus Co chose the Duple body for all but one of the Titans delivered in 1929 and 1930. GK892, descending Ludgate Hill among LGOC NSs and the inevitable horse-drawn lorry, was one of six licensed in 1930. Alan B. Cross

Another operator who used single-deckers on the Lonesome route from Streatham was Reliance whose number 16 was a Leyland Tiger TS4 with a thirty-one seat Dodson body, new in October 1932.

This elderly looking bus on route 38E at Chingford was actually new to FAR (Rasey) in October 1929. The chocolate and yellow Birch body was mounted on a Dennis HS chassis. Dennis Odd collection

93

Reliance number 11 (Later TD 122), a 1929 Dodson bodied Leyland Titan TD1, is working between Stratford and Chingford Mount on route 511. This service had been a creation of the Independents, no fewer than sixteen of whom had run it in their heyday; of these, eight were still operating between 1930 and 1933. Reliance quixotically attempted to get authority for a new service in May 1934 but unsurprisingly failed.

This Leyland Titan TD2, at 'The Bakers Arms', Leyton, was new to Pro Bono Publico in 1932 and carried the final design of Dodson body, a fifty-three seater, which had been launched at the Commercial Motor Show the year before.

The only non-Leyland in the January 1930 intake was a Daimler CF6 for Red Line (GC1684) which also had the only body not by Dodson and had an interesting subsequent career. The fifty-six seat open staircase bodywork was by Birch and had an experimental enclosed driver's windscreen. The CF6 was to prove too light for the arduous conditions encountered in London and it was withdrawn two years later. Its body was then transferred to an AEC Regent chassis with fluid flywheel and preselector gearbox, then an unusual specification and unique among AECs operated by London Independents. The opportunity was taken to bring the body more up to date by enclosing the stairs, fitting roller blinds instead of boards and improving the cab. The original staircase was retained, the enclosure being achieved by building a wall around it, and the extra weight of this and the other modifications enforced a reduction in the seating capacity to fifty-one. The new bus eventually became STL 558 (GW2294) in the London Transport fleet. In between these happenings, Red Line took delivery of a heavier duty Daimler CH6 (GO5538) which was licensed in April 1931 to replace one of the two-year old Dennis Hs. It was the first bus to run in London with fluid transmission and preselector gearbox. This too had a Birch body but with enclosed staircase and fifty-two seats. The CH6, which eventually became DST 5, proved to be troublesome too and a repeat order which was believed to be in the offing never materialised.

The standard Birch body was similar to the Dodson product but could be distinguished by its downward sloping canopy and shallower saloon windows. Hawkins's 1930 TD 1 compares well with the LGOC NS as it crosses Trafalgar Square on route 59B on its way to South Croydon 'Swan & Sugar Loaf'.

Red Line's 1932 AEC Regent GW2294 (later STL 558) had a second-hand Birch body dating from 1930, removed from its unsuccessful Daimler CF6 and with a rear wall built around the previously open staircase. Red Line ran exclusively on route 218E from this terminus in Wharfedale Road, King's Cross to Sudbury. Dennis Odd Collection

Another CF6 with a Birch body identical to the Red Line vehicle was licensed by Eagle in March 1930 (GC7388). It replaced a Dennis 4-ton but Eagle may have regretted letting it go, as the Daimler is reputed to have given them even more trouble than its Brickwoods sibling, needing a new engine on average every three months in its first year and a half. When a TD2 model Titan arrived in July 1932, the CF6, which became DST 4 with LT, was relegated to being a spare in place of a single-deck Dennis E.

The writ of the Metropolitan authorities did not run in Romford, where the prosperous business of A.E. Blane's Imperial Bus Service continued to thrive. By 1930, the area was shaking off its old rural character and was well on the way towards becoming a dormitory suburb. The steadily increasing population caused passenger traffic to grow beyond the capacity of Blane's smaller vehicles and his first step to overcome their inadequacy was to buy a twenty-five seater in February 1930. This was an AJS Pilot (VX4253), unusual in being a forward control model, and was bodied by the local firm of Metcalfe. The other three buses purchased in 1930 were the last very small buses delivered to Blane, all being fourteen seaters on Dennis 30cwt chassis (VX6739/7354/7401) and their principal use as the larger vehicles began to come into the fleet was to be on contract work along with the earlier displaced 'minis', notably for Gidea Park College and, later, Ford Works. All subsequent buses were larger and, like the five delivered in 1930, were used not to replace older buses but to increase the size of the fleet. The first, a Metcalfe bodied Morris Commercial Dictator licensed in March 1931 (VX9932), was a twenty-six seater but the next two vehicles took a further leap in size to thirty-two seats and brought yet another model into this distinctly varied fleet, the Dennis Lancet (EV4760/6168). Imperial's last two vehicles were second-hand Gilford 1680Ts with twenty-six seat Metcalfe bodywork (TR8754/8755), purchased in April and June 1933, somewhat belatedly but demonstrating Blane's determination to stay in the bus business, despite the looming approach of the new Board.

The Imperial Yard in Marlborough Road, Romford, with its three Dennis 30cwt fourteen seaters. The two at the front are 8 and 9 which had bodies by Thurgood of Ware and the partly obscured one is Metcalfe bodied number 10. They became DM 6, 8 and 7 in the LPTB fleet. D.W.K. Jones

The Eagle Omnibus Company bought this Birch bodied Daimler CF6, which was identical to the ill-starred Red Line vehicle, in March 1930. It later became DST 4 in the LPTB fleet but was withdrawn in 1934. Malcolm E. Papes collection

Right **The Miller Traction Co Ltd bought five Leyland Titans all with Dodson bodywork, of which VX8835 was one of the 1931 pair of open staircase TD1s. It is seen in Duncannon Street against the familiar backdrop of St Martin in the Fields working on trunk route 15A.**

In nearby Dagenham, there was a lot of discontent among residents about the failure of bus companies to provide adequate services to the new and expanding estates in the area. At the end of 1929 the Minister of Transport's help was sought and he decreed that the four Independents working in the area (Martin, Miller, Peraeque and Renown) should have a conference with the LGOC to consider how best to provide adequate and co-ordinated bus services. The result was that Miller, Peraeque and Renown withdrew from routes 26D, 266 and 292 after 6th November 1930 and the following day started a new route 293, with a few General peak hour runnings, between Dagenham 'Church Elm' and Becontree Heath via Rippleside. Other developments in the area by the LGOC are given in chapter two.

Above **Dodson** introduced this more modern body at the Commercial Motor Show in 1931. Although obviously a more up-to-date product than the earlier designs, the clumsy stepped arrangement at the front compared ill with other contemporary models, including the Combine's efforts. Miller's number 9 was licensed in September 1932 and, among other things, worked on the newly created 293.

Left **Martin's** number 12 (VX97), which later became DH 14 in the LPTB fleet, was one of the four Dennis Hs licensed during 1929 which were the first Independent buses to have enclosed staircases, although the Hickman fifty-five seat bodywork looks as antique as the visible chassis components. Martin worked mainly on the 23 group and this photograph was taken at Aldgate, the western terminus of route 123A. D.W.K. Jones

Left **UR9997, one of the unwanted Duple bodied Guy OND twenty-seaters bought by Royal Highlander in 1931, at work in Watford on hire to Premier. It eventually became G 4 in the LGOC and London Transport fleets.** J.F. Higham

Below left **Former Royal Highlander route 225 disappeared as a result of changes in November 1932. MV933, a fourteen-seat Birch bodied Bean, was the last new bus to be licensed by the company, in December 1931, although another was being built at the time of the takeover. It became BN 1.** J.F. Higham

H.A. Martin's Paterson Omnibus Company followed a rather conservative vehicle policy and remained resolutely loyal to the Dennis. Even so, it had been the first Independent to specify an enclosed staircase on its new buses in 1929 and it was therefore something of a surprise that the Birch body on the Dennis H licensed in April 1930 reverted to an open staircase design (VX5533). This proved to be its last new bus, although two second-hand vehicles were bought later, one to run an additional schedule granted in the summer of 1932 and the other to replace a Dennis H written-off after a collision with a tram in Ilford in February 1933. The additional schedule was the outcome of a long, slightly tangled, sequence of events starting way back in 1925 when an operator called Maxton was forced off the 27 by a retrospective Restricted Streets Order. Martin, discovering that there might be a legal case for overturning this decision, did a deal with Maxton to take over his rights and put a bus out on the 27 in June 1930. The Police took proceedings against him which he lost but on appeal he was granted a schedule on route 525, ironically the route which had been offered to but found unacceptable by Maxton. The operation was transferred on 17th September 1932.

The City Motor Omnibus Co was a little slow in getting on with modernising its fleet but it made a start in May 1930 with a remarkable sixty-two seat six-wheeler, numbered CS 1. The chassis was built by City from Leyland parts, including the engine and radiator from a five year old LB5 (A 22) whose registration (XX9060) it took. The body, supplied by Dodson to City designs, was only the second covered top double-decker in the fleet and it had to wait nearly a year before it was joined by any others. CS 2-6 arrived in March 1931, bearing bodywork by Ransomes Sims and Jefferies of Ipswich identical in appearance to that on CS 1. Side-by-side with these came a group of six four-wheelers which were also peculiar to City in having Leyland Tiger TS3 chassis, although known as Titan TD 'special' (T 1-6). Their fifty-six seat bodies were supplied by Dodson, again to City's own design and were readily identifiable by the different arrangement of the front upper deck whose potentially modern two window arrangement was flanked by curved corner glasses giving the finished vehicle a rather old-fashioned look. This impression was given further force by the adoption of a high skirt line. Another five identical vehicles arrived in February (T 7-11) and one on 29th April 1932. The latecomer was T 12 which had the distinction of being the first oil-engined bus to be operated by a London Independent.

A new operator entered the lists in March 1930, Mrs W.M. Winter who operated a Bean with eighteen-seat London type bodywork by Birch on a newly licensed route between Pinner 'Red Lion' and Pinner Hill Golf Club. It started on 28th March but did not last long under Mrs Winter's suzerainty as General took it over, with the Bean (BN 4; MY3496), on 10th September and ran it from Harrow Weald garage. The Bean was replaced by a Dart in January 1931. This is a curious little episode and Mrs Winter's true independence must be in doubt because her bus was given a body number by the LGOC and they also helped out by lending her one of their Darts (DA 2) when her own bus was off the road between 19th and 29th May.

Another operation in this area which had been around only since September 1929 (although there had been a spell of illegal operation in 1928) was the Grundel brothers' Loumax bus, working between South Harrow and Harrow Council Estate. They sold out to a Mrs Sayers in March 1930 and she embarked on a course of expansion, for which she acquired two twenty-seat Guy ONDF forward control buses in March and April 1930 (MY3390/4117). These were very unusual in London for having bodywork by United Automobile Services, whose Lowestoft factory eventually became Eastern Coach Works. These were used to open up a new service 210B between Greenford ('Hare &

Hounds') and Hanwell Station which started on 8th November 1930. This was eventually absorbed into a new route 211 which ran through Gordon Road to Ealing Broadway. There were width restrictions in Gordon Road because of overhanging trees and the three Beans bought for the 211 had special bodies built by Birch which did not project beyond the wheels and were only 6ft 6ins wide. They were licensed in March 1931 (HX3466/3467) and December (MV933) and later became BN 1-3.

The next six buses, which were intended for a new route 181A between Uxbridge and Pinner, were financed by a new associate of Mrs Sayers, one Ernest Hewitt who already had bus interests in Watford encompassing Premier and West Herts. Hewitt ordered six Guy Victorys with twenty-seat Duple bodywork and these were licensed two at a time in March, June and July (UR9195/9196/9899/9900/9997/9998) and carried the fleetname 'Royal Highlander'; they eventually became G 1-6. The 181A started in April 1931 but only three licences had been obtained and Hewitt used the unwanted vehicles on his Watford services. There was a somewhat stormy relationship between the partners and Mrs Sayers got into financial difficulties which eventually led to Loumax and Royal Highlander being acquired by General on 15th September 1932, as described in chapter two.

City's Leyland LB5 number A 35, although first licensed in 1925, was a comparative youngster in the City fleet in 1930. It is shown here at Edmonton Town Hall on the rarely photographed route 294 which City shared with Ambassador.
K.W. Glazier collection

The rest of the 1932 deliveries to City comprised nine Guy FCX six-wheelers G 2-10), which were particularly interesting as they were second-hand, having been part of the fleet of the London Public Omnibus Company which passed to the LGOC in 1929. General had withdrawn them and they had been sold to various operators, from whom City now acquired them. All had sixty-two seat Dodson bodywork and were licensed by City in March and April 1932. The high capacity theme was continued in 1933 but this time with new Leyland Titanic TT1 chassis fitted with eight litre Leyland direct-injection oil engines (TS 1-3). Despite the forward-looking chassis specification, City's conservatism was only too apparent in the bodies which were open staircase, among the last to be delivered new to any operator anywhere. The vehicles replaced in all cases were Leyland LBs, of which ten remained in stock when the programme came to an end in 1933.

Centre **City's brown and cream Leyland Titanic (TS 3) looks gigantic compared with the much shorter General STL following it, yet its Dodson body seats only two more because of the old-fashioned style favoured by City, with its open staircase and projecting cab canopy. Compare this with the handsome body supplied by the same manufacturer on the almost contemporary Westminster Sunbeam illustrated on page 101.**
H.C. Casserley

Right **City's T 12, whose Leyland chassis was actually a Tiger TS3 but known as a 'Titan Special' was the first oiler in any Independent fleet. The bodywork, although by Dodson, was built to City's own design with a high skirt and rather old-fashioned upper deck front which gave it the look of an earlier generation. Highgate Hill was the northern terminus of the long and important route 536 which was operated by a consortium comprising Birch, City and United.**
K.W. Glazier collection

Route 202, still an unrestricted route, was the object of an attempt at some expansion by Renown who put its spare thirty-two seat PLSC3 model Leyland Lion into service there on 26th January 1931. Unfortunately, the Lion suffered a fire which destroyed its body while on a garage run through Rotherhithe Tunnel on 16th May and as it was the company's only single-decker, this brought the venture to an abrupt end. Meanwhile the 202 had become restricted on 29th April. Renown's final piece of expansion came surprisingly late and was indeed the last new operation for any Independent in London. The Minister made an Amendment Order in April 1933 which allowed Renown to work a new route 234 between Dagenham Docks and Heathway Station, subject to the surrender of the two schedules on route 202. The new route started on 4th April 1933, just nine days before the London Passenger Transport Act received the Royal Assent. The bus acquired for this was Renown's last, a TD2 licensed in April 1933 and almost certainly the last open staircase vehicle to enter service anywhere (HV2822). It was also the last body to be turned out from the factory of Christopher Dodson, who had decided to close down his business when the activities of Independents were cancelled by the LPT Act. Like a similar one supplied to the St George company, it was probably assembled from spare parts held in stock to help in the process of running down the factory. Perhaps as a result, it had a curious mixture of roller blinds on the side, old-fashioned indicator boards at the front and an open driver's cab.

In November 1930, Birch Bros licensed the first of twelve Titan TD1s delivered between then and April 1932 (B 29-40), the last two carrying the final style of body already described.

Birch's continuing efforts to expand and to get approval for double-deckers on route 231 were always frustrated. An application in June 1931 to extend the route to Park Royal was refused but a Sunday extension was introduced in August. Then, in 1933, the company offered to build double-deckers of a special design with an inward sloping upper deck to make them safe for operation in the tree-lined roads which were used by the 231. By now they were dealing with a new authority, the Metropolitan Traffic Commissioner, who refused their application on the grounds that the company was to be taken over by another new authority, the LPTB and that their compensation claim might be affected.

Into battle? Birch B 16, a 1928 Dennis E, makes one of route 231's rare main road appearances as it turns from Maida Vale into Clifton Road. The conductor is standing on the platform, withdrawing his arm from the right turn signal he has just given across the back of the bus. The external cantilevered platform steps can be seen hanging down at the rear nearside.
The Omnibus Society

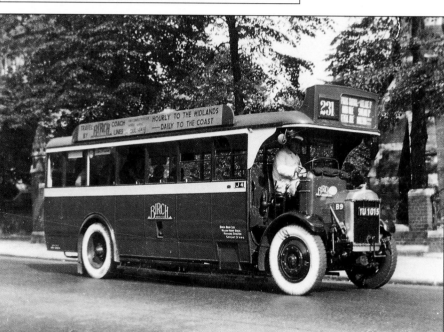

The 231 was a constant battle ground between the Metropolitan Police and Birch, who wanted to expand it and run specially modified double-deckers but were perpetually frustrated. B 9, a 1927 Dennis E carrying the company's own thirty-seat bodywork, was photographed at Belsize Park in September 1933. D.W.K. Jones

Route 202 was an unrestricted route which attracted Renown to try it in January 1931. Two other operators worked the route, G.H. Allitt and Nil Desperandum, whose 1928 Birch bodied Leyland PLSC3, which later became LN 5 in the LPTB fleet, was photographed at Surrey Docks in 1934. D.W.K. Jones

What must surely qualify as the most startling new vehicles put into service by anyone in 1932 were the five long wheelbase AEC Regents licensed by Chas. H. Pickup between January and July, which eventually became STL 553-557 in the LPTB fleet. Technically these were as advanced as anything running in London and they had modern enclosed staircase bodies by Park Royal, but what made them unique was that they were open toppers. Pickup apparently believed that there was a future for this arrangement and was undoubtedly influenced by their particular suitability as an attraction for summer outings on routes 37B and 73 to Richmond and 70 to Dorking, all routes he operated. Looking back from the 1990s, with brand new open top tours buses in abundance, he could be seen as about sixty years ahead of his time.

A surprising event occurred in November 1932; a new operator appeared in the London Traffic Area. H.F. Phillips sought approval to run a service from the newly opened Heathway station in Dagenham to the Ford Works. This was refused and he sought instead a route between Dagenham Docks station on the LMSR's Tilbury line and Ford Works over roads of such poor quality that the LGOC was not interested in them. He got approval and route 232 started on 23rd November 1932, using a Bean bought second-hand. This was not quite the last development by an Independent, as the Renown route 234, already mentioned, started five months later.

There was plenty of proof that the Independents were still very much in business and interested in improving their product right up to the end and one event which demonstrated this with real force was the entry into service with the Westminster Omnibus Co in February 1933 of a new sixty-four seat double-decker, the largest then to operate in London. This was a new model from the Sunbeam company, known as the Sikh, a handsomely majestic six-wheeler carrying perhaps the ultimate in Dodson's body designs (JJ9215). Unfortunately, its modern appearance was severely marred by its open driver's cab, an arrangement reminiscent of early 1930 rather than 1933 insisted upon by the Managing Director who thought enclosed cabs were unsafe and a health hazard. There had been an earlier Sikh painted in Westminster colours but it was not operated by them. It was built for the Sphere Omnibus Co but never operated by them either, despite successfully passing the Police tests for routes 73 and 76.

Charles H. Pickup took five of these eccentric Park Royal bodied open top Regents during 1932, with an eye to pleasure traffic to, among other places, Richmond, which is where GW1744 (later STL 553) leads this line-up comprising an Independent Titan, two LGOC NSs and an LT. J.B. Gent collection

Although most famous for its open top Regents, Charles Pickup also bought three Leyland Titan TD1s. Two of them had covered top fifty-six seat Dodson bodywork with this unusual arrangement of indicators in which the destination blind was carried in the roof dome. New in 1931, GO4367 (fleet number 11) ended life as TD 32 in the LPTB fleet. Omnibus Society

The Westminster Omnibus Company's Sunbeam Sikh was the largest bus operating in the capital when it started running in February 1933 and its majestic Dodson sixty-four seat body was probably the finest produced by that doomed manufacturer, marred only by the anachronistic open driver's cab which was required by Westminster's Managing Director. It was licensed to run on the 76, as in this photograph at Edmonton, and the 73 but had a short life and although numbered SM 1 by the LPTB was withdrawn almost immediately on takeover in 1934.

With the passing into law of the London Passenger Transport Act in April 1933, it might have been expected that further expansionist activities by the scheduled Independents would come to an end. For the most part this was true but a remarkably cheeky application was made by Reliance in May 1934, ten months after the Board's monopoly powers came into being, for a route 510 between Chingford Mount and Waltham Cross, using two buses. Not surprisingly this was refused because the company was to be taken over soon afterwards. The motive for what seems on the face of it to have been a quixotic application is lost in time but it could have been an attempt to test the Board's willingness to use its consents procedure to allow operators to run services in which it might itself not be interested.

Before leaving the Independent bus scene, it is appropriate to look at the only company working entirely outside the Metropolitan Traffic Area which was accorded the dubious accolade of being named in the Second Schedule of the London Passenger Transport Act. The Lewis Omnibus Company of Watford achieved this distinction because of its special association with the Metropolitan Railway Company which, despite its vigorous claims to the status of a Main Line Railway, was primarily an underground and suburban operator and therefore one of the scheduled companies.

The Lewis Omnibus Company had been incorporated as recently as 22nd November 1929 and came into being as a result of an agreement between Lewis and the Metropolitan to operate services to feed the railway, in exchange for which the North West Lands and Transport Company took a fifty per cent stake in Lewis. The North West Lands company had been formed by the Metropolitan as a device to enable it to continue to have an interest in bus services, despite its failure to obtain bus operating powers in 1928. They had already set up an agreement with the Aylesbury Motor Co but a possible approach to Amersham & District for a similar arrangement was shelved because the Met had got wind of the impending agreement with the LGOC. It was its reluctance to get involved with General that led to its looking at Lewis as a possible partner in Watford; an earlier agreement with National, which never seems to have worked very satisfactorily, had lapsed when the railway company realised that the bus company was working under an agreement with LGOC.

The Met also wanted to develop feeder services in the Harrow and Pinner areas and still had lingering hopes of resurrecting its earlier ideas for similar operations around Neasden, Kingsbury, Wembley Park, Sudbury, Greenford and Ruislip. Negotiations with A & W for them to operate these services had got to an advanced stage when A & W suddenly found what the Met Board described as 'spurious' reasons for not completing the agreement and the attempt collapsed. The Metropolitan's negotiators seemed blissfully unaware of the wish of the A & W partners to sell their business, which they did, to LGOC, in June 1930. The approach to Lewis was altogether more fruitful. One attraction was that Lewis could use his existing licence to provide

the long-sought link from Watford Junction LMS station to the Metropolitan, which would open up the possibility of feeding off the potentially lucrative traffic from the north.

The agreement with Lewis included the operation of the proposed services from Wealdstone ('The Case Is Altered') to Harrow station via Headstone Drive and Harrow View; and from Harrow to Northwood via Pinner, Pinner Hill Road and Potter Street. The NW Lands and Transport Company Board had already approved expenditure of £10,000 for the purchase of seven buses but Lewis persuaded them instead to invest £8,950 in five double-deck buses for a new service from St Albans to Watford and a further £3,000 for two coaches for a service to Southsea.

The buses were AEC Regents with enclosed staircase forty-eight seat bodywork by Short Bros, numbered R 1-5 (UR5506-5510) by Lewis and later ST 1133-1137 by London Transport. They were licensed in January and the route for which they were obtained started running on 11th March

1930. A spare was obtained in October and this took the number R 8 (UR7879) and eventually ST 1138. The two coaches were AEC Regals with Harrington rear entrance thirty-one seat bodywork and were licensed in June 1930 as R 6 and 7 (UR6802/6801), becoming T 360 and 363 with London Transport. Three more coaches were bought in 1932, two more Harrington bodied Regals but this time with front entrance thirty-one seat bodywork and a Morris Viceroy with Duple twenty-seat front entrance body. The Regals were numbered R 9 and 10 (JH1915/1916) and the Morris M 1 (JH2585); London Transport gave them the numbers T 367/368 and MS 1.

It is a matter of conjecture whether the services planned by the Met would eventually have started had the LPTB not been formed. Either way, Lewis's recommendation to go for the St Albans route ensured that the prospect of his company becoming a major operator in north-west Middlesex was never realised and another interesting chapter in bus history was closed when the Lewis concern was absorbed by the Board on 1st October 1933.

The last bus to be purchased by the Prince Omnibus Co, in December 1931, was this Leyland Titan TD1 with Duple thirty-one seat bodywork, finished in the company's handsome chocolate and cream colour scheme. It was photographed at 'The Angel' Edmonton on route 551, another creation of the Independents, on which nine companies had once operated.

The disappearance of the Independents from London removed an alternative source of employment for those who fancied the idea of being a busman but who preferred to avoid the strictly ordered, impersonal environment of a large organisation. (There was no such thing as a 'buswoman' in those days.) There were obviously good and bad employers among the fifty-four companies but in almost every case the atmosphere was more relaxed and 'family like' than could be found in the garages of the 'Combine' companies. What is more, nearly every Independent offered better pay than the LGOC and its associates, although their working conditions may often have been inferior. The actual rates varied from company to company but on average if you worked for an Independent you were likely to get something in excess of ten per cent more pay than someone working for the 'Combine', even though their rates were very high compared to most other available jobs.

Most Independents ran things very informally, although it would be a mistake to equate this with laxity or undue leniency; the working life was rigorous and demanding. The eight hour working day and six day working week were widely accepted and some companies paid enhancements of various kinds but it was not uncommon for staff to be instructed to work well beyond these limits, without further rewards, often at risk of losing their jobs if they refused. Discipline was tough, often summary and there was no appeal against the governor's decision. There was no formal protection against injustice and there were undoubtedly companies in which unfairness or favouritism weighed the scales unfairly against individuals. In most companies, however, the proprietor was very close to his men, knew their good and bad points and could usually make a fair judgement of the rights and wrongs of a case. In some the boss was like a father figure and staff of all grades would go to him with their personal problems, as well as any gripes they might have about the job.

By contrast, like most big undertakings the Underground Group had modelled its organisation and administration on military precedents and all employees were governed by a mass of written rules underpinned by a strict disciplinary code. Disciplinary procedures were based loosely on the system operated by the courts of justice and misbehaving staff could find themselves caught up in a labyrinth of inquiries, often heard by officials they either did not know or knew only at a distance. To protect individuals from injustice the Group had agreements with various Trades Unions, who represented staff in all matters. These agreements covered all aspects of the business and set the limits within which managers and supervisors were expected to work; but the very impersonality of the organisation could allow infringements to occur which in a similar company would be noticed and, in the better ones, stopped.

People who worked for the Independents appear to have been a fiercely loyal lot who valued their own independence from the 'big battalions' and they shared their proprietors' sadness when they were obliged to transfer to the monolithic Board. There was many a 'wake' in the months following the formation of the LPTB, none more grand than the farewell gathering of the staff of Claremont Omnibus Services. After a dinner at Gennaro's restaurant, they were all taken in four-wheeled and hansom cabs to the Garrick Theatre where they saw Old Time Varieties, finishing up with tear-stained farewell drinks at the Cafe Monaco. Nothing could better sum up the close relationship between John Pike, the proprietor, and his men than the leaving present they bought him. They found the largest cocktail cabinet they could and stuffed it full of bottles of all kinds; he said later it was one of his prized possessions. It was hardly surprising that the driver and conductor of the very last independent bus in London, belonging to the Prince Omnibus Co, were close to tears when they pulled into Ponders End in the early hours of Wednesday 5th December 1934, to be welcomed home for the last time by Arthur Gannon, the proprietor, and his wife.

Symbolically putting a stop to Independent operation, this traffic policeman was caught by the Post Card cameraman fortuitously holding up this red and cream Daimler CF6 owned by the Eagle Omnibus Co, one of only two of the model to be found in London. It was not a great success and although it became DST 4 in the LPTB fleet, it was withdrawn in 1934. Capital Transport collection

CHAPTER SIX

TRAMS AND TROLLEYBUSES BEFORE 1933

Development of the tramway system was still very much in progress at the beginning of 1930. A new LCC line was under construction linking Well Hall with Grove Park, partly along a section of the new South Circular Road, and plans were well advanced for the enlargement of Kingsway Subway to take double-deckers. The County Council of Middlesex, whose agents were the Metropolitan Electric Tramway Company, had obtained a Light Railway Order for a tramway linking their system at Tottenham with the Walthamstow Corporation tracks at Ferry Lane and work on this was expected to start imminently. In association with this, the council intended to extend its Higham Hill tramway to Chingford Road, so that through cars could be run from Chingford Mount to Finsbury Park. Nearby, the MET had plans to construct a tramway along Mayes Road, Wood Green and to link the two Alexandra Palace terminals, so that double-deck trams could be run from Wood Green to Hornsey. Another, rather more modest, MET scheme was for a tramway interchange station at Golders Green, either by means of a loop through the bus station or a siding off Finchley Road. This was later developed into a more ambitious layout in a new traffic roundabout with a bridge connection to the Underground station. The South Metropolitan company was preparing to seek powers to extend its

tramway from Mitcham to St Helier, in association with the LCC, whose estate it would serve. There were also smaller projects, like the installation of a new junction at Stanstead Road to allow cars to turn from Brockley towards Catford.

Weighing the balance in the other direction was the decision of the LCC Highways Committee in July 1930 to seek no further Parliamentary Powers for the time being. This had particular reference to powers to run over the new Lambeth Bridge and prospective new bridges at Waterloo and Charing Cross. Meanwhile, the structure of Lambeth Bridge was designed to be suitable for conduit track at a later date if needed,

Just as they wielded considerable leverage on the design of motor buses, so too did the Metropolitan Police exercise a strong influence over the development of the tramcar in London. The London County Council also had a significant influence over the design of other operators' cars which it exercised by exploiting its position when entering into through running agreements. The effect of this was that many of the municipal and company fleets contained some bogie cars conforming in most respects to the basic LCC design exemplified by the ubiquitous E1 class. For their own local services, however, most of the municipalities standardised on the four-wheel car and in the case of Bexley, Erith and

Ilford, which had no through running agreements, the entire fleets were so composed. Although the LCC set very high standards, its design policy was not very progressive and the vehicles being produced at the beginning of the 1930s differed very little in appearance from the earliest covered top cars dating from 1906. The companies were also bound by LCC requirements on through running services but were rather more independent and, by using the financial strength of the Underground Group, were instrumental in setting the pace for the development of modern trams for London. A number of experimental cars had gone into service between 1927 and 1930 leading ultimately to the production of the superb 'Feltham' model which put to shame the contemporary LCC E3 and HR2 designs.

Above **Looking down onto Victoria Embankment from Waterloo Bridge, the tram on the left is 562, a 'reconstructed subway' car of class E1 with a new English Electric body mounted on Mountain & Gibson maximum traction trucks and using electrical equipment salvaged from the F & G class subway single-deckers. It is shown running to Wimbledon on the short-lived extension introduced to replace the LUT Haydons Road route in April 1931. There is a standard E1 on route 72 in the distance and the car on route 26 about to negotiate the junction for Kingsway Subway is an E class.** B.J. Cross collection

Right **Metropolitan Electric Tramways bogie car 211 (later LPTB 2301)** was a type C1 seventy-four seater with Brush bodywork and Mountain & Gibson maximum traction trucks. Originally an open topper dating from 1909, it had been fitted with a top cover in 1929, when it also received B.T-H high speed motors. It is at Hornsey on route 51, one of many worked jointly with the LCC.
C. Carter

Below **The MET's single-deck cars** were used exclusively on the services to Alexandra Palace where they used this section of reserved track. Car 148 (later LPTB 2314) was a type E car built in 1905 with both bodywork and radial four wheel truck by Brush.
K.W. Glazier collection

Below right **Half the cars operated by Bexley Council** were these four wheelers built by Dick Kerr in 1903 and mounted on Peckham P22 trucks. They were class B cars purchased from the LCC between 1915 and 1917 to help carry the heavy First World War munitions traffic and to replace the burnt out Dartford fleet. They did not survive long enough to receive LPTB numbers.
K.W. Glazier collection

Bottom right **Route 63** was good example of a joint route into the County of London on which the trams used had to conform to LCC design standards. East Ham Car 55, at the top of Ilford Hill by Station Road, was one of twenty Brush seventy-two seat bogie cars built for the corporation in 1927/1928 which were almost identical to the LCC's E1 class. This car became number 85 in the LPTB fleet and in common with all but one of the others was still in service when the London system closed in July 1952.
M.J. O'Connor

The LCC had been heavily involved since 1926 in what was unofficially known as the 'Pullmanisation' programme, under which virtually its entire fleet of E, E1 and M class cars had been modernised, with more powerful motors and improved seating and other passenger amenities. The last 133 were turned out by Charlton Central Repair depôt during the first quarter of 1930. Its first 'new' trams in this period were what were known as the 'reconstructed subway cars'. These fifty cars (552-601) consisted of new double-deck bodies, built by English Electric at a cost of £2,040 each, mounted on the Mountain and Gibson trucks from the single-deck cars of classes F and G which would become redundant with the rebuilding of the tunnel. The body design was similar to the experimental HR1 car built in 1928 and as such was something of a hybrid combining features of earlier E1 designs and of the new E3 and HR2 classes which were to appear later in the year. The lower deck was of timber construction and similar in appearance to standard E1s with an inward sloping lower half, while the upper deck was made of aluminium alloy. The main distinguishing features of these cars were the large route number stencil which occupied over half the front upper saloon window and the wide pillar at the centre of the lower deck. Unlike all previous cars, these were the first to have half-drop opening windows on the upper deck which could be operated individually by passengers.

The subway closed after the morning peak on 2nd February 1930 and a replacement bus service, operated by the LGOC, started the following day. Route 175 ran from Chapel Street, Islington to Charing Cross Underground station (on the Embankment), following a loop from Aldwych via Norfolk Street, Embankment and Northumberland Avenue. Nunhead and Tottenham garages supplied a total of seventeen covered top NS-type buses. The severing of the through link seems to have had a detrimental effect on trade as the Sunday service was withdrawn on 23rd March and the weekday service was reduced from 16th May.

LCC class F bogie car number 557 was one of those built for the new Kingsway Subway in 1906 by Dick Kerr on Mountain & Gibson maximum traction trucks which were withdrawn in 1930. The northern terminus of route 33 was then at a stub end crossover in St Paul's Road, Highbury, where a K-type bus operating under the insignia of the Tramways (MET) Omnibus Co passes by on route 30. Dr Hugh Nicol

The lower deck interior of 581, a 'reconstructed subway' car, shows the style and standard of finish common to LCC rolling stock of this period. Other than the upholstered seats, the overall appearance is old fashioned and compares ill with contemporary buses and the Underground Group's Felthams. B.J. Cross collection

New HR2 class car 1871 fulfils its destiny as it climbs the four-track section on Dog Kennel Hill, where the LCC estate of flats has yet to be built and a semi-rural atmosphere still prevails. The first fifty cars of this class were built without drivers' windscreens. B.J. Cross collection

Below **The cars replaced by the HR2s on the Dulwich routes were M-class four wheelers, like 1690 on peak hour route 60 at Dulwich Library, a high powered Brush car with unusual Heenan & Froude trucks, built specially for hilly routes in 1910.** Malcolm E. Papes collection

In the meantime, the first of a new generation of LCC tramcars went into service in the summer of 1930. In March 1929 the Council had authorised the purchase of one hundred and fifty new cars, fifty of class HR2 at a final cost of £3,450 per car and one hundred E3s, which cost £2,990 each. The HR2 class was designed specifically for operation on steep hills and the first order for fifty (1854-1903), was intended for the Dulwich routes, where they were to replace the ageing C and M class four-wheel cars specially equipped for use on Dog Kennel Hill. The two class 6 maximum traction bogies, supplied by the Electro-Magnetic Brake Co Ltd (EMB), had equal size wheels and each axle carried a 35hp Metropolitan Vickers motor, the pairs on each truck being permanently connected in series. This made them impressively powerful cars, the full 140hp providing enough pulling power to lift the $17\frac{1}{2}$ ton car up a 1 in 11 gradient at 12mph. Special equipment for use on steep hills included an electrically operated run-back preventer. With the arrival of these cars the glades of Dulwich were introduced to the wonderful new sound of the four motors working in tuneful harmony, something quite distinctive which cannot be captured in mere words but once heard was never forgotten. The E3s (1904-2003) were intended particularly for use through Kingsway Subway when it re-opened and had an improved design of the maximum traction bogie employing SKF roller bearings for the first time on an LCC tram. There was one $57\frac{1}{2}$hp English Electric motor on each truck.

The contract to supply the bodywork for the E3s went to Hurst Nelson & Co of Motherwell, while that for the HR2s was placed with the English Electric Co. Although very similar in appearance to the 'reconstructed subway cars', they differed in the important matter of having all metal bodies, as pioneered on experimental HR2 car 1853 in 1929, which made them suitable for operation anywhere on the system, including the

Kingsway Subway. The new cars seated seventy-four passengers, standard LCC moquette being used as a seat covering on the lower deck and red flame-proof leathercloth in the upper saloon. 'Ashanco' ventilation was provided on the lower deck through a series of ventilators, situated above the saloon windows. Internal finishings were smoother and neater than earlier designs and the overall effect was clean, airy and pleasant.

As with contemporary buses, the police and Ministry of Transport were reluctant to authorise the fitting of windscreens (or 'vestibles' as they were always then known on trams) and all 150 cars were delivered with open fronts. In 1930 the LCC was granted a six month licence to operate three cars with weather protection for the driver and the first car to appear with a 'vestible' screen was E1 class number 1506. A different type of screen was tried at each end of the car, one with one adjustable louvre with a 'Klaxon' windscreen wiper and the other with two louvres but no wiper. The other two cars had only partial screening: No.1248 had screens covering only the dash plates; and 1539 had only part of the dashplate area protected. Trials were successful, the style of screen used on 1506 winning approval. In consequence, the E3s and HR2s were fitted with screens of the two louvre variety in the second half of 1931.

The HR2s were the first to go into service, at the beginning of June 1930, in time for the Whitsun holiday, at Camberwell depôt, where all fifty were soon operating. The E3s followed from July onwards and at first went to New Cross, then to Holloway and, temporarily, to Abbey Wood and Streatham but with the re-opening of the subway, they assumed their intended rôle and settled down at Camberwell, Hackney, Holloway, Jews Row (Wandsworth) and Norwood as the exclusive rolling stock for routes 31, 33 and 35. Twenty-five of the M class cars which were replaced by the HR2s were sent to Leyton, to replace older four-wheelers, initially on route 8. Surprisingly, there was some criticism in the Press about the harshness of the noise made by the E3s when they were new but those who remember the cars in service in later years will recall a very sweet sounding and smooth running vehicle.

The Hurst Nelson HR2s were the first to be delivered new to the LCC with enclosed driver's windscreens but were identical in all other essentials to the English Electric cars, except that no trolley booms were fitted. Most went to Holloway for route 11 but 103, which is at Blackwell Tunnel terminus, was one of a number sent to Camberwell. The sloping top to the destination indicator box, which was also carried on the E3s, contained an illuminated glass panel reading 'Via Kingsway Subway' which was concealed under a metal plate when not required.
K.W. Glazier collection

There was one further batch of each class. At the end of the 1930-1931 financial year, the LCC needed 1,707 trams for service, including spares. There were 1,602 modern cars available, including those which had been 'Pullmanised', leaving a difference of 105; fifty of these were cars owned by Leyton Council and operated by the LCC on their behalf. Thirteen additional cars would be needed for the new Grove Park to Woolwich route when construction was completed, bringing the shortage up to 118. The 115 cars of classes A and D, dating from 1903/1904, still then in service were not in good enough condition to be modernised. It was estimated that if authority could be obtained for the operation of the larger HR2 cars on Highgate Hill in place of the specially equipped four-wheel M class vehicles, and the opportunity also taken to order enough new cars to replace the remaining peak hour runnings of Ms on the Dulwich routes, the extra capacity of the seventy-four seaters would enable a saving of eight trams.

Following a satisfactory test of one of the first batch of HR2s on 3rd September 1930, the Ministry of Transport authorised their use on Highgate Hill. At the end of the month, the Council agreed to the purchase of another sixty cars at a final price of £2,884 each, £566 cheaper than the first batch. Bodywork was by Hurst Nelson and these were the first LCC cars to be delivered new with drivers' windscreens. No trolley poles were fitted as they were intended for use on routes which ran exclusively on conduit track. Otherwise, apart from a few minor modifications in all essentials they were identical. The first HR2 started work on route 11 up Highgate Hill on 31st March 1931 and all sixty were in service, at Holloway and Camberwell by December 1931. They were given the fleet numbers 101-160.

The balance of old cars was represented by the fleet operated on behalf of Leyton Council but the agreement was due to expire on 30th June 1931 and the LCC's conditions and proposed charges for a renegotiated agreement became a matter of dispute; in fact, at one point there seemed to be a real risk that the arrangement might lapse. Eventually a compromise was reached and the supplemental agreement covered the twenty-five years to 30th June 1956 and, apart from changes in the financial arrangements, included the installation by the LCC of a traverser at Leyton depôt and the purchase of fifty new E3 class cars. They were built by English Electric at a cost of £2,916 each and were to the same specification as the LCC cars, except that they had drivers' screens from the start. They were numbered 161-210 and put onto the three London routes: 55, 61 and 81.

One of the Leyton E3s on home territory on the reserved track alongside Epping Forest at Whipps Cross. B.J. Cross collection

The grand re-opening of the enlarged Kingsway Subway by the Prince of Wales was originally planned for 17th December 1930 and, in preparation for the event, the E3 car numbered 1930 was painted in a splendid livery of royal blue lined out in gold. Unfortunately 1930's moment of glory never materialised as the tunnel was not ready even for trial running until 4th January 1931 and the formal opening had to be deferred until 14th January. The Chairman of the Council, Major Tasker stepped into the rôle intended for the Prince of Wales and the place of tram 1930 was taken by 1931, attired in a livery, suitably modified for its more plebeian guest, of ghostly white lined out in blue. Accompanied by another E3 and an E1 (1506, presumably to show off its vestibule screen) it made a ceremonial run from the Embankment to Theobalds Road and back to Holborn station.

The new stations at Holborn and Aldwych were attractive and well appointed havens, the one at Holborn, with its cream coloured Travertine marble being particularly reminiscent of contemporary Underground practice. To economise on space, an island platform layout was used, which required offside loading and unloading. The old single-deckers had been designed to cope with this by having steps on both sides of each platform but the presence of the staircase prevented a similar arrangement on the double-deckers and passengers had to board and alight instead by the driver's platform at the front of the tram. This procedure introduced a whole series of sound effects which were peculiar to the subway, starting with the echoing 'clenching' sound of the brakes and followed by the clatter of the doorway chain being removed, the clunking noise of the steps being lowered and then the whole procedure again in reverse. If an HR2 ventured into the subway its identity would be immediately apparent as it would add its own brand of motor noise to the melody, creating a distinctively greater din than an E3. All this and the pervasive smell of ozone gave the subway its own special atmosphere which was to fascinate several generations of schoolchildren.

The entry and exit of trams at each end was signal controlled because in both cases they had to cross other traffic. At the Theobalds Road end, there was also the need to ensure that no more than one car in each direction was on the 1 in 10 slope at any one time. This limited the capacity of the subway to thirty cars an hour in each direction and various ideas for increased through running were to fall foul of this restriction. Three new routes started the public service through the subway on 15th January 1931: 31 (Hackney - Wandsworth); 33 (Highbury - Brixton Water Lane, peak hours only); and 35 (Archway - New Cross Gate via Kennington). With later modifications the 33 and 35 became two of the most financially successful tram routes in London.

Specially painted in white, elegantly lined out in blue, Hurst Nelson E3 car 1931 poses for an official photograph at the entrance to Holloway depôt before being used for the ceremonial opening of the enlarged Kingsway Subway.
Greater London Record Office

Like the LCC, many tramway operators were in the process of replacing their first generation electric tramcars, which by now were between twenty-five and thirty years old, although in most cases heavily modified over the years. The County Borough of West Ham was taking delivery of a batch of twenty-seven bogie cars (69-85), to replace some of its oldest four-wheelers, built to the exacting standards required by 'through-running', with seventy-three seat bodywork by either Brush or, in the case of car 75, the Corporation. Externally they made no concessions to modern ideas in styling and had much in common with the LCC's E1 class cars. Throughout their working lives these cars could always be distinguished from those of other origins by the small route number box below the front upper saloon window which contained a very cramped route number. Internally a warm atmosphere was created by the generous use of varnished woodwork. West Ham took one further, similar car in May 1931 (numbered 68), which proved to be the last built in their own workshops. It was also their first with vestibule screens, a feature which was extended to the 69-85 batch in 1932.

Undoubtedly the greatest positive tramway event of the 1930s was the arrival of the 'Felthams', so called because they were built at the Feltham works of the Union Construction Co Ltd. Following a series of experiments between 1927 and 1930, the Underground Group decided to invest in one hundred tramcars of a radically new and modern design, forty-six for London United Tramways and fifty-four for Metropolitan Electric Tramways. At £3,150 per car, they were slightly more expensive than the E3s and the second batch of HR2s. The purchase of the MET cars was conditional on the renewal of the lease by Middlesex County Council, which at the beginning of 1930 was by no means a certainty as the company were seeking a reduced rental and the County Council had been considering taking over the operation of the tramways themselves. Thanks to Frank Pick's remarkable negotiating skills and strongly influenced by the company's forward looking policy on tramcar development, the County relented and a new forty-two year lease was signed in the nick of time to come into force on 1st January 1931.

Top **The last car to be built by West Ham at its Greengate Street works, in 1931, E1-style car 68 was also the first to receive a driver's windscreen. As number 295 in the LT fleet it survived until the system closed in 1952.** M.J. O'Connor

Centre **Deep in LCC territory in Caledonian Road, all three cars in this photograph are owned by the MET. Two of them are new UCC type Felthams whose splendid appearance must have been a severe embarrassment to the managers at County Hall. The nearer UCC is 360 and the car next to it is H-type number 271.** M.J. O'Connor

Right **The 'Cinderella' of the company tramways was the South Metropolitan company which worked routes radiating from Croydon. In 1931 it borrowed ten cars of the U-type from London United, one of which, 268, is on the terminal stub in Tamworth Road, West Croydon. These were originally open top W-type dating from 1902-1904 which were later fitted with fully enclosed top decks. The tram on the main road is a Croydon Corporation bogie car.** J.B. Gent collection

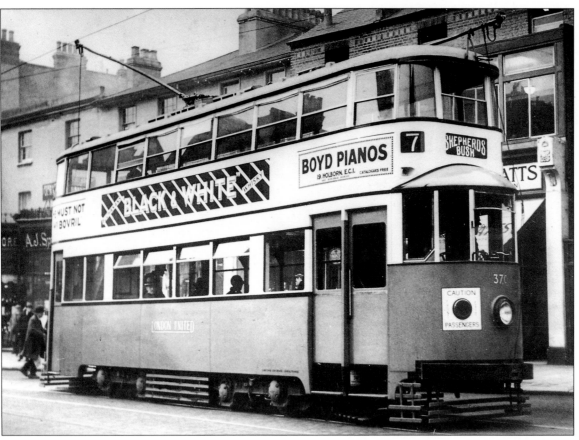

Design work on the Felthams had been entrusted to the London Electric Railway at Ealing Common and many of the details were similar to those adopted on contemporary tube rolling stock. This family resemblance was to be carried through into the first London trolleybuses too. At 40ft 6ins over bumpers and 7ft 1in wide, they were by far the largest cars built for London and were designed to carry a total of eighty-four passengers. The influence of both Underground railway practice and the American ancestry of the design concept were apparent in the arrangement of two large vestibules, one at each end of the lower deck, to accommodate twenty standing passengers, ten in each, from which the stairs rose in a straight flight. The main passenger entrance was fitted with hand operated folding doors and opposite this was a single-leaf air-operated sliding door through which passengers could alight when it was at the leading end of the tram. The driver's cab was fully enclosed, in a sort of pod extending beyond the main structure. These features combined to give a very efficient passenger flow through the vehicle, with both staircases in use at all times and the minimum of conflict in the saloons.

The lower passenger saloon had seats for twenty-two, while upstairs there were forty-two. There were no internal bulkheads upstairs, as the stairwells followed bus practice by being within the saloon. The downstairs seats were covered in the same grey 'lozenge' moquette as used on buses and those upstairs were covered in red 'Rexine'. The interior finishings and passenger amenities were of the highest standard yet seen on a London tram and showed a determination to establish the tram as a luxurious form of

transport. Extensive use was made of blue scratchproof grained 'Rexine' arranged in panels surrounded by polished grey wood and the metal grabrails maintained the harmony by being covered in blue 'Doverite'. Electric tubular radiator heaters were fitted under the longitudinal seats in the upper saloon, a facility with which MET had been experimenting on earlier cars for about a year.

The bogie sets were made by EMB, with SKF axle boxes and each truck carried one seventy horse power motor, made by British Thomson-Houston for the MET cars and by GEC for the LUT cars, giving the same power as the HR2s. The magnetic and screw brakes were supplemented in these trams by air brakes supplied by the Consolidated Air Brake and Engineering Co Ltd.

The external appearance of the 'Felthams' was unique and unmistakable. The main body structure was curved at each end and the upper deck curved inwards, all round, giving the car a slightly streamlined look. Literally the most outstanding feature was the driver's cab which projected beyond the main body and had its own curved roof. Above this was a roller blind destination display and in each corner curve was a stencil route number displayed behind glass. Beneath these were the statutory 'police' lights, inset into the panels and on the front dash was a single headlamp, which could be dipped mechanically. There was also a red light on the 'nearside' dash panel to warn approaching drivers that passengers were alighting at the front end of the tram. The cars had the livery style adoped for LT 1, with red lower panels and cream above the waist.

The MET 'Felthams' were numbered 319, 321-329 and 332-375 and all were delivered

new to Finchley depôt. The first went into service on route 40 on 1st February 1931 and later deliveries went to route 21. When the Finchley allocation of route 21 was completed, earlier cars were transferred to Wood Green for routes 21 and 29. On the latter, their superior performance compared with the LCC's through running E1s, put them to shame. Although a trial with one of Clapham's higher powered E1s was carried out, nothing could be done about it in LCC days. The cars released by the Felthams were the four-wheel D type dating from 1906. This brought to an end the operation of open-top trams in central London.

The London United Felthams (numbered 351-396) were acquired specifically to work the long straight run out from Shepherds Bush to Uxbridge on route 7 and indeed they were probably too large for most of the rest of its system. For this job, though, their speed and smooth running made them ideal and, like their MET counterparts, they were immensely successful with the travelling public from the day they went into service in the first week of January 1931. They were part of a two-pronged strategy developed by the LUT to deal with its fleet renewal: heavily trafficked and highly profitable routes were to be given new high performance trams with superior passenger facilities; poor earning routes were to be converted to 'trackless trolley' operation. Unfortunately, this policy was effectively stillborn because the Royal Commission on Transport, whose final report appeared in 1930, gave the thumbs down to trams. It saw no place for them in modern cities and recommended that existing systems should be abandoned gradually as the need for renewal arose and that no new systems should be developed. This became public policy.

The opening of the LUT's first section of trolleybus route between Twickenham and Teddington ('Savoy') on Saturday 16th May 1931, therefore proved to be the first stage in the total abandonment of London's trams instead of the start of the complementary system originally conceived. The system was introduced in stages, as work was completed and vehicles became available, the last section from Norbiton to Wimbledon being completed on 31st August 1931. While the turning loop at Wimbledon was being connected up on 31st August and 1st September, LUT trams terminated at Worple Road. The trolleybus service, route 4, started on 2nd September but up to four trams continued to operate for a time while the remaining trolleybuses were delivered. This conversion isolated the LUT tracks between Wimbledon and Merton and via Haydons Road to Summerstown. In anticipation of this, the LCC entered into its last through running agreement and took over the operation of the Haydons Road line on 16th April 1931 with an extension of route 14 to Wimbledon. For this, the lines of the two operators had to be linked and a change-pit installed at Summerstown.

The sixty trolleybuses ordered for the conversion were a true product of the Combine. They had 27ft 7½ins long AEC 663T chassis, an electrically powered version of the Renown motor bus, and fifty-six seat half-cab bodywork by the Union Construction Company. The interior layout of the bodies was similar to the contemporary LT and ST designs (except in the case of number 60 which had a curved staircase) but the finishings and seats were virtually identical to the Feltham trams. Externally, the similarity to the Felthams was even more striking, particu-

larly in the arrangement of the front upper saloon windows and in the shape of the driver's cab roof canopy. The colour scheme also followed the Felthams' example. Number 1 was delivered with an unusual arrangement of board indicators but all subsequent deliveries had roller blinds, although from number 3 onwards the rear display was supressed and

a tram type route board carried in the rear window instead. For reasons buried in the sands of time, these vehicles were later given the nickname 'Diddler'.

Ten of the U-type trams replaced by the trolleybuses were lent to the South Metropolitan company for use on the Croydon to Mitcham route.

While trolleybuses were taking south-west London by storm, in south-east London work was in progress to build a new tramway line along the newly built Westhorne Avenue, the first part of a planned South Circular Road. The track from Well Hall Road as far as Briset Road was completed and opened to traffic on 1st October 1931, when half the service on route 44 was diverted away from Eltham Church. The remainder, as far as Eltham Road, opened on 30th June 1932 and was served by route 72 which was so heavily modified as to be effectively a new route. It now ran from Beresford Square, Woolwich to Savoy Street via Westhorne Avenue, Lewisham, New Cross and Kennington. The old route of the 72 from Forest Hill through Brockley and via Walworth Road and St Georges Circus was covered by route 35, which was extended from Brockley Rise to Forest Hill and diverted via Walworth Road instead of Kennington. Route 66, which had been the companion Embankment loop service to the 72, was curtailed to operate from John Carpenter Street to Forest Hill via Blackfriars Bridge.

The fiercely independent Ilford Borough Council tramways took delivery of eight new trams in 1932. These cost £2,154 each and were long wheelbase four-wheelers with Brush bodywork seating sixty-eight. Mr L.E. Harvey, the General Manager was obviously a soulmate of the Westminster Omnibus Company's MD, as he thought enclosed drivers' cabs would create draughts and give his drivers lumbago, in consequence of which these eight cars (numbers 33-40) were delivered without windscreens. They also had longitudinal seating on the lower deck, another of Mr Harvey's outdated preferences. They replaced open top four-wheelers which were as old as the system itself, having been put into service in 1903.

The penultimate through running agreement signed by the London County Council was with Walthamstow Corporation for the extension of route 81 from the 'The Rising Sun' to Woodford, a mile-and-a-half run of dubious traffic value through attractive woodlands. The tracks were joined early in 1931 and the through service started running on 5th March 1931. One of the requirements of the agreement was that Walthamstow should buy additional vehicles of a type suitable for running into the County of London and the eight cars needed to fulfil this commitment were delivered in 1932. Numbered 39-46, they had sixty-nine seat Brush bodywork similar in general appearance to the latest LCC E1s but with enclosed windscreens, mounted on Brush bogies of LCC design, with one 63hp motor on each truck. They were powerful cars with a breathtaking performance and a turn of speed which was very useful on route 57, where they were put to work under the terms of a fresh agreement signed in March 1932.

Above **One of the new Ilford four-wheelers built by Brush on Peckham pendulum trucks in 1932 with open platforms on the insistence of the General Manager. These cars had an experimental type of passenger operated opening window on the upper deck which occupied the upper two-thirds of the frame and slid in a horizontal direction.** B. J. Cross collection

Left **LCC E class car 650 at the 'Napier Arms' terminus of newly extended route 81, the result of a through running agreement between County Hall and Walthamstow Corporation.** Charles F. Klapper

Right **One of the new bogie cars bought by Walthamstow Corporation in 1932 to fulfil its part of the new agreement with the LCC, number 43 (which became LPTB 2058) works a local route between 'Bakers Arms' and Chingford Mount. The specification of these Brush cars was similar to the LCC E1s but their two 63hp motors gave them greater power.** K.W. Glazier collection

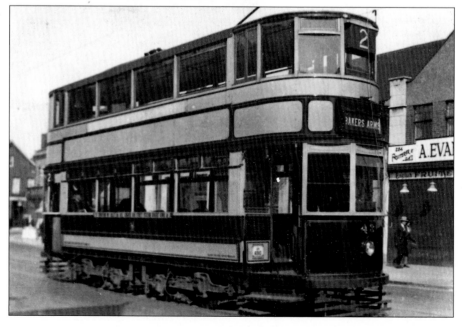

At the end of 1929, the London County Council, probably inspired by the experiments being conducted by the company tramways, had given approval to the expenditure of £5,000 to build an experimental new tramcar of advanced design, with built-in vestibule ends to enable twenty standing passengers to be carried. The remit to the designers included consideration of alternative positions for the passenger doorway, including a centre entrance and one in the extreme rear of the car so that boarding passengers would be protected from passing traffic. The intention was that 150 such cars should be built. In the event, the car which appeared in the spring of 1932 was conventional in layout, with end platforms but in little else could it be described as conventional.

To avoid costly depôt alterations, the length of the car was limited to thirty-six feet but a capacity of sixty-six seated passengers, two more than the Felthams, was nevertheless achieved. There were twenty-eight deeply sprung seats downstairs, all transverse in reversible pairs and thirty-eight in the upper saloon, twenty-four in reversible pairs and seven at each end facing inwards around the stairwells. They were covered in a handsome blue moquette and the blue theme was carried through to the 'Rexine' covering on the side panels which was complemented by the use of blue 'battleship' linoleum on the floors. There were no doors or steps between the platform and the lower saloon and no stairwell bulkheads upstairs, so that, at both ends whatever the direction of travel, passengers and the conductor had free access to the stairs, which were built in straight flights. The general airiness and spaciousness of the passenger saloons was enhanced by the use of concealed lighting. The driver was given his own cabin, reached through a door from the platform, where his equipment included air brakes, an air-operated windscreen wiper and an electric warning gong.

Few, if any, double-deck trams built in later years surpassed number 1, as it was called, in appearance and quality of design. Unlike the Felthams, the driver's cab was built into the main body structure which, combined with the smooth panelling, flush-fitted metal framed windows, rounded ends and inward sloping upper-deck, resulted in a truly handsome and majestic finished product. Its route number and destination displays also marked a radical shift away from boards and stencils to roller blinds including number and intermediate point displays on the side of the car. The specialness of the car was recognised in the choice of its livery of royal blue on the main body panels and white around the upper saloon windows.

The original intention had been to mount this body on a new set of experimental trucks but these proved a failure when tried on E3 car 1986 and, instead, the bogies from HR2 class car 160 were used. As a result 160 became an E3, the only one of the class not to have trolley booms. The combination of these powerful and smooth running trucks with the improved body features of number 1 was a joy to experience. Car number 1, which earned itself the nickname 'Bluebird' made its first public appearance at Charlton Works on 19th May 1932, on display to delegates attending the Annual Congress of the Tramways, Light Railways and Transport Association. Following trials, it entered revenue earning service in July from Holloway depot on routes 33 and 35. Nothing came of the intention to order 150 but the council did order another three of the Alpex aluminium top decks of the type fitted to number 1 with the intention of putting them onto existing cars.

The council now turned its attention to the rehabilitation and modernisation of existing cars, the main target being the one thousand standard E1 class cars. Before they were tackled various experiments were carried out, the most obviously revolutionary being the

trials with bow collectors (cars 835, 1023 and 1360) and pantographs (cars 844, 1172 and 1219). Others were electro-pneumatic contactor control (cars 1103 and 1104), aluminium body panelling (car 795) and 'bucket' type swivelling seats for the lower saloon. Finally, a small programme was undertaken in 1932 of lengthening and modernising three redundant M class cars using spare class-4 bogies from stock at Charlton, possibly as a pilot for the main programme. The lengthening was accomplished by slicing the bodies in half and inserting an additional bay and the refurbishment work comprised flush side panelling, white enamelled ceilings, linoleum floor coverings, moquette covered seats throughout, passenger operated opening windows on the upper deck and drivers' windscreens. The completed cars were classified ME/3. The first two, cars 1441 and 1444, retained their old style upper decks but 1446 was fitted with the first of the three Alpex upper decks, which transformed its appearance to that of a thoroughly new and modern car. For insurance reasons, the completed car took the number of an E1 car, 1370, which had been damaged beyond economical repair in an accident at Kennington Oval. This proved to be the LCC's vehicular last gasp but the glory of putting 1370 into service went to the new LPTB, who did so on 2nd July 1933.

Above **The ultimate in LCC design and its 'swan song' was the blue car number 1 which glistens with sleek newness in this scene at 'The Angel' Islington. This was the only London tram to have entirely roller blind indicator displays, in which respect it was ahead of the motor bus by some twenty-four years.** L. Burrows

APPENDIX ONE

(A) LIST OF BUS ROUTES OPERATING IN THE METROPOLITAN POLICE DISTRICT ON 1ST JANUARY 1930

The following list contains details of all routes operating in the Metropolitan Police District and other routes operated by the London General Omnibus Company elsewhere. All routes were operated by the LGOC unless otherwise stated; on routes operated by Independents or LGOC associated companies, these are shown in the entries for the individual routes. To simplify the presentation of seasonal variations, any changes which took place between 1st January and 28th May 1930 are also shown. The number allocated on 3rd October 1934, when the 'Bassom' system was dismantled, is also shown where the route, or a comparable one, was still operating by that date.

Route Number	1934 Number	Route	Route Number	1934 Number	Route
G1	109/248 *	Collier Row ('White Hart') – Cranham (P.O.) via Romford, Roneo Corner, Upminster.	14A	14	Hornsey Rise ('Favourite Hotel') – Putney ('Railway Hotel') via Holloway, Kings Cross, Tottenham Court Rd, Piccadilly, Knightsbridge, Sth Kensington, Fulham Rd; extended to Kingston Vale via Putney Heath, Roehampton (Monday to Friday peaks) as 14F; and to Hampton Court (Vrow Walk) Summer Sundays as 14. (Also operates Saturday peaks Kings Cross – Hampton Court as 14D). *(Also: Enterprise, Omega, Red Rover, Triumph.)*
G5	246	Romford ('Parkside Hotel') – Hornchurch L.M.S. Station via Roneo Corner.			
G40	370	Romford – Grays via Upminster, Ockendons, North Stifford.			
1C	1	Willesden (Pound Lane) – Lewisham (Rennell St) via Kilburn, Marylebone, Tottenham Court Rd, Charing Cross, Waterloo, Bermondsey, Deptford; extended Summer Sundays to Chislehurst via Lee, Eltham, Mottingham as 1B. *(Joint with Tilling.)*	15A	15	East Ham ('White Horse') – Ladbroke Grove via Barking Rd, Poplar, Aldgate, Bank, Charing Cross, Regent St, Oxford St, Paddington; extended Sundays to Acton Vale ('Kings Arms') via Wormwood Scrubs, as 15. *(Also: Chariot, Eagle, Miller, Peræque, Renown.)*
2	2*	North Finchley ('Swan & Pyramids') – Catford ('George Inn') via Finchley Rd, Park La, Victoria, Vauxhall, Brixton, Herne Hill, West Norwood, Crystal Palace, Sydenham. (On Mondays to Saturdays in two sections: N. Finchley – W. Norwood (2D); Golders Grn – Catford (2A).	16A	16*	Victoria (S.R. Station Forecourt) – Cricklewood ('The Crown') via Marble Arch, Kilburn.
3B	3	Camden Town Station – Crystal Palace ('White Swan') via Albany St, Regent St, Westminster Bridge, Kennington, Brixton, Herne Hill, Croxted Rd. *(Also City.)*	17	17	London Bridge (S.R. Station Forecourt) – Southall (Norwood Road) via Bank, Holborn, Marble Arch, Shepherds Bush, Ealing. (Sundays.) *(Independent route: Summerskill.)*
4	N/O	Hadley Woods ('Cock') – Greenwich via Southgate, Wood Green, Finsbury Park, Highbury, Islington, Aldersgate, Elephant & Castle, Bermondsey, Surrey Docks (Summer Sundays).	18	18	London Bridge (S.R. Station Forecourt) – Harrow Weald Garage via Southwark Bridge, Ludgate Cir, Holborn, Kings Cross, Marylebone, Harrow Rd, Wembley, Sudbury, Harrow.
4A	4	Finsbury Park Station – Bermondsey ('Queen Charlotte').	19D	19	Finsbury Park (Rock Street) – Upper Tooting ('Wheatsheaf') via Highbury, Islington, Bloomsbury, Piccadilly, Sloane Sq, Battersea, Clapham Junction, Trinity Rd; extended Sundays to Streatham Common ('The Greyhound') as 19. *(Also: Chocolate Express.)*
5A	15*	Raynes Park ('Junction Tavern') – Upton Park (Forest Gate Garage) via Merton, Tooting, Balham, Clapham, Kennington, London Bridge, Aldgate, Poplar. *(NOTE: withdrawn Raynes Park to Clapham Common 30/5/30 – renumbered 5C.)*	20	21A*	Wood Green ('The Wellington') – Shooters Hill ('Red Lion') via Newington Grn, Moorgate, London Bdg, Old Kent Rd, New Cross, Lewisham, Blackheath Village.
5B	5*	Clapham Common (Old Town) – Wanstead ('The George') via route 5A and Wanstead Flats (Summer Saturdays and Sundays) *(Introduced 2/6/30.)*	21	21	Wood Green ('The Wellington') – Farningham ('Bull Hotel') via route 20 to Lewisham, Eltham, Sidcup, Swanley. (Joint with Tilling.) *(Also: Carswool, Pickup, Raper.)*
6	6	Hackney Wick ('Victoria Hotel') – Alperton ('Fox & Goose') via Shoreditch, Bank, Strand, Regent St., Marble Arch, Warwick Ave., West Kilburn, Willesden, Wembley. *(NOTE: withdrawn Alperton to Willesden ('White Hart') 29/1/30.)* *(Also Empress, Premier.)*	22	22	Putney Common ('The Cricketer') – Homerton ('Clapton Park Tavern') via Kings Rd, Sloane Sq, Piccadilly, Holborn, Bank, Dalston
7	7	Liverpool Street (Und Stn) – Acton Vale ('Kings Arms') via Bank, Holborn, Marble Arch, Paddington, Ladbroke Grove, East Acton (Mondays to Saturdays).	23	23*	Marylebone Station (Gt. Central St) – Rainham (Clock Tower) via Baker St, Oxford St, Holborn, Bank, Aldgate, Poplar, Barking, Dagenham (Mondays to Saturdays). *(Also: Martin.)*
8	8*	Colindale Station – Old Ford ('Lady Franklin') via Hay Lane, Kingsbury, Neasden, Willesden, Kilburn, Marble Arch, Holborn, Bank, Liverpool St, Bethnal Green.	24	24	Hampstead Heath (South End Green) – Pimlico ('King William IV') via Camden Town, Tottenham Court Rd, Whitehall, Victoria. *(British route.)*
9	9*	Liverpool Street (Und Stn) – Barnes (Avondale Road) via Bank, Charing Cross, Piccadilly, Kensington, Hammersmith, Castelnau (Mondays to Saturdays).	25	25*	Victoria (S.R. Station Forecourt) – Seven Kings (Hotel) via Bond St, Holborn, Aldgate, Stratford, Ilford. *(Also: Victory.)*
10A	10*	Elephant & Castle (Tarn St) – Abridge ('Blue Boar') via London Bdg, Aldgate, Stratford, Wanstead, Woodford Bdg; extended Summer Saturdays and Sundays to Chipping Ongar ('Cock Hotel') via Stanford Rivers. *(Also: Summerskill.)*	26	25A*	Victoria (S.R. Station Forecourt) – Chigwell Row ('Maypole') via 25 to Ilford, Gants Hill, Barkingside. *(Also: Empress, Enterprise, Martin, Peræque, Renown, Westminster.)*
11E	11	Liverpool Street (Und Stn) – Shepherds Bush (Wells Road) via Bank, Charing Cross, Victoria, Sloane Square, Chelsea, Fulham, Hammersmith *(Also: Chocolate Express, Cleveland.)*	27	27*	Highgate (Und Stn) – Hounslow Garage via Camden Town, Euston Rd, Marylebone Rd, Paddington, Notting Hill Gate, Kensington, Hammersmith, Chiswick, Kew, Richmond, Twickenham, Whitton. *(Also: The Adelaide, Martin.)*
12A	12*	South Croydon ('Red Deer') – Oxford Circus via Addiscombe, Penge, Forest Hill, Peckham, Elephant, Westminster Bdg.; extended Sundays to Shepherds Bush ('Princess Victoria') via Notting Hill Gate as 12. *(Joint with Tilling.)* *(Also: Raper, St. George.)*	28E	28 *	Wandsworth Bridge (Tavern) – Hendon ('The Bell') via Walham Grn, Kensington, Notting Hill Gate, Westbourne Park, Kilburn, West Hampstead, Golders Green; extended Sundays to Hendon (Station Road) as 28.
13	13	London Bridge (S.R. Station Forecourt) – Hendon ('The Bell') via Cannon St, Charing Cross, Oxford St, Baker St, Golders Green (Mondays to Saturdays).	29	29*	Victoria (S.R. Station Forecourt) – Hadley Woods ('The Cock') via Charing Cross, Tottenham Court Rd, Camden Town, Finsbury Park, Wood Green, Southgate. *(Also: Ambassador.)*
			30	30	South Hackney ('Queens Hotel') – Roehampton ('Montague Arms') via Hackney, Dalston, Highbury, Islington, Kings Cross, Baker St, Marble Arch, Brompton Rd, Lillie Rd, Putney, Doverhouse Rd.

Route Number	1934 Number	Route	Route Number	1934 Number	Route
31	31	Camden Town ('Mother Red Cap') – Chelsea ('Stanley Arms') via Swiss Cottage, Kilburn, Notting Hill Gate, Kensington, Earls Court.	47	47	Shoreditch (Calvert Avenue) – Green Street Green ('Rose & Crown') via London Bdg, Rotherhithe, Deptford, Lewisham, Catford, Bromley (Mondays to Saturdays and Summer Sundays). (Winter Sunday service: Shoreditch – Farnborough, as 47A.) See also 147. (Joint with Tilling.) (Also: Allitt.)
32	32	Lampton ('Black Horse') – Wimbledon Common via Gt West Rd, Chiswick, Goldhawk Rd, Shepherds Bush, Marble Arch, Regent St, Whitehall, Gt Smith St, Vauxhall, Clapham, Tooting, Merton (Mondays to Saturdays). (NOTE: altered 28/5/30 to run Turnham Green – Raynes Park.)	48	48	Blackheath ('Royal Standard') – Golders Green Station via New Cross, Old Kent Rd, Elephant, Waterloo, Charing Cross Rd, Oxford St, Baker St, Swiss Cottage.
33A	33*	Waterloo Station (Alaska St) – Richmond (Wakefield Rd) via Charing Cross, Piccadilly, Kensington, Hammersmith, Barnes; extended Summer Saturdays to Hampton Court (Vrow Walk) via Twickenham, Teddington, as 33. Sundays works Aldwych – Richmond as 33B. (Also: Chocolate Express, Premier.)	49C	49	Shepherds Bush (The Lawn) – Lewisham (Rennell St) via Holland Rd, Kensington, South Kensington, Battersea, Clapham Junction, Streatham, Church Rd., Crystal Palace, Sydenham, Forest Hill, Brockley Rise.
34	N/O	Liverpool Street (Und Stn) – South Croydon ('Swan & Sugar Loaf') via Bank, Elephant, Kennington, Streatham, London Rd. (Independent route: Peræque.)	50	5	Streatham Common ('The Greyhound') – Mitcham Common ('Horse & Groom') via Greyhound Lane, Manor Rd. (Also: Reliance.)
35	35*	Clapham Common Station – Highams Park Station via Brixton, Camberwell, Elephant, London Bdg, Dalston, Hackney, Leyton, Wood St.	51A	N/O	Putney Bridge Station – Oxford Circus via Wimbledon, Tooting, Stockwell, Vauxhall, Great Smith St, Charing Cross; extended Sundays to Colindale Station via Kilburn, Cricklewood, as 51. (NOTE: After 27/5/30 Monday to Saturday service withdrawn and 51 diverted to operate from Raynes Park, via Merton Park.)
36	36	West Kilburn ('The Falcon') – Hither Green Station via Harrow Rd, Paddington, Marble Arch, Victoria, Camberwell, New Cross, Lewisham, Catford. (Tilling route.) (Also: City.)	52	52*	Ladbroke Grove ('Earl Percy') – Victoria (S.R. Station Forecourt) via Kensington, Hyde Park Corner.
37	37	Peckham ('Lord Hill') – Hounslow Heath ('The Hussar') via East Dulwich, Herne Hill, Brixton, Clapham Junction, Putney, Richmond, St Margarets, Isleworth. (Also: City, Glen, Pickup, Puttergill.)	53A	53	West Hampstead (West End Green) – Plumstead Common (Park Road) via St Johns Wood Rd, Baker St, Wigmore St, Regent St, Westminster Bridge, Elephant, Old Kent Rd, New Cross, Greenwich, Woolwich; extended Sundays to Bostall Woods (Plumstead Garage), as 53.
38	38	Victoria (S.R. Station Forecourt) – Epping Forest ('Wake Arms') via Piccadilly, Bloomsbury, Islington, Dalston, Clapton, Leyton, Walthamstow, Chingford (Daily in summer months only; during winter works: Victoria – Chingford (Royal Forest Hotel) as 38E). (Also: Gordon, Rasey.)	54	54	Plumstead Common ('Woodman') – Selsdon (Farley Rd) via Woolwich, Blackheath, Lewisham, Catford, Beckenham, Elmers End, Shirley, Croydon, Normanton Rd, Upper Selsdon Rd.
39	39	Southfields Station – Edmonton ('The Angel') via Wandsworth, Clapham Junction, Battersea, Royal Hospital Rd, Victoria, Charing Cross, Tottenham Court Rd, Camden Town, Tottenham (Mondays to Fridays). (Also: Convey & Clayton.)	55	55*	Chiswick (Edensor Road) – Hanwell (HW) Garage via Grove Park, Turnham Green, Acton, Northfields.
39D	290	Charing Cross (Trafalgar Square) – Tottenham Garage via 39. (Nights).	56	56	Mile End Station – Cubitt Town (Stebondale Street) via West India Dock, Millwall.
40B	40*	West Norwood ('The Rosendale') – Wanstead ('The George') via Herne Hill, Loughborough Junction, Camberwell, Elephant, London Bridge, Aldgate, Poplar, Forest Gate.	57	57	Cubitt Town (Stebondale Street) – Poplar (Blackwall Tunnel) via Prestons Rd.
40D	N/O	Camberwell Green – Epping Forest ('Warren Wood House') via 40B to Wanstead, Woodford, Epping New Rd. (Summer Saturdays and Sundays.)	58	59	Camden Town (Camden Gardens) – Chipstead Valley Road (How Green Lane) via Albany St, Regent St, Westminster Bridge, Kennington, Brixton, Streatham, Thornton Heath Pond, Croydon, Coulsdon. (Joint with Tilling.) (Also: Summerskill.)
§41A	232	Muswell Hill Bdy – Crouch End Bdy (Clock Tower) via Muswell Hill Rd, Archway Rd, Hornsey Rise. (NOTE: withdrawn Muswell Hill to Highgate Und Stn 9/4/30.)	59	N/O	Camden Town (Camden Gardens) – Reigate (West Street) via 58 to Coulsdon, Merstham, Wray Common. (Joint with Tilling.) (Also: Hawkins, Holliday & Bangs, Pembroke, Summerskill.)
41B	41*	Crouch End (Middle Lane) – Tottenham Hale ('White Hart') via Turnpike Lane, West Green, Tottenham.	60	60	Colindale Station – Old Ford ('Lady Franklin') via Cricklewood, Marble Arch, Charing Cross, Bank, Liverpool St, Bethnal Green (Mondays to Saturdays). (Also: Premier.)
42A	42	Finsbury Park (Station Road) – Camberwell Green via Manor House, Hackney, Whitechapel, Aldgate, Bricklayers Arms, Albany Road; extended Saturdays and Sundays to Clapham Common Station via Brixton as 42. (Also: Empress, Hawkins.)	§61	217	Kingston (Bus Station) – Staines (Bridge Street) via Esher, Walton, Addlestone, Chertsey
43D	43	Whetstone ('The Bull') – London Bridge (S.R. Station Forecourt) via Friern Barnet, Muswell Hill Bdy, East Finchley, Archway Rd, Holloway, Islington, Moorgate; extended Sundays to South Croydon ('Swan & Sugar Loaf') via Kennington, Streatham, Thornton Heath Pond, as 43C. (NOTE: Altered 9/4/30 to run: North Finchley ('Swan & Pyramids') – London Bdg Mondays to Saturdays as 43C; and South Croydon, Sundays, as 144C. Also diverted via Muswell Hill Bdy.)	§62	218	Kingston (Bus Station) – Staines (Bridge Street) via Esher, Walton, Shepperton, Laleham.
			63A	63	Honor Oak ('Forest Hill Tavern') – Chalk Farm Station via Peckham, Trafalgar Rd, Old Kent Rd., Elephant, Blackfriars, Farringdon Rd, Kings Cross, Crowndale Rd; diverted Saturday afternoons and Sundays via Malden Rd to Hampstead Heath (South End Green), as 63.
44	44	Victoria (S.R. Station Forecourt) – Kings Cross ('Duke of York') via Piccadilly, Leicester Sq, Covent Garden, Russell Sq, Euston. (Mondays to Saturdays.)	64	6A	Waterloo Station (Mepham Street) – Hackney Wick ('Victoria Hotel') via Strand, Bank, Shoreditch, Hackney Rd, (Monday to Saturday peaks).
45	45	Kings Cross ('Duke of York') – Clapham Common Station via Gray's Inn Rd, Ludgate Cir, Elephant, Camberwell, Brixton. (Mondays to Saturdays.)	65	65	Ealing (Argyle Road) – Leatherhead ('New Bull Inn') via Brentford, Richmond, Kingston, Surbiton, Hook.
46	46	Kensal Rise Station – Victoria (S.R. Station Forecourt) via Harrow Rd, Westbourne Park, Notting Hill Gate, Kensington, Knightsbridge, Sloane Sq. (NOTE: extended Kensal Rise to Alperton ('Fox & Goose') via Willesden, Neasden, Wembley Park, Park Lane on 29/1/30.)	66	66	Leytonstone ('Green Man') – Gidea Park Station via Eastern Ave, Romford, Victoria Rd.
			67A	67	Stoke Newington (Northwold Road) – Earlsfield ('Leather Bottle') via Newington Grn, Islington, Chancery Lane, Waterloo, Elephant, Kennington, Clapham, Nightingale Lane; diverted Summer Sundays to Wimbledon Common via Plough Lane, Alexandra Rd, as 67.
			68C	68	Chalk Farm Station – South Croydon ('Red Deer') via Kingsway, Waterloo, Elephant, Camberwell, Norwood, Thornton Heath, West Croydon.
			69	69	Camberwell Green – Wormley ('Queens Head') via Elephant, London Bridge, Dalston, Edmonton, Waltham Cross. (Also: Earl, Reliance.)

Route Number	1934 Number	Route	Route Number	1934 Number	Route
70	70	Clapham Common Station – Dorking ('Falkland Arms') via Tooting, Morden, Ewell, Epsom, Leatherhead. (Also: Pickup, St. George.)	93	93*	Willesden (Pound Lane) – South Wimbledon Station via Harlesden, Wood Lane, Hammersmith, Putney, Wimbledon, Merton Park. (NOTE: re-routed and extended to Morden as 93D from 28/5/30.)
71	N/O	Finsbury Park Station – St Albans (St Peters Street) via Wood Green, New Southgate, North Finchley, Barnet. (Summer Sundays.)	94	294	Cricklewood Garage – Liverpool Street (Und Stn) via Marble Arch, Charing Cross, Bank (Nights).
72	N/O	Finsbury Park Station – Rye House ('Temperance Hotel') via Tottenham, Waltham Cross, Hoddesdon. (Summer Sundays.)	95	95*	Hounslow Garage – Hayes ('Crown Inn') via Harlington.
			96A	96/96A	Putney Common ('The Cricketer') – Wanstead ('The George') via Fulham Rd, Piccadilly, Strand, Bank, Aldgate, Stratford; extended Summer Saturdays and Sundays to Loughton via Woodford, as 96F; and on Summer Sundays to Epping Forest ('Wake Arms') as 96.
73A	73	Stoke Newington (Northwold Road) – Richmond (Wakefield Road) via Newington Green, Islington, Kings Cross, Oxford St, Hyde Park Corner, Hammersmith, East Sheen; extended Summer Saturday afternoons and Sundays to Hampton Court (Vrow Walk) via Kingston, as 73. (Also: Cardinal, Cleveland, Glen, Peræque, Pickup, Premier.)	96D	N/O	Leytonstone ('Green Man') – Loughton ('Crown') (Monday to Friday).
74B	74	Camden Town (Camden Gardens) – Putney ('Railway Hotel') via Zoo, Baker St, Hyde Park Cnr, Cromwell Rd, Earls Court, Lillie Rd; extended Summer Sundays to Roehampton ('Montague Arms') via Putney Heath, as 74.	97B	97*	Sudbury Hill ('Rising Sun') – Brentford (Half Acre) via Greenford, Argyle Rd, Ealing, Northfields.
75D	75*	Woolwich ('Crown & Anchor') – Caterham Valley via Blackheath, Lee, Catford, Anerley, Penge, Croydon, Purley, Whyteleafe; extended Summer Sundays to Godstone ('Hare & Hounds'), as 75. (Tilling route.)	98	N/O	Aldwych – Beaconsfield ('Royal Saracens Hotel') via Regent St, Oxford St, Shepherds Bush, Uxbridge, Gerrards Cross (Summer Sundays).
			99A	99	Woolwich ('Earl of Chatham') – Erith ('Prince of Wales') via Upper Belvedere.
76	76	Victoria (S.R. Station Forecourt) – Edmonton ('Angel') via Westminster, Waterloo, Blackfriars, Bank, Hoxton, Dalston, Tottenham. (Also: Westminster.)	§99C	499	Erith ('Wheatley Arms') – Dartford (Westgate Road) via Crayford.
76A	76	Victoria (S.R. Station Forecourt) – Liverpool Street (Und Stn) via 76 to Bank (Monday to Saturday peaks).	100A	10A	Elephant & Castle (Tarn St) – Epping Town ('Cock Hotel') via route 10 to Wanstead, Woodford, Loughton. (Also: Miller.)
77A	77*	Kings Cross ('Duke of York') – Tooting ('Mitre') via Kingsway, Charing Cross, Westminster Bridge, Vauxhall, Clapham Junction, Earlsfield; extended Sundays to Belmont ('California') via Sutton, as 77C; and Summer Sundays to Burgh Heath ('Surrey Yeoman'), as 77.	100C	N/O	Stratford Bdy ('King Edward VII') – Harlow ('Green Man') (Summer Sundays). (On Summer Saturdays starts from Leytonstone as 100E.)
78A	78*	Shoreditch (Calvert Avenue) – Dulwich ('Grove Hotel') via Aldgate, Bermondsey, Peckham, Barry Rd. (Joint with Tilling.)	101A	101	North Woolwich (Free Ferry) – Wanstead ('The George') via East Ham; extended Summer Saturday afternoons and Sundays to Lambourne End via Manor Rd, as 101. (Also: Miller, Powell & Whybrow.)
§79	219	Kingston (Bus Station) – Woking Station via Esher, Hersham, Weybridge, Addlestone, Byfleet, Old Woking.	102	N/O	Aldwych – Windsor (Castle Hill) via Piccadilly, Hammersmith, Chiswick, Gt West Rd, Bath Rd, Slough. (Summer Sundays.)
80	80	Charing Cross (Trafalgar Square) – Lower Kingswood ('The Fox') via Gt Smith St, Vauxhall, Clapham, Tooting, Mitcham, Sutton, Belmont. (NOTE: withdrawn Charing Cross to St. Helier and diverted to operate from Morden Station, 28/5/30.)	103	N/O	Hammersmith Bdy – Acton Vale via Shepherds Bush (Monday to Saturday peaks). (NOTE: Withdrawn after 27/5/30.)
81	417	Langley Village – Windsor Castle via Slough, Eton.	104C	240*	Golders Green Stn – Burnt Oak (Edgware Rd) via Hendon, Mill Hill, Edgware.
81C	81	Hounslow Garage – Windsor Castle via Bath Rd, Colnbrook, Slough.	105A	N/O	Mitcham ('The Cricketers') – Forest Gate Garage via Tooting and route 5 (Mondays to Saturdays). (NOTE: Withdrawn after 27/5/30)
82	N/O	East Acton (Ducane Road) – West Wickham ('The Wheatsheaf') via Old Oak Rd, Shepherds Bush, then route 12 to Penge, Elmers End. (NOTE: renumbered 82B 29/1/30; then extended Summer Sundays East Acton to Harlesden ('Willesden Junction Hotel'), as 82, from 9/4/30.)	106B	106	Finsbury Park Station – Becontree (Chittys Lane) via Lordship Park, Stoke Newington, Bethnal Grn, Mile End, Limehouse, Poplar, Barking By-Pass, Barking; extended Summer Sundays to Upminster ('Bell') via Rush Green, Hornchurch, as 106.
83	83	Golders Green Station – Kew Gardens ('Coach & Horses') via Hendon Central, Kingsbury Green, Wembley, Alperton, Ealing.	108B	108	Bromley-By-Bow ('Seven Stars') – Forest Hill (Waldram Rd) via Blackwall Tunnel, Blackheath, Lewisham, Catford.
84	84	Golders Green Station – St Albans (St Peters Street) via North Finchley, Barnet, London Colney.	§108D	208	Clapton (Millfield Rd) – Bromley-By-Bow ('Seven Stars') via Hackney Wick.
85	85	Putney Bridge Station – Kingston (Bus Station) via Roehampton.	§109	227*	Penge ('Crooked Billet') – Eltham (High Street) via Bromley, Chislehurst. (Joint with Tilling.)
86	86	Stratford Broadway ('King Edward VII') – Brentwood ('Robin Hood & Little John') via Ilford, Romford, Brook Street. (Also: B.B.P., Martin, Powell & Whybrow, Victory.)	§110	210	Finsbury Park Station – Golders Green Station via Hornsey Rise, Highgate, Hampstead Heath.
§87	234	Streatham Common ('The Greyhound') – Purley ('Railway Hotel') via Mitcham, Wallington, Foxley Lane.	§111	212	Finsbury Park Station – Muswell Hill Bdy via Crouch End.
88	88	Acton Green ('Duke of Sussex') – Belmont ('California') via Shepherds Bush, Marble Arch, Charing Cross and route 80.	112	N/O	Park Royal – Lower Sydenham (Southend Lane) via East Acton, Shepherds Bush, route 12 to Forest Hill, Perry Rise (Sundays). (On Mondays to Saturdays, operates: Park Royal – Dulwich ('Grove Hotel'), as 112A; East Acton (Ducane Rd) – Lower Sydenham, as 112E. (NOTE: Park Royal services extended to Harlesden daily from 29/1/30.) (Joint with Tilling.) (Also: Raper.)
89	N/O	Charing Cross (National Gallery) – Wallington ('Melbourne Hotel') via route 80 to Mitcham, Hackbridge, Carshalton, Parkgate Rd.	§113	213	Kingston (Bus Station) – Banstead via Coombe Lane, Malden, Cheam, Sutton, Belmont. (NOTE: withdrawn Belmont – Banstead after 27/5/30.)
90	90/237*	Richmond Station – Chertsey ('Kings Arms') via Twickenham, Hanworth, Sunbury, Shepperton.	114B	114*	South Harrow Station – Edgware Station via Harrow, Harrow Weald, Stanmore, Edgware Rd.
91	291	Willesden Garage – Liverpool Street Und Stn via Harlesden, Paddington, Marble Arch, Charing Cross, Bank (Nights).	§115	215	Kingston (Bus Station) – Guildford ('Horse & Groom') via Esher, Ripley. (Mondays to Fridays). (See also route 620.)
92	9	Barnes (Avondale Road) – Romford ('New Mill Inn') via route 9 to Bank, Aldgate, Poplar, Barking, Becontree Heath (Sundays).	116A	116*	Hounslow Garage – Staines (Bridge Street) via Bedfont; extended Monday to Saturday afternoons in summer months to Virginia Water ('The Wheatsheaf'), as 116B; and Summer Sundays to Ascot ('Royal Ascot Hotel') as 116.

Route Number	1934 Number	Route	Route Number	1934 Number	Route
117D	117*	Hounslow Garage – Slough Station ('Royal Hotel') via Feltham, Ashford, Staines, Egham, Windsor.	144A	N/O	Arkley ('Arkley Hotel') – London Bridge (S.R. Station Forecourt) via Barnet, N. Finchley, E. Finchley and route 43; extended Sundays to South Croydon ('Swan & Sugar Loaf') via route 134 to Thornton Hth Pond, West Croydon, as 144E. (NOTE: withdrawn after 8/4/30.)
118	18A	London Bridge (S.R. Station Forecourt) – Acton Station via route 18 to Harlesden, Park Royal, Gipsy Corner (Monday to Saturday peaks).	145B	145*	Becontree ('Five Elms') – Woodford Wells ('Horse & Well') via Bennett's Castle La., Green La., Ilford, Gants Hill, Gates Corner; extended Summer Saturdays p.m. and Sundays to High Beach ('Kings Oak'), as 145.
120	120*	Feltham ('Red Lion') – Hayes ('Railway Arms') via Hounslow Heath, Lampton, Norwood Grn, Southall, Coldharbour Lane (Mondays to Saturdays p.m. and Sundays); Mondays to Saturdays a.m. operates Hounslow Heath – Hayes as 120B.	146	146	Lewisham (Rennell St) – Westerham Hill ('Fox & Hounds') via Bromley Rd, Bromley, Hayes Lane, Leaves Green, Biggin Hill. (Tilling route.) (Also: Glen.)
121A	121	Mill Hill Broadway – Peckham Rye ('Kings Arms') via Hendon Central, Swiss Cottage, Baker Street, Oxford Circus and route 12; extended Mondays to Saturdays to Dulwich ('Grove Hotel') as 121. (NOTE: From 29/1/30, split at Hendon Central Mondays to Saturdays.)	147	47	Shoreditch (Calvert Avenue) – Knockholt Pound ('The Three Horseshoes') via route 47 to Green Street Green, Rushmore Hill.
122	23	Wormwood Scrubs ('Pavilion Hotel') – Rainham (Clock Tower) via Ladbroke Gve., Westbourne Gve., Paddington, Oxford St., then route 23 to Dagenham (Sundays).	148	148*	Leytonstone ('Green Man') – Dagenham ('The Chequers') via Gants Hill, Ilford, Green Lane, Bennett's Castle Lane, Valence Av, Wood Lane
123	23A	Marylebone Station (Gt Central St) – Gidea Park ('The Plough') via route 23 to Barking, Becontree Heath, Romford, Chelmsford Rd. (Mondays to Saturdays.)	149A	149*	Ilford (Ley Street) – Little Heath ('Haw Bush') via Eastern Av (Mondays to Saturdays).
125	25B	Ebury Bridge ('The Monster') – Becontree Heath via Warwick St, Victoria, then route 25 to Ilford, Green Lane (Also: B.B.P.)	150	101A	Upton Park ('Boleyn') – North Woolwich via East Ham Town Hall, Manor Way (Mondays to Saturdays a.m. peak).
126	25C	Victoria (S.R. Station Forecourt) – East Ham ('White Horse') via route 25 to Manor Park, East Ham Town Hall (Mondays to Saturdays).	153	153	Plumstead Common (Park Rd) – West Hampstead (West End Green) via route 53 but via Marylebone High Street and Paddington St (Mondays to Saturdays).
127A	27A	Highgate Und Stn – Teddington ('Clarence Hotel') via route 27 to Twickenham, Cross Deep. (NOTE: withdrawn from 9/4/30 between Highgate and Camden Town (Camden Gardens).)	§154	233	Finsbury Park Station – Muswell Hill ('Victoria Hotel') via Ferme Park Rd, Middle Lane.
127C	27A	Camden Town (Camden Gardens) – Hampton Court (Vrow Walk) via 127A to Teddington, Bushy Park (Summer Thursdays, Saturdays and Sundays).	§155	245	Morden Station (Circular) via North Cheam, Worcester Park, Kingston By-Pass, Bushey Rd, South Wimbledon. (NOTE: withdrawn S. Wimbledon – Morden after 27/5/30, renumbered 155B.)
128	N/O	Elephant & Castle ('The Rockingham') – Lower Kingswood ('The Fox') via Camberwell, Brixton, Clapham and route 80 (Summer Sundays).	156	156*	Morden Station (Circular) via North Cheam, Sutton, Angel Hill.
129	N/O	North Finchley ('Swan & Pyramids') – Victoria (S.R. Station Forecourt) via Woodhouse Rd, New Southgate, Bounds Green, Wood Green and route 29 (Mondays to Saturdays).	157	157*	Morden Station – Wallington ('Melbourne Hotel') via St Helier, Sutton, Carshalton.
130A	39*	Raynes Park ('Junction Tavern') – Edmonton ('Angel') via Hartfield Road, Wimbledon, Durnsford Rd. and route 39 (Sundays); extended Summer Sundays to Chingford ('Royal Forest Hotel') via Hall Lane, Chingford Mount, as 130.	158	158	Watford Junction ('The Clarendon Hotel') – South Harrow Station via Bushey Heath, Harrow, Lower Rd.
132A	132	Lewisham (Rennell St) – Bexley ('Kings Head') via Eltham, Blackfen; extended Saturday p.m. and Sundays to Dartford (Westgate Rd) via Dartford Heath, Shepherds Lane, as 132.	159A	159	Camden Town (Camden Gardens) – Thornton Heath ('Prince of Wales') via Albany St, Regent St, Westminster Bridge, Kennington, Streatham, Green Lane; extended Saturdays to South Croydon ('Swan & Sugar Loaf') via Whitehorse Rd, W.Croydon as 159. Operates Sundays Oxford Circus – Sth Croydon as 159C.
133	133	Liverpool Street (Und Stn) – South Croydon ('Swan & Sugar Loaf') via London Bridge, Kennington, Brixton, Norbury, Melfort Rd, Whitehorse Rd (Mondays to Saturdays).	160	8A	Old Ford ('Lady Franklin') – London Bridge (S.R. Station Forecourt) via Bethnal Green, Liverpool St Stn (Monday to Saturday peaks).
134	133A	Liverpool Street (Und Stn) – Addiscombe ('Black Horse') via 133 to Norbury, St James's Rd (Mondays to Saturdays).	161	N/O	Islington (Parkfield St) – Waterloo Station (Alaska St) via Bloomsbury (Mondays to Saturdays) – temporary replacement for Kingsway Subway tram services. (NOTE: introduced 14/5/30.)
135	35A	Camberwell Green – High Beach ('Kings Oak') via route 35 to Leyton, Whipps Cross, Woodford, Epping New Rd (Summer Sundays).	§162B	462	Slough Station ('Royal Hotel') – Leatherhead ('The New Bull') via Chertsey, Weybridge, Cobham, Fetcham.
136	136*	West Kilburn ('The Falcon') – Bromley Common ('The Crown') via Royal Oak, Queensway, Bayswater Rd, Marble Arch, route 36 to Lewisham, Lee, Grove Park. (Tilling route.)	163	23C	Upton Park ('Boleyn') – Creekmouth (Power Station) via Barking, Mover's Lane, River Rd (Monday to Saturday peaks). Operates off-peak Barking (Blakes Corner) – Creekmouth as 163B.
137	N/O	Golders Green Station – Welwyn (High Street, The Plain) via Hendon Central, Barnet By-Pass, Great North Rd. (Summer Sundays).	164	164	Morden Station Circular via St. Helier, Sutton, Belmont, Banstead, Firtee Rd, Reigate Rd, Ewell, Cheam. (NOTE: From 30/5/30, withdrawn Firtree Rd – Morden and diverted to Epsom Stn via College Rd.)
138	38A	Victoria (S.R. Station Forecourt) – Loughton ('Crown') via route 38 to Leyton, Woodford, Buckhurst Hill.	165D	164A	Raynes Park ('Junction Hotel') – Burgh Heath ('Surrey Yeoman') via South Wimbledon, Morden, Sutton, Belmont and Banstead Village; extended Summer Sundays to Walton-on-the Hill ('Chequers'), as 165. (NOTE: From 28/5/30 withdrawn Raynes Park – Morden, renumbered 165C and Sunday service becomes all-year.)
139	N/O	Finsbury Park Station – High Beach ('Kings Oak') via route 106 to Clapton, Lea Bridge Rd., Whipps Cross, Epping New Rd. (Summer Saturdays p.m. and Sundays).	166	166	London Bridge (S.R. Station Forecourt) – Waterloo Station (Alaska Street) via Bank, Holborn, Kingsway (Mondays to Saturdays).
§141	241	Edgware Station – Borehamwood (Film Studios) via Edgwarebury Lane, Spur Rd, Brockley Hill, Elstree.	167	34B*	Edmonton ('Angel') – Sparklet's Works via Angel Rd (Monday to Saturday peaks).
142B	142	Kilburn ('The Falcon') – Watford Junction ('The Clarendon Hotel') via Cricklewood, Edgware, Stanmore, Bushey.	168D	68	Kings Cross ('Duke of York') – Waterloo Station (Alaska St) via Kingsway (Monday to Saturday peaks).
143A	143	Hendon Central Station – London Bridge (S.R. Station Forecourt) via East Finchley and route 43; extended Sundays to South Croydon ('Swan & Sugar Loaf') via route 133, as 143.	169B	169*	Kilburn Park Station – Norwood Junction Station via Swiss Cottage, Adelaide Rd, Regents Park Rd, Albert Terrace, St Marks Square, Camden Town, then route 68 to Upper Norwood; extended Summer Sundays to West Wickham Station ('Railway Hotel') as 169A.

Route Number	1934 Number	Route
§171	214*	Kingston (Bus Station) – Chertsey (Windsor St) via Springfield Rd, Beaufort Rd, Maple Rd, Balaclava Rd, Effingham Rd, Ewell Rd, Thames Ditton, Ember Court, East & West Molesey, Walton. *(Extended Sundays to Staines from 13/4/30; Monday to Saturday service renumbered 171C.)*
173A	73A	Stoke Newington (Northwold Rd) – Roehampton ('Montague Arms') via route 73 to Barnes Common; extended Saturdays p.m. and Summer Sundays to Kingston (Bus Stn) via Kingston Hill, as 173.
175	N/O	Islington (Parkfield St) – Charing Cross Und Station via Holborn, Aldwych, Nothumberland Av (return Norfolk St). (Temporary replacement for Kingsway Subway tram services.) *NOTE: Started 3/2/30.*
176	76A	Victoria Station (S.R. Station Forecourt) – Crouch End Broadway via route 76 to Tottenham, West Green Rd, Turnpike Lane, Tottenham Lane.
177	77A	Kings Cross ('Duke of York') – Raynes Park ('Junction Tavern') via route 77 to Clapham Junction, Wandsworth, Durnsford Rd, Wimbledon, Hartfield Rd.
178	178	Croydon (Katherine St) – Addiscombe ('Black Horse') via Cherry Orchard Rd.
179	N/O	Croydon ('Katherine St.') – Addiscombe ('Black Horse') via Addiscombe Rd, Shirley Rd.
180	80A	Charing Cross (Trafalgar Square) – Walton-on-the-Hill ('Chequers') via route 80 to Burgh Heath, Tadworth. *(NOTE: Withdrawn Charing Cross – St Helier and diverted to operate from Morden Station, also withdrawn Sundays from 28/5/30.)*
181	N/O	Charing Cross (Trafalgar Square) – Epsom Market Place via route 80 to Belmont, Banstead Village, Firtree Rd, College Rd (Saturdays and Sundays). *(NOTE: withdrawn after 25/5/30.)*
182	82	Stepney Station – Rotherhithe (Odessa St) via Rotherhithe Tunnel, Surrey Docks, Redriff Rd.
183B	183	Golders Green Station – Pinner Green ('The Starling') via Hendon Central, Kingsbury, Harrow; extended Sundays to Northwood Station, as 183.
184	17	London Bridge (S.R. Station Forecourt) – Southall (Western Rd) via Bank, Holborn, Marble Arch, Shepherds Bush, Ealing.
185	N/O	London Bridge (S.R. Station Forecourt) – Sudbury Hill Station ('Rising Sun') via 184 to Hanwell, Greenford (Saturdays peaks and a.m.). Saturday p.m. service operates Oxford Circus – Sudbury Hill as 185A. *(NOTE: introduced 31/5/30.)*
186	86A	Stratford Broadway ('The Swan') – Upminster ('The Bell') via route 86 to Romford, Hornchurch. *(Also: B.B.P., Chadwell, Martin, Victory)*
§187	247/A*	Chadwell Heath (Station Rd) – Brentwood ('Yorkshire Grey') via Romford, Brentwood Road, Gidea Park, Harold Wood. (Operates in two sections: Chadwell Hth – Harold Wood/Romford – Brentwood.)
189	N/O	Ludgate Circus – Turnham Green via Charing Cross, Oxford Circus, Shepherds Bush, Goldhawk Rd (Nights: one journey only.)
190	U/N	Wimbledon Station (circular via Southfields). Special service operated during Wimbledon Tennis Championships. (In 1930: 23rd June to 5th July; in subsequent years unnumbered.)
191	U/N	South Wimbledon Station – Wimbledon Tennis Ground. Special service operated during Wimbledon Tennis Championships. (In 1930: 23rd June to 5th July; in subsequent years unnumbered.)
194	194*	West Wickham Station ('Railway Hotel') – Cheam ('Plough') via Shirley, Croydon, Denning Ave, Beddington, Carshalton, Sutton. *(NOTE: Sunday shorts W. Wickham – Croydon (Katherine St) from 13/4/30 as 193.)*
§195	228*	Sidcup Station – Chislehurst ('Queens Head') via Perry Street
196	N/O	Putney Common ('The Cricketer') – High Beach ('Kings Oak') via route 96 to Wanstead, Woodford, Epping New Rd (Summer Sundays).
197	197	Croydon (Katherine St) – Norwood Junction (Clifford Rd) via Dingwall Rd, Lansdowne Rd, Morland Rd.
§199A	N/O	Erith ('Wheatley Arms') – Dartford (Westgate Rd.) via Crayford Rd, Thames Rd, Burnham Rd (Saturdays).
200	N/O	Becontree (Chittys Lane) – Dagenham ('Church Elm') via Bennett's Castle Lane, Barking, Rippleside (Monday to Friday peaks and Saturdays).
§201C	N/O	Stroud Green ('Stapleton Hall Tavern') – Edmonton (Sparklet's Works) via Finsbury Park, Harringay, Westbury Ave, Gt Cambridge Rd, Silver St.
§202	202	New Cross (Clifton Rise) – Rotherhithe ('Red Lion') via Trundley's Rd, Bush Rd. *(Independent route: Allitt, Gordon, Hawkins.)*
§203	N/O	Belsize Park (Belsize Lane) – Kensal Rise via Besize Park Gdns, Primrose Hill Rd, Adelaide Rd, Ordnance Hill, Hall Road, Maida Vale, Warwick Ave, West Kilburn. *(Independent route: Westminster.)*
§204	238A/204*	Gordon Hill Station – Tottenham LCC Estate (Devonshire Stores) via Lancaster Rd, Baker St, Enfield, Church St, Great Cambridge Rd. (Mondays to Saturdays); Sunday service operates Gordon Hill – Edmonton (Weir Hall), as 204A.
§206	206	South Harrow (Northolt Road) – Harrow Council Estate (Hamilton Crescent.) via King's Rd. *(Independent route: Loumax.)*
§207	207	Barnes Common – Richmond Park (Golf Club) via Priory Lane, (return Clarence Lane, Roehampton Lane.) *(Independent route: H. Turner.)*
§210	N/O	Ealing Broadway – Greenford ('Hare & Hounds') via West Ealing, Drayton Green. *(Independent route: Royal Highlander.)*
212C	N/O	Waltham Cross – Charing Cross (Trafalgar Square) via Edmonton and route 39 (Mondays to Saturdays) *(Also: Ambassador.) (NOTE: withdrawn by LGOC after 8/4/30.)*
213	89	Plumstead Common ('The Woodman') – Westerham Hill ('Fox & Hounds') via Woolwich, Blackheath, Lewisham, Catford, Bromley, Leaves Grn (Sundays).
§214A	N/O	Hendon Central Station – Edgware (Premier Parade) via Watford Way, Mill Hill, Hale Lane; extended Mondays to Saturdays to Canons Park (Watford Way) via Edgwarebury Lane, as 214. *(Independent route: Birch.) (NOTE: withdrawn Canons Park – Edgware after 22/4/30.)*
217B	N/O	Hanwell (HW) Garage – East Ham ('White Horse') via route 184 to Oxford Circus and 15 to E. Ham (Sundays). *(NOTE:withdrawn after 19/1/30.)*
218	18C*	London Bridge (S.R. Station Forecourt) – Hanwell (HW) Garage via route 18 to Sudbury, Greenford (Mondays to Saturdays); Sunday service operates Kings Cross ('Duke of York') – Hanwell as 218A. *(Also: Brickwood, Pioneer.)*
222	23D	Wormwood Scrubs ('Pavilion Hotel') – Dagenham ('Church Elm') via route 122 to Dagenham 'Chequers', Heathway (Sundays).
223	N/O	Marylebone Station (Great Central St) – Dagenham ('Church Elm') via route 23 to Dagenham ('Chequers'), Heathway (Mondays to Saturdays). *(Also: Essex.)*
227	N/O	Hadley Highstone – Hampton Court (Vrow Walk) via North Finchley, Highgate and route 127. (Sundays) *(Independent route: The Adelaide)*
228	N/O	Morden Station – Lower Kingswood ('The Fox') via North Cheam, Epsom, Epsom Downs, Tadworth (Summer Sundays).
229C	N/O	Brixton Station – Stoke Newington (Northwold Rd) via Kennington, London Bridge, Shoreditch. *(Independent route: Prince.)* Extended Sundays to Wormley ('Queen's Head') as 229 *(Independent route: Claremont.)*
§231A	231	Kensal Rise – Hampstead (Town Hall) via West Kilburn, Warwick Ave, Circus Rd, Ordnance Hill, Adelaide Rd, Englands Lane, (return Belsize Pk Gdns); extended Sundays to Hampstead Heath (South End Green), as 231. *(Independent route: Birch.)*
233	N/O	East Ham ('White Horse') – Hampton Court (Vrow Walk) via Aldgate, Bank, Aldwych and route 33 (Summer Sundays). *(Also: Premier.)*
255	155	Chiswick (Edensor Rd) – Turnham Green Station via Chiswick Lane, Mawson Lane, Corney Rd (Monday to Friday peaks and Saturdays).
263A	236	Finsbury Park (Rock St) – Leyton (Essex County Ground) via Highbury Barn, Mildmay Grove, Shacklewell Lane, St Marks Rd, Queens(bridge) Rd, London Fields, Victoria Park Rd, Hackney Wick, Grove Green Rd, Fairlop Rd, Hainault Rd; extended Sundays to Chingford Mount ('Prince Albert') as 263B.
266	N/O	Leytonstone ('Green Man') – Chadwell Heath (Billet Rd) via Eastern Ave, Hainault Rd, Billet Rd. *(Independent route: Miller, Renown, Summerskill.)*

Route Number	1934 Number	Route
284A	134*	Victoria Station (Buckingham Palace Rd) – Hadley Highstone ('Two Brewers') via Whitehall, Tottenham Court Rd, Kentish Town, Highgate, North Finchley, Barnet; extended Summer Sundays to Hatfield ('Dray Horse') via Potters Bar, Brookmans Park, as 284. *(Overground route.)*
285A	135*	Victoria Station (Buckingham Palace Rd) – Arkley ('Arkley Hotel') via route 284A to Barnet, Wood St; extended Summer Sundays to Borehamwood, as 285. *(Overground route.)* *(NOTE: started 9/4/30.)*
289A	89	Plumstead Common ('The Woodman') – Bromley Common ('Chatterton Arms') via route 213; extended Summer Sundays to Green Street Green, as 289.
290A	N/O	Aldwych – Windsor via route 9 to Hammersmith, Chiswick, Kew, Richmond, St Margarets, Isleworth, Hounslow, Bath Rd, Slough, Eton (Saturdays). *(NOTE: withdrawn after 24/5/30.)*
291	91*	Liverpool Street (Und Stn) – Hounslow Heath ('The Hussar') via route 290 to Hounslow. (Mondays to Saturdays). *(NOTE: altered from 28/5/30 to run: Victoria Station – Lampton ('Black Horse') via Hyde Park Corner, Hammersmith, Chiswick, Great West Rd)*
292	N/O	Becontree Heath – Poplar (Blackwall Tunnel) via Longbridge Rd, Barking, Mover's Lane, Barking By-Pass. *(Independent route: Martin, Miller, Peræque, Renown.)*
294	N/O	Edmonton (Town Hall) – Pimlico (Grosvenor Rd) via Tottenham, Lordship Lane, Wood Green, then route 29 to Victoria, Belgrave Rd *(Independent route: Ambassador, City.)*
§297A	239	Tufnell Park (Hotel) – King's Cross (Albion Street) via Brecknock Rd; extended Sundays to Charing Cross (Trafalgar Square) via Euston, Kingsway, Strand, as 297 *(NOTE: withdrawn Kings Cross – Charing Cross after 12/1/30.)*
299	124*	Victoria (S.R. Station Forecourt) – Edmonton (Weir Hall) via route 29 to Harringay, Westbury Ave, Gt Cambridge Rd; extended Summer Sundays to Wormley ('Queen's Head') via Gt Cambridge Rd, Waltham Cross. *(NOTE: Victoria – Edmonton service renumbered 299D from 11/4/30, on introduction of summer programme.)*
301	301	Watford Heath – Aylesbury via Kings Langley, Boxmoor, Berkhamsted, Tring. *(National route.)*
302	302	Watford Heath – Hemel Hempstead via Kings Langley. *(National route.)*
303	303	New Barnet Station – Hitchin Station via Potters Bar, Hatfield, Welwyn, Stevenage. *(National route.)*
§304	304	Borehamwood ('The Crown') – St Albans via Allum Lane, Radlett. *(National route.)*
§306E	306	Watford Junction – Enfield Town ('The George') via Bushey, Elstree, Borehamwood, Barnet, Enfield Chase. *(National route.)*
§306F	242	Waltham Cross (Eleanor Cross Rd) – Waltham Abbey ('Green Man'); extended Tuesdays and Thursdays to Epping Forest ('Volunteer') as 306B and Summer Sundays to 'Wake Arms' as 306D.
§307A	N/O	Harrow Weald ('Red Lion') – Northwood Station ('Northwood Hotel') via Harrow, Pinner (Mondays to Saturdays).
308	103*	Aveley ('The Ship') – Stapleford Abbots ('Royal Oak') via Wennington, Rainham, Rainham Rd, Becontree Heath, Old Church Rd, Romford, Collier Row, Havering.
§309	309	Watford (Market Place) – Harefield ('King's Arms') via Rickmansworth, Harefield Rd, Rickmansworth Rd. *(National route.)*
310A	310	Enfield Town (Cecil Rd) – Hertford via Ponders End, Hoddesdon, Ware; extended Sundays to Stevenage via Watton, as 310. *(National route.)*
§311	311	Watford Junction Circular via Bushey Station, Radlett, Shenley, Borehamwood, Elstree, Bushey. *(National route.)*
312A	N/O	Waltham Cross – Ware (Post Office) via Hoddesdon. *(National route.)*
313	313	Enfield Town (Cecil Rd) – St Albans (St Peters St) via Botany Bay, Potters Bar, London Colney. *(National route.)*
316	316	Enfield Town (Cecil Rd) – Royston via 310 to Ware, Buntingford *(National route.)*
§354	354	Harefield Cross Road – Rickmansworth. *(Independent route: Filkins and Ainsworth.)*
§355A	355A	St Albans – Radlett. *(Independent route: Charles Russett & Son.)*
§357	357	Uxbridge – Northwood via Harefield. *(Independent route: Filkins & Ainsworth.)*
366	N/O	Leytonstone ('Green Man') – Brentwood ('Yorkshire Grey') via Eastern Ave, Gallows Cnr, Brook Street. *(Independent route: Reliance.)*
369B	69	Herne Hill ('Half Moon Hotel') – Edmonton Station via Denmark Hill, Camberwell Grn and route 69 (Monday to Saturday peaks).
401	401	Bexleyheath (Market Place) – Sevenoaks via Dartford Heath, Dartford, Farningham, Otford. *(East Surrey route.)*
402	402	Bromley North Station – Sevenoaks via Farnborough, Knockholt, Dunton Green. *(East Surrey route.)*
403	403	West Croydon Station – Sevenoaks via High St, Selsdon Rd, Normanton Rd, Sanderstead, Chelsham, Westerham, Riverhead. *(East Surrey route.)*
405	405	West Croydon Station – Handcross via Redhill, Horley, Crawley. *(East Surrey route.)* *(NOTE: withdrawn between Crawley ('George') and Handcross and renumbered 405A, 15/4/30.)*
406	406*	Kingston Station – Redhill Station via Surbiton, Tolworth, Ewell, Epsom, Tadworth, Lower Kingswood. *(East Surrey route.)*
407	407	Sidcup Station – Orpington ('Maxwell Arms') via North Cray, Bexley, Dartford, Swanley. *(East Surrey route.)*
408	408	West Croydon Station – Guildford ('Horse & Groom') via Beddington, Sutton, Epsom, Leatherhead. *(East Surrey route.)*
409	409	West Croydon Station – Uckfield via Caterham, Godstone, East Grinstead, Nutley. *(East Surrey route.)*
410	410	Bromley North Station – Reigate via Biggin Hill, Westerham, Godstone, Redhill. *(East Surrey route.)*
411	51	Bromley North Station – Sidcup Station via Farnborough, Orpington, St Mary Cray. *(East Surrey route.)*
412	N/O	West Croydon Station – Horsham via Redhill, Horley, Crawley. *(East Surrey route.)* *(NOTE: withdrawn 15/4/30.)*
414	414	West Croydon Station – Horsham Station via Coulsdon, Redhill, Betchworth, Dorking, Capel. *(East Surrey route.)*
415	415	West Croydon Station – Farleigh via Park Lane, Normanton Rd, Sanderstead, Chelsham. *(East Surrey route.)*
416	416	West Croydon Station – Esher via 408 to Leatherhead, Oxshott. *(East Surrey route.)*
§418	418	Effingham – West Ewell (Horton Lane) via Leatherhead, Ashtead Station, Epsom, Horton Lane *(NOTE: extended to Tolworth, 16/4/30.) (East Surrey route.)*
420	420	West Croydon Station – Chelsham (Mental Hospital) *(Note: 'Warlingham Park Hosp.')* via route 415 to Chelsham, South Rd *(East Surrey route.)*
421	421	West Croydon Station – Epsom Downs via route 408 to Epsom, Ashley Rd, Summer Saturdays and Sundays *(East Surrey route.)*
494	194*	West Wickham Station – Wallington ('Melbourne Hotel') via route 194 to Wallington Green (Mondays to Saturdays).
§501	222	Uxbridge ('New Inn') – Hounslow Central Station ('Bulstrode Hotel') via Cowley, Sipson, Bath Rd.
502	98/455	West Wycombe (Post Office) – Hayes Station ('Railway Arms') via Beaconsfield, Gerrards Cross, Uxbridge, Hillingdon, Coldharbour Lane (Sundays). On Mondays to Saturdays operates in two sections: West Wycombe – Uxbridge ('Eight Bells') as 502A and Uxbridge Garage – Hayes as 502B.
§503	458	Uxbridge ('Eight Bells') – Windsor Castle via Iver, Langley, Slough
504A	N/O	Amersham Station – Uxbridge ('Eight Bells') via Chalfonts, Gerrards Cross extended Sundays to Hayes via 502, as 504.
§505	223*	Uxbridge ('Eight Bells') – Richings Park ('Tower Arms Hotel') via Cowley, Iver, Thorney Lane.
§506	224*	Uxbridge ('New Inn') – Staines (Bridge St) via Cowley, Harmondsworth, Wraysbury.
511B	34A	Stratford Broadway – Chingford ('Royal Forest Hotel') via 'Thatched House', Leyton, Walthamstow, Chingford Mount; extended Summer Sundays to High Beach as 511. *(Independent route: City, Empire (Kirk), Gordon, Nelson, Prince, Pro Bono Publico, The Reliance, Supreme.)*
515	69A	Enfield Highway – Brimsdown Station via Green Street (Monday to Saturday peaks).

Route Number	1934 Number	Route	Route Number	1934 Number	Route
516	69B	Ponders End ('The Alma') – Southbury Road (Monday to Saturday peaks).	§602	102	Muswell Hill Broadway – Chingford ('Royal Forest Hotel') via Bounds Green, Bowes Road, Edmonton, Hall Lane.
522A	N/O	Aldgate – Cricklewood ('Crown') via Bank and route 60 (Monday – Saturday peaks).	604	34B*	Edmonton Station – Stratford Broadway ('King Edward VII') via North Circular Rd, Crooked Billet, Leyton, 'Thatched House'.
522E	N/O	Aldwych – Edgware (Church Lane) via 60 to Colindale, Burnt Oak (Monday to Saturday peaks). *(Also: Premier, on 522.)*	605	N/O	Golders Green Station – Hendon (Station Rd) via The Burroughs (Mondays to Saturdays).
525	N/O	Enfield Town – Cubitt Town via Ponders End, Edmonton, Tottenham, Stamford Hill, Hackney, Bethnal Green, Grove Rd, Limehouse, West Ferry Rd *(Independent route: Ambassador, Martin, Peræque, Prince.)*	606	N/O	Ilford (Ley St) – Woodford Bridge ('Crown & Crooked Billet') via Barkingside, Manor Rd (Mondays to Saturdays).
526D	26	North Finchley ('Swan & Pyramids') – Wandsworth Bridge ('Tavern') via Golders Green, Cricklewood, Willesden, Harlesden, Acton, Shepherds Bush, Holland Rd, North End Rd, Walham Green. *(Also: Birch.)*	608	58	Stonebridge Park ('Coach & Horses') – Hampstead Garden Suburb via North Circular Rd. *(NOTE: extended to Hornsey Rise ('Favourite') via Archway Rd and St Johns Way, 9/4/30.)*
529	N/O	Pimlico ('King William IV') – Winchmore Hill ('Green Dragon') via Belgrave Rd, Victoria, route 29 to Palmers Green. *(Also: Perkins.)*	612	N/O	Dulwich ('Grove Hotel') – Kew Gardens ('Coach & Horses') via route 12 to Shepherds Bush, Goldhawk Rd, Chiswick (Summer Sundays).
536	137	Highgate (Und Station) – Elmers End via Camden Town, Euston Rd, Great Portland St, Oxford St, Hyde Park Cnr, Vauxhall, Camberwell, New Cross, Brockley, Catford, Beckenham. (Independent route: Birch, City, United.) *(NOTE: extended to West Wickham on Sundays from 25/5/30.)*	614	297	Turnham Green Garage – Liverpool Street (Und Stn) via Hammersmith, Walham Green, South Kensington, Hyde Park Cnr, Strand, Bank. (Nights)
537	N/O	Acton Vale ('Kings Arms') – Rainham via route 15 to East Ham, Barking, Dagenham. (Saturdays and Sundays.) *(Independent route: Chariot)*	615	292	Aldwych – Liverpool St (Und Stn) via Holborn, Bank, Moorgate (Nights).
§538	238	Stroud Green ('Stapleton Hall Tavern') – Forty Hill via Finsbury Park, Wood Green, Winchmore Hill, Enfield, Chase Side.	616	293	Aldwych – Liverpool Street (Und Stn) via Holborn, Bank, Fenchurch St, Aldgate (Nights).
549	71*	Southall (Western Rd) – Stoke Newington (Northwold Rd) via routes 184, to Oxford Street, then 73 (Sundays).	617	298*	Charing Cross (Trafalgar Square) – Forest Gate Garage via Piccadilly Circus, Holborn, Bank, Aldgate, Stratford (Nights).
550	73C*	Islington (Chapel St) – Finsbury Park (Rock St) via Liverpool Rd, Drayton Park (Mondays to Saturdays). *(NOTE: renumbered 273 and extended to Roehampton ('Montague Arms') from 9/4/30.)*	618	N/O	Kensal Rise Station – Waterloo Station via route 6 to Aldwych (Monday to Saturday a.m. peaks).
§551	34/251*	Edmonton (Sparklet's Works) – Totteridge (Barnet Lane) via Palmers Green, Oakleigh Rd. *(Also: Prince.)*	619	N/O	Putney Bridge Station – Leatherhead ('New Bull Inn') via Putney Heath, Roehampton, Kingston By-Pass, Hook, Chessington (Summer Sundays).
573	N/O	Stoke Newington (Northwold Road) – Hampton Court (Vrow Walk) via route 73 to Richmond, Twickenham, Teddington. *(Independent route: Earl, Premier.)*	620	20	Kingston (Bus Stn) – Guildford ('Horse & Groom') via Portsmouth Rd, Brighton Rd, Hook, Esher, Portsmouth Rd (Saturdays and Sundays.) See also route 115.
601	299	Ludgate Circus – Leyton ('Bakers Arms') via Bank, Shoreditch, Dalston, Clapton (Nights).	§621A/B	243	Peckham ('Lord Hill') Circular via Peckham Rye, Nunhead La., Evelina Rd (621A via Nunhead Lane, Evelina Rd; 621B the reverse.)
			623	100	Barking Broadway (Axe St) – Beckton Gas Works (Irregular).

N/O Route or section of route no longer operating on 3/10/34 or not continued by LPTB
* Route altered by 3/10/34
§ Single-deck route

B) TRAM ROUTES OPERATING ON 1ST JANUARY 1930

The following lists contain details of all tram services operating in London on 1st January 1930. Each operator is shown separately but routes operated jointly with the London County Council appear only in the LCC list. The many minor variations (notably the various 'EX' services operated by the LCC) are omitted for the sake of simplicity.

MUNICIPAL TRAMWAYS

LONDON COUNTY COUNCIL

Route Number	1934 Number	Route	Route Number	1934 Number	Route
2/4	2/4	Wimbledon Hill – Victoria Embankment loop via Tooting, Clapham, Kennington; then 2 via Westminster, Blackfriars, Elephant; 4 the reverse. On Saturday afternoons and Sundays, extended from Wimbledon to Hampton Court via Raynes Park, New Malden, Norbiton, Kingston.	9	9	Moorgate – North Finchley via Angel, Highgate. *(Joint with MET but operated by LCC cars.)*
			10	10	Tooting Broadway – City (Southwark Bridge) via Streatham, Kennington, Borough. (Tooting – Borough Saturday afternoons and evenings.)
2A/4A	2A/4A	Streatham Library – Victoria Embankment via Tooting, then as 2/4 (Monday to Friday peaks).	11	11	Moorgate – Highgate Village via New North Rd, Highbury.
3	3	Holborn – Hampstead via Grays Inn Rd, Kings Cross, Royal College St, Prince of Wales Rd.	12	12	Hop Exchange – Tooting Junction via St Georges Circus, Vauxhall, Battersea, Wandsworth, Garratt Lane.
5	5	Moorgate – Hampstead via Angel, Kings Cross, Crowndale Rd, Camden Town, Malden Rd.	13	13	Highgate ('Archway Tavern') – Aldersgate via Angel, Goswell Rd (Monday to Saturday peaks).
6	6	City (Southwark Bridge) – Mitcham (Cricket Green) via Borough, Elephant, Kennington, Clapham, Tooting.	14	14	Hop Exchange – Wandsworth via Southwark Street, Blackfriars Bridge, Westminster Bridge, Vauxhall, Battersea (Mondays to Saturdays); extended peaks to Earlsfield; Saturdays p.m. to Tooting Junction.
7	7	Holborn – Parliament Hill Fields via Grays Inn Rd, Kings Cross, Royal College St, Kentish Town.			
8/20	8/20	Victoria (Clock Tower): circular via Vauxhall, Stockwell, Clapham, Tooting, Streatham, Brixton, Stockwell. (20 works reverse loop.)	15	15	Moorgate – Parliament Hill Fields via Angel, Kings Cross, Royal College St, Kentish Town.

Route Number	1934 Number	Route	Route Number	1934 Number	Route
					Saturdays).
16/18	16/18	Purley – Victoria Embankment loop via Croydon, Streatham, Kennington then 16 via Westminster, Blackfriars, Elephant; 18 the reverse. *(Joint with Croydon Corporation.)*	51	51*	Bloomsbury – Muswell Hill (Alexandra Park) via Rosebery Ave, Angel, Essex Rd, Manor House, Turnpike Lane (Mondays to Saturdays). *(Joint with MET; operated by MET cars.)*
17	17	Farringdon St Station – Highgate ('Archway Tavern') via Kings Cross, Holloway.	52	52	City (Southwark Bridge) – Grove Park Station via Borough, Old Kent Rd., New Cross, Lewisham, Catford (Monday to Saturday peaks).
19	19	Tottenham Court Rd – Barnet via Camden Town, Highgate, North Finchley. *(Joint with MET; operated by MET cars.)*	53	53	Tottenham Court Rd – Aldgate via Camden Town, Manor House, Clapton, Cambridge Heath.
21	21	Holborn – North Finchley via Grays Inn Rd, Kings Cross, Holloway, Manor House, Wood Green, New Southgate. *(Joint with MET; operated by MET cars.)*	54	54	Victoria (Clock Tower) – Grove Park Station via Vauxhall, Camberwell, New Cross, Lewisham, Catford.
22/24	22/24	Tooting Broadway – Victoria Embankment loop via Streatham, Brixton, Kennington: then 22 via Westminster, Blackfriars, Elephant; 24 the reverse (Monday to Saturday peaks).	55	55	Bloomsbury – Leyton (L.M.S. Stn) via Shoreditch, Hackney, Lea Bridge; extended Summer Sundays to Wanstead Flats and from 'Bakers Arms' to Epping Forest ('Rising Sun').
25	25	Tottenham Court Rd – Parliament Hill Fields via Camden Town, Kentish Town (Mondays to Saturdays).	56/84	56/84	Peckham Rye (Stuart Rd) – Victoria Embankment loop via Goose Green, Camberwell, Elephant, St Georges Circus; then 56 via Westminster, Blackfriars; 84 the reverse (Mondays to Saturdays). On Sundays 56 works Peckham Rye – Savoy Street via Westminster
26	26	Hop Exchange – Kew Bridge via Blackfriars, Westminster, Vauxhall, Clapham Junction, Wandsworth, Putney, Hammersmith.	57	57	Liverpool St Station – Chingford Mount via Hackney, Leyton, Walthamstow. *(Joint with Walthamstow.)*
27	27	Tottenham Court Rd – Edmonton Town Hall via Camden Town, Manor House, Tottenham (Mondays to Saturdays). *(Joint with MET.)*	58	58	Victoria (Clock Tower) – Blackwall Tunnel (South Side) via Camberwell, Dulwich, Forest Hill, Catford, Greenwich.
28	28	Victoria (Clock Tower) – Harrow Road (Scrubs Lane) via Vauxhall, then route 26 to Hammersmith, Shepherds Bush.	59	59	Holborn – Edmonton Town Hall via Grays Inn Rd, Kings Cross, Manor House, Tottenham. *(Joint with MET; operated by MET cars.)*
29	29	Tottenham Court Rd – Enfield (Church St) via Camden Town, Manor House, Wood Green, Winchmore Hill. *(Joint with MET.)*	60	60	City (Southwark Bridge) – Dulwich Library via Borough, Elephant, Camberwell, Dog Kennel Hill (Monday to Saturday peaks).
30	30	Tooting Junction – Harrow Road (Scrubs Lane) via Wandsworth, Putney, Hammersmith, Shepherds Bush; extended Monday to Saturday peaks to Wembley Church.	61	61	Aldgate – Leyton ('Bakers Arms') via Stratford, Leytonstone, Whipps Cross. *(Joint with Leyton and West Ham Corporations.)*
32	32	Clapham Common ('Plough') – Chelsea Bridge (South Side) via Queens Rd.	62	62*	Grove Park Station – Savoy Street via Catford, Forest Hill, Dog Kennel Hill, Camberwell, Elephant, Westminster (Mondays to Saturdays). *(NOTE: withdrawn Grove Park to Southend Village 3/4/30.)*
§33	33*	Elephant & Castle – Highbury Station via Westminster, Kingsway Subway, Angel (Monday to Saturday peaks). *(NOTE: withdrawn 2/2/30.)*	63	63	Aldgate – Ilford via Stratford, Manor Park. *(Joint with East Ham and West Ham Corporations.)*
34	34/48*	Kings Road, Chelsea (Beaufort St) – City (Southwark Bridge) via Battersea, Clapham Junction, Cedars Rd, Clapham Common, Stockwell, Brixton, Camberwell, Elephant, Borough.	64	N/O	New Cross Gate – Victoria Embankment loop via Camberwell, Walworth Road, Blackfriars and Westminster or the reverse. Some journeys operate inward via Kennington Rd and Westminster; and certain journeys operate beyond New Cross Gate to Crofton Park (Monday to Saturday peaks).
§35	35*	Elephant & Castle – Highgate ('Archway Tavern') via Westminster, Kingsway Subway, Angel, Holloway. *(NOTE: withdrawn Elephant – Bloomsbury 2/2/30.)*	65	65	Bloomsbury – Poplar (Blackwall Tunnel) via Clerkenwell, Great Eastern St, Limehouse; extended Monday to Saturday peaks to East Ham Town Hall.
36/38	36/38	Abbey Wood – Victoria Embankment loop via Woolwich, Greenwich, New Cross, Old Kent Rd, Elephant; then 36 via Blackfriars, Westminster, St Georges Circus; 38 the reverse.	66/72	N/O	Forest Hill – Victoria Embankment loop via Brockley, New Cross, Camberwell, Elephant; then 72 via Westminster, Blackfriars; 66 the reverse (Mondays to Saturdays). (On Sundays, 72 works Forest Hill – Savoy Street via Westminster.)
37	51*	Manor House – Aldersgate via Newington Green, Essex Rd, Angel, Goswell Rd. (Monday to Saturday peaks).	67	67	Aldgate – Barking Broadway via Poplar, East Ham. *(Joint with East Ham and West Ham Corporations.)*
39	71*	Bruce Grove Station – Aldersgate via Wood Green, Manor House, Holloway, Angel, Goswell Rd. (Mondays to Saturdays). *(Joint with MET.)*	68	68	Waterloo Station – Greenwich Church via Elephant, Tower Bridge Rd, Rotherhithe, Deptford.
40	40	Abbey Wood – Savoy Street via route 36 to New Cross, Camberwell, Kennington, Lambeth North, Westminster.	69	19	North Finchley – Tottenham Court Road via Archway, Kentish Town, Camden Town (Monday to Saturday peaks). *(NOTE: diverted at Mornington Crescent to run to Farringdon Street Station via Kings Cross and introduced off-peak 8/5/30.)*
41	41	Moorgate – Manor House via Hoxton, Newington Green; extended Mondays to Saturdays to Wood Green; and Monday to Saturday peaks to Palmers Green. *(Joint with MET.)*	70	70	London Bridge Station (Tooley St) – Greenwich Church.
43	43	Stamford Hill – Holborn via Shoreditch, Clerkenwell, Grays Inn Rd.	71	71	Aldgate – Bruce Grove via Cambridge Heath, Hackney, Clapton, Stamford Hill, Tottenham; extended Monday to Saturday peaks and Sundays to Wood Green.
44	44	Woolwich (Beresford Square) – Eltham Church (Monday to Friday peaks).	74	74	Forest Hill – Blackfriars (John Carpenter St) via Brockley, Old Kent Rd, Elephant & Castle; extended Sundays to Savoy Street. (NOTE: diverted at Brockley Rise to operate daily from Grove Park via Catford, 8/4/30.)
46	46	Woolwich (Beresford Square) – City (Southwark Bridge) via Eltham, Lewisham, New Cross, Old Kent Rd, Borough.	75	75	Holborn – Stamford Hill via Rosebery Ave, Essex Rd., Dalston (Mondays to Saturdays).
47	47	Stamford Hill – London Docks via Shoreditch, Leman St.			
49	49	Liverpool Street Station – Edmonton (Town Hall) via Dalston, Tottenham; extended Monday to Saturday peaks to Ponders End. *(Joint with MET but operated by LCC cars.)*	76/80	N/O	West Norwood ('Thurlow Arms') – Victoria Embankment circular; 76 via Herne Hill, Brixton, Kennington, Westminster, Blackfriars, Elephant, Camberwell, Loughborough Junction, Herne Hill; 80 the reverse (Mondays to Saturdays). On Sundays route 80 works
50	58	Blackwall Tunnel (South Side) – Forest Hill Station via Greenwich, Catford, Stanstead Rd (Mondays to			

Route Number	1934 Number	Route
77	77	Aldersgate – West India Dock via Angel, Essex Rd, Dalston, Hackney, Burdett Rd.
78	78	Victoria – West Norwood ('Thurlow Arms') via Vauxhall, Brixton, Herne Hill.
79	79	Smithfield – Waltham Cross via Angel, Holloway, Tottenham, Edmonton. *(Joint with MET; operated by MET cars.)*
81	81	Bloomsbury – Epping Forest ('Rising Sun') via Angel, Essex Rd, Dalston, Hackney, Leyton.
83	83	Moorgate – Stamford Hill via Hoxton, Dalston (Mondays to Saturdays).
89	89	Acton – Hammersmith via Askew Rd; extended Mondays to Saturdays to Putney (High St). *(Joint with LUT.)*

LEYTON CORPORATION *(operated by the LCC)*

Route Number	1934 Number	Route
7	97	Victoria & Albert Docks – Chingford Mount via 'Abbey Arms', Stratford, 'Thatched House', Leyton, Walthamstow. *(Joint with Walthamstow and West Ham Corporations.)*
8	87	Victoria & Albert Docks – Leyton ('Bakers Arms') via 'Abbey Arms', Forest Gate, Wanstead Flats, 'Thatched House'. *(Joint with Walthamstow and West Ham Corporations.)*

BEXLEY – DARTFORD JOINT TRAMWAYS COMMITTEE

Route Number	1934 Number	Route
	96	Woolwich – Horns Cross via Welling, Bexleyheath, Crayford, Dartford.

CROYDON CORPORATION TRAMWAYS

Route Number	1934 Number	Route
2	42	Croydon ('Greyhound') – Thornton Heath (High St) via Brigstock Rd.
4	N/O	West Croydon Station – Penge via Selhurst, Norwood Junction. *(Joint with SouthMET.)*

EAST HAM CORPORATION TRAMWAYS

Route Number	1934 Number	Route
	73	Royal Albert Docks – Wanstead Park via East Ham High Street.

ERITH URBAN DISTRICT COUNCIL TRAMWAYS

Route Number	1934 Number	Route
	98	Abbey Wood – Bexleyheath (Market Place) via Erith.

ILFORD URBAN DISTRICT COUNCIL

Route Number	1934 Number	Route
	93	Barking Broadway (East St) – Chadwell Heath via Ilford.
	91	Barkingside – Ilford Broadway via Newbury Park, Ilford Lane; extended Monday to Friday peaks, all day Sats and Sundays p.m. to Barking Broadway (East St).

WALTHAMSTOW CORPORATION LIGHT RAILWAYS

Route Number	1934 Number	Route
2	2	Leyton ('Bakers Arms') – Chingford Mount (Monday to Friday peaks and Saturday afternoons).
3	23	Ferry Lane ('The Ferry Boat Inn') – Woodford ('Napier Arms') via Forest Rd.
5	85	Markhouse Road (Lea Bridge Rd) – Higham Hill via Blackhorse Rd.

WEST HAM CORPORATION TRAMWAYS

Route Number	1934 Number	Route
1	1	Stratford Broadway – East Ham Town Hall via Plashet Grove.
2	1A	Stratford Broadway – Upton Park ('Boleyn') via Portway, Green St.
5	95	Canning Town – Wanstead Flats via Green St.
6	69	Canning Town – Stratford Broadway via Hermit Rd.
9	99	Victoria & Albert Docks – Stratford Broadway via Prince Regents Lane, Plaistow.
10	10	Stratford Broadway circular via Romford Rd, Green St, Barking Rd, Greengate St, Plaistow.

COMPANY TRAMWAYS

LONDON UNITED TRAMWAYS

Route Number	1934 Number	Route
7	7	Shepherds Bush – Uxbridge via Ealing, Southall.
55	55	Brentford – Hanwell via Boston Manor; extended Mondays to Saturdays to Ealing.
57	57	Shepherds Bush – Hounslow via Chiswick, Brentford.
63	63	Shepherds Bush – Kew Bridge via Chiswick; extended Monday to Saturday peaks to Isleworth fire station.
65	65	Shepherds Bush – Hampton Court via Chiswick, Brentford, Twickenham (Bank Holidays only).
67	67	Hammersmith – Hampton Court via Chiswick and route 65.
69	T/B 1*	Kingston – Twickenham via Hampton Wick, Teddington.
71	T/B 4	Hampton Court – Wimbledon Station via Kingston, New Malden, Raynes Park.
73	T/B 2*	The Dittons – Kingston Hill via Surbiton, Kingston, Norbiton.
77	T/B 3*	Tolworth – Richmond Park Gates via Surbiton, Kingston, Kings Rd.
81	Bus 67*	Summerstown – Merton High Street (Haydons Rd.) via Haydons Rd.

METROPOLITAN ELECTRIC TRAMWAYS

Route Number	1934 Number	Route
18	39A	Wood Green – Bruce Grove.
26	49A	Ponders End – Enfield Town Station.
32	37	Wood Green Und Stn – LNER Station; extended afternoons and evenings to Alexandra Palace.
34	39	Bruce Grove – Muswell Hill (Alexandra Park) via Wood Green, Turnpike Lane; extended afternoons and evenings to Alexandra Palace.
40	45	Cricklewood Broadway – North Finchley via Golders Green; extended Mondays to Saturdays to Whetstone.
60	60	Paddington (Edgware Rd) – North Finchley via Harlesden, Willesden, Cricklewood, Golders Green; extended Summer Sundays to Barnet.
62	62	Paddington – Sudbury ('Swan') via Harlesden, Wembley.
64	64	Edgware (High St) – Paddington (Edgware Rd) via West Hendon, Cricklewood, Harlesden (Monday to Saturday peaks).
66	66	Acton (Market Place) – Canons Park via Harlesden, Cricklewood.
68	68	Acton (Market Place) – Harlesden (Jubilee Clock) (Mondays to Saturdays).

SOUTH METROPOLITAN ELECTRIC TRAMWAYS

Route Number	1934 Number	Route
5	5	West Croydon Station – Crystal Palace via Selhurst, Anerley.
6	30*	West Croydon Station – Mitcham (Fair Green) via Mitcham Common.
7	7	West Croydon Station – Sutton (Benhill St) via Waddon, Carshalton.

APPENDIX TWO

SUMMARY OF LICENSED BUSES AND COACHES 1930-1933

The following tables show the number of vehicles of each type owned by the LGOC which were licensed for service on 1st January each year from 1930 to 1933 and on 30th June 1933, the last day of General ownership. They include vehicles operated on behalf of General by associated companies, each of whom, other than National, also owned vehicles on their own account. Unfortunately, no comparable records exist for them, nor for London General Country Services Ltd, which is why no figures can be shown for those vehicles not owned by LGOC, nor for country and Green Line operations after 1st January 1932. *(SOURCE: Chiswick Works stock books.)*

CLASS	1.1 1930	1.1 1931	1.1 1932	1.1 1933	30.6 1933
LGOC					
K (DD)	798	56	10	—	—
K (SD) 20seat	56	51	—	—	—
K (SD) 22seat	2	8	—	—	—
K (SD) 24seat	25	27	—	—	—
K (SD) 30seat	12	11	—	—	—
S (DD)	776	776	—	—	—
S (SD)	50	50	18	6	23
NSo §	61	61	64	30	144
NSc #	2113	2114	2164	1843	1643
NSc/clerestory	25	25	25	25	25
LS (DD)	11	11	11	11	11
LS (SD)	1	1	1	1	1
O (SD)	12	—	—	—	—
O (DD)	119	122	40	—	—
DA	—	20	31	37	40
D (SD) 20seat	4	4	4	4	4
D (SD) 24seat	5	5	—	—	—
D (SD) 25seat	20	20	—	—	—
D (SD) 26seat	19	19	—	—	—
D (SD) 30seat	23	23	—	—	—
L (DD)	28	—	—	—	—
Guy '6'	14	—	—	—	—
LT (DD) p	1	151	866	1120	1120
LT (DD) o	—	—	21	106	106
LT (SD)	—	—	199	199	199
ADC416	10	—	—	—	—
R	20	—	—	—	—
ST	1	514	713	787	787
DST	—	—	3	3	3
STLp	—	—	—	—	75
Q (SD)	—	—	—	1	1
T (Bus)	44	50	46	48	48
T (Coach)	—	11	—	—	—
BN	—	1	—	4	2
Guy (SD)	—	—	—	7	—
TOTAL	4565	4399	4350	4216	4232

§ Includes 16 solid tyred (1930); 7 (1931); figures for subsequent years not available.
# Includes 1,765 solid tyred (1930); 1,716 (1931); figures for subsequent years not available.

MET	1st January 1930	1931	1932	1933
K (DD)	162	104	—	—
S (DD)	58	58	—	—
NSo/pneum	8	8	—	—
NSc/solid	77	77	—	—
NSc/pneum	10	10	34	—
ST	—	22	100	—
TOTAL	315	279	134	—

OVERGROUND	1st January 1930	1931	1932	1933
D (DD)	—	—	3	3
ST	—	—	27	27
TOTAL	—	—	30	30

TILLING	1.1 1930	1.1 1931	1.1 1932	1.1 1933	30.6 1933
O (DD)	112	102	102	55	18
O (SD)	—	12	12	—	—
STL	—	—	—	17	80
T (SD)	—	—	—	12	12
TOTAL	112	114	114	95	110

GREEN LINE	1st January 1930	1931	1932
T	—	135	255
R	—	15	25
AW	—	—	33
LT (DD)	—	—	1
TOTAL	—	150	314
To LGCS 7.4.32			

EAST SURREY	1st January 1930	1931	1932
LS (DD)	1	—	—
S (DD)	32	32	—
K (DD)	23	—	—
K (SD)	4	4	—
NSo	20	20	25
NSc	1	1	1
AEC 202 (SD)	2	—	—
Commer	—	—	3
Morris	—	—	4
ADC416 (DD)	1	1	1
ADC416 (SD)	11	11	11
R (SD)	1	1	1
TSM (SD)	—	—	1
Thornycroft (SD)	—	—	8
Daimler (SD)	—	—	2
AJS (SD)	—	—	1
T (Bus)	—	6	14
T (Coach)	—	17	—
ST	1	37	71
TOTAL	97	130	143
To LGCS 7.4.32			

NATIONAL	1st January 1930	1931	1932
S (DD)	19	4	—
S (SD)	13	13	13
NSo	31	31	31
Lancia (SD)	4	—	—
ADC 416 (SD)	39	49	53
Guy (SD)	6	6	6
Dennis (SD)	3	—	—
Morris (SD)	1	1	—
R (SD)	14	9	5
ADC 427	—	—	2
ADC (Cab)	9	11	9
ST	—	15	19
TOTAL	139	139	138
To LGCS 7.4.32			

	1st January 1930	1931	1932
AUTOCAR			
T	—	9	—
AEC			
NSc	—	—	3

INDEPENDENT NEW BUSES TAKEN INTO STOCK 1930-1933

COMPANY	REG. No.	CHASSIS	BODY		DATE	Final LPTB No.
Adelaide	GC3354	Leyland Titan TD1	Dodson	H28/24RO	1/30	TD 3
AGS	GC5781	Leyland Titan TD1	Birch	H30/26RO	2/30	TD 36
	GW1285	Leyland Titan TD2	Birch	H30/26RO	2/32	TD 37
Allitt	GK6337	Leyland Titan TD1	Birch	H30/26RO	11/30	TD 39
	GN3185	Leyland Titan TD1	Birch	H30/26RO	1/31	TD 40
	UU1907§	Dennis ES	Birch	B30R	6/32 (ex Eagle)	DE 25
Ambassador	GK7167	Dennis Lance	Birch	H30/26R	12/30	DL 29
	GX143	Dennis Lance	Dodson	H28/26R	3/32	DL 30
BBP	VX7702	Dennis HV	Birch	H30/26RO	9/30	DH 8
Birch	GK6431	Leyland Titan TD1	Birch	H30/26RO	11/30	TD 74
	GK8660/9718	Leyland Titan TD1	Birch	H30/26RO	12/30	TD 75-76
	GN4380-4381	Leyland Titan TD1	Birch	H30/26RO	1/31	TD 77-78
	GN5880-5881	Leyland Titan TD1	Birch	H30/26RO	2/31	TD 79-80
	GO1526	Leyland Titan TD1	Birch	H30/26RO	3/31	TD 82
	GO1525	Leyland Titan TD1	Birch	H30/26RO	4/31	TD 81
	GP7289	Leyland Titan TD1	Birch	H30/26RO	7/31	TD 83
	GX131	Leyland Titan TD1	Birch	H30/26R	3/32	TD 85
	GX132	Leyland Titan TD1	Birch	H30/26R	4/32	TD 84
Blane	VX4253	AJS Pilot	Metcalfe	B25F	2/30	AJS 1
	VX6739	Dennis 30cwt	Thurgood	B14F	7/30	DM 6
	VX7354	Dennis 30cwt	Thurgood	B14F	8/30	DM 8
	VX7401	Dennis 30cwt	Metcalfe	B14F	10/30	DM 7
	VX9932	Morris Dictator	Metcalfe	B26F	3/31	M 50
	EV4760	Dennis Lancet	Metcalfe	B32F	2/32	DL 35
	EV6168	Dennis Lancet	Metcalfe	B32F	5/32	DL 34
	TR8754/8755§	Gilford 1680T	Metcalfe	B26F	6/33	GD 1-2
Capitol	KX3852/3854	Tilling Stevens B10A	?	B26F	1/31	N/O
Chariot	GJ8501	AEC Regent 661	Birch	H30/26RO	6/30	ST 1028
City	XX9060	Leyland/City	Dodson	H34/28RO	5/30	LM 1
	GN5819/GO1559	Leyland/City	RSJ	H34/28RO	3/31	LM 2-3
	GO1346/1348/ 1930/1932-3/7571	Leyland Titan TDsp	Dodson	H30/26RO	3/31	TD 114/111/115/113/112/110
	GP127	Leyland/City	RSJ	H34/28RO	5/31	LM 4
	GP4336	Leyland/City	RSJ	H34/28RO	6/31	LM 5
	GP 93	Leyland/City	RSJ	H34/28RO	8/31	LM 6
	GW2758-2762	Leyland Titan TDsp	Dodson	H30/26RO	2/32	TD 116-120
	YT8954/YX1833/ 4101/YU4431/7375	Guy FCX	Dodson	H34/28RO	3/32	GS 21/17/20/19/18
	YW7838/YX1834/ 4098/4100	Guy FCX	Dodson	H34/28RO	4/32	GS 22-25
	GX1839	Leyland Titan TDsp	Dodson	H30/26RO	4/32	TD 121
	AGH149-151	Leyland Titanic TT1	Dodson	H34/28RO	3/33	TC 1-3
Claremont	GK8667	Dennis Lance	Dodson	H28/24RO	12/30	DL 26
Cleveland	GC6664	Leyland Titan TD1	Dodson	H28/24RO	2/30	TD 55
Daisy/CC	HX2171	Dennis Lance	Dodson	H30/24RO	12/30	DL 27
Eagle	GC7388	Daimler CF6	Birch	H30/26RO	2/30	DST 4
	MV6306	Leyland Titan TD2	Dodson	H28/24R	7/32	TD 30
Earl	MY2806	Leyland Titan TD1	Dodson	H28/24RO	2/30	TD 35
Empire	VX7487	AEC Regent 661	Dodson	H28/24RO	9/30	ST 1029
Empress	GX2692-2693	Leyland Titan TD2	Dodson	H28/26R	6/32	TD 72-73
Enterprise	GJ3435	Leyland Titan TD1	Dodson	H28/24RO	5/30	TD 47
	GH1100	Leyland Titan TD1	Dodson	H28/24RO	6/30	TD 48
	GH1101	Leyland Titan TD1	Dodson	H28/24RO	7/30	TD 49
	GK8925	Leyland Titan TD1	Dodson	H28/24RO	12/30	TD 50
	GO8472	Leyland Titan TD1	Dodson	H28/24RO	5/31	TD 51
Express	GC6087	Leyland Titan TD1	Dodson	H28/24RO	2/30	TD 102
	GO1636	Leyland Titan TD1	Dodson	H28/24RO	3/31	TD103
Glen	GJ8489	Leyland Titan TD1	Dodson	H28/24RO	6/30	TD 2
Golden Arrow	GN5896	Dennis HV	Dodson	H30/26RO	1/31	DH 4
	JJ1836-1837	Dennis Lancet	Duple	C32R	1/33	DL 29-30
Gordon	VX5169	Leyland Titan TD1	Dodson	H28/24RO	4/30	TD 57
	EV3403	Maudslay ML7C2	Dodson	H26/26R	11/31	MY 1
H & B	GJ5506	Dennis HS	Birch	OT30/26RO	5/30	DH 6
Hawkins	GH7079	Leyland Titan TD1	Birch	H30/26RO	8/30	(sold)
	GX1955	Leyland Titan TD1	Birch	H30/26R	5/32	TD 87
Loumax	MY3390	Guy ONDF	United	B20F	2/30 (sold to LGOC 9/32)	
	MY4117	Guy ONDF	United	B20F	4/30 (sold to LGOC 9/32)	
Martin	VX5533	Dennis H	Birch	H30/26RO	4/30	DH 15
	GH5342§	Dennis HV	Birch	H30/26RO	8/32	DH 16 (ex Red Rover)
	HM7855§	Dennis 4ton	Dodson	OT26/22RO	2/33	D 194 (ex Miller)
Miller	VX4269	Leyland Titan TD1	Dodson	H28/24RO	2/30	TD 104
	VX5859	Leyland Titan TD1	Dodson	H28/24RO	5/30	TD 105
	VX8831/8835	Leyland Titan TD1	Dodson	H28/26RO	1/31	TD 106-107
	EV7308	Leyland Titan TD2	Dodson	H26/26R	9/32	TD 108

COMPANY	REG. No.	CHASSIS	BODY		DATE	Final LPTB No.
Nelson	GC1804	Leyland Titan TD1	Dodson	H28/24RO	1/30	TD 6
	GC7493	Leyland Titan TD1	Dodson	H28/24RO	2/30	TD 5
	GX1914	Leyland Titan TD2	Dodson	H30/24R	5/32	TD 4
Nil Desperandum	YX7703§	Leyland Lion PLSC3	Birch	B32R	4/30	LN 6 (ex Pembroke)
	GN7512	Leyland Lion LT2	Birch	B30R	8/30	LN 7
	GH7079§	Leyland Titan TD1	Birch	B30R	5/32	TD 86 (ex RH)
Omega	GP3379	Leyland Titan TD1	Dodson	H30/26RO	7/31	TD 28
Pembroke	GJ3020	AEC Regent 661	Birch	H30/26RO	5/30	ST 1031
Peræque	GK8779-8780	Leyland Titan TD1	Dodson	H30/26RO	12/30	TD 43-44
	GK9384	Leyland Titan TD1	Dodson	H30/26RO	1/31	TD 45
	GT1083	Leyland Titan TD1	Dodson	H30/26RO	11/31	TD 46
Phillips	RO9162	Chevrolet LO	?	C14F	10/31	w/d 11/32
	DV5364§	Bean	Tiverton	B20F	7/32	BN 5
Pickup	GO4367/5424	Leyland Titan TD1	Dodson	H30/26RO	1/31	TD 32-33
	GW1224/1785	AEC Regent 661	Park Royal	OT30/26R	1/32	STL 554-5
	GW1744	AEC Regent 661	Park Royal	OT30/26R	2/32	STL 553
	GX167	AEC Regent 661	Park Royal	OT30/26R	3/32	STL 556
	GY839	AEC Regent 661	Park Royal	OT30/26R	7/32	STL 557
Pinner Bus	MY3496	Bean	Birch	B18F	2/30	BN 4
	GF493	Dennis Dart	LGOC	B18F	4/30	DA 2 (on loan from LGOC)
Pioneer	HX2492	Leyland Titan TD1	Dodson	H28/24RO	1/31	TD 54
Premier	GJ7536-7538	Leyland Titan TD1	Duple	H28/24RO	6/30	TD 58/59/62
	GH889/890/2491	Leyland Titan TD1	Duple	H28/24RO	7/30	TD 61/63/64
	GK891-896	Leyland Titan TD1	Duple	H28/24RO	11/30	TD 67/68/66/71/70/69
Prince	MY2663	Leyland Titan TD1	Dodson	H28/24RO	1/30	TD 127
	MY2917	Leyland Titan TD1	Dodson	H28/24RO	2/30	TD 128
	MY4043	Leyland Titan TD1	Dodson	H28/24RO	4/30	TD 129
	MV1019	Leyland Titan TD1	Duple	B31R	12/31	TD 131
	MV1376	Leyland Titan TD2	Dodson	H27/26R	1/32	TD 130
Pro Bono Publico	VX7553	AEC Regent 661	Dodson	H30/23RO	9/30	ST 1030
	EV5860	Leyland Titan TD2	Duple	H27/26R	4/32	TD 29
Red Line	GC1684	Daimler CF6	Birch	H30/26RO	1/30	w/d 1/32
	GO5538	Daimler CH6	Birch	H28/24R	4/31	DST 5
	GW2294	AEC Regent 661	Birch	H26/25R	3/32	STL 558
Red Rover	GH5342	Dennis HV	Birch	H30/26RO	8/30	to Martin 8/32
	GY1961	Dennis Lance	Birch	H29/25R	8/32	DL 28
Reliance	VX8363/8364	Dennis Lance	Dodson	H27/24R	11/30	DL 33/32
	EV6510/6692	Leyland Titan TD2	Dodson	H28/26R	6/32	TD 123/124
	EV8334	Leyland Tiger TS4	Dodson	B31R	10/32	TR 1
	EV8335	Leyland Titan TD2	Dodson	H27/26R	10/32	TD 125
Renown	HV453	Leyland Titan TD1	Dodson	H28/24RO	3/30	TD 22
	HV702	Leyland Titan TD1	Dodson	H28/24RO	6/30	TD 23
	HV898	Leyland Titan TD1	Dodson	H28/24RO	8/30	TD 24
	HV1188	Leyland Titan TD1	Dodson	H28/24RO	2/31	TD 25
	HV1540§	Leyland Titan TD1	Dodson	H30/26RO	7/31	TD 26
	HV2822	Leyland Titan TD2	Dodson	H30/26RO	4/33	TD 27
Romford District	GJ2307	Dennis GL	Duple	B19F	5/30	DM 3
	VX9897	Dennis GL	Duple	B20F	3/31	DM 4
	EV4010	Dennis 30cwt	Metcalfe	B14F	1/32	DM 2
	EV4011	Dennis Dart	Metcalfe	B20F	1/32	DA 43
	EV5909	Dennis Dart	Metcalfe	B20F	5/32	DA 44
	ANO794	Dennis Dart	Metcalfe	B20F	8/33	DA 45
Royal Highlander*	UR9195-9196	Guy OND	Duple	B20F	3/31	G 1-2
	HX3466-3467	Bean	Birch	B14F	3/31	BN 2-3
	UR9899-9900	Guy OND	Duple	B20F	6/31	G 6/3
	UR9997-9998	Guy OND	Duple	B20F	7/31	G 4-5
	MV933	Bean	Birch	B14F	12/31	BN 1
	* - all to L.G.O.C. 16/9/32					
Ryan	MY4650	Leyland Titan TD1	Dodson	H28/24RO	5/30	TD 13
St George	GO5448	Leyland Titan TD1	Dodson	H30/26RO	5/31	TD 97
	JJ1269	Leyland Titan TD2	Dodson	H30/26RO	1/33	TD 98
Sphere	GK7166	Dennis Lance	Dodson	H30/26R	12/30	DL 31
Standard	GN4832	Leyland Titan TD1	Dodson	H28/24RO	2/31	TD 10
	GW550	Leyland Titan TD2	Dodson	H27/26R	12/31	TD 11
	GY2042	Leyland Titan TD2	Dodson	H26/26R	7/32	TD 12
Supreme	MY2742	Leyland Titan TD1	Dodson	H28/24RO	1/30	TD 7
	HX2643	Leyland Titan TD1	Dodson	H30/26RO	1/31	TD 8
Triumph	YL417	Leyland LB5	Dodson	OT26/22RO (ex City)	7/31	L 51
United	GC1679/4321	Leyland Titan TD1	Dodson	H28/24RO	1/30	TD 15/14
	GK607/608	Leyland Titan TD1	Dodson	H30/26RO	10/30	TD 16-17
	GP168	Leyland Titan TD1	Dodson	H30/26RO	5/31	TD 18
	GP2512	Leyland Titan TD1	Dodson	H30/26RO	6/31	TD 19
	GW738	Leyland Titan TD1	Dodson	H30/26RO	12/31	TD 20
Victory	VX4261	Leyland Titan TD1	Dodson	H28/24RO	2/30	TD 126
Westminster	GC3170-3172	Leyland Titan TD1	Dodson	H28/24RO	1/30	TD 92-94
	GN184	Leyland Titan TD1	Dodson	H30/26RO	1/31	TD 95
	GX2602	Leyland Titan TD1	Dodson	H30/26RO	5/32	TD 96
	JJ9215	Sunbeam Sikh	Dodson	H36/28R	2/33	SM 1

No new buses were delivered to the following companies during this period: Astoria, Carswool, Chadwell, Essex, F.A.R., Perkins, Star (Glen).
§ Secondhand.

APPENDIX FOUR

SUMMARY OF LICENSED BUSES, LONDON AREA INDEPENDENTS: 1930-1933

The following table shows the number of vehicles of each make, owned by Independent companies working in the London Traffic Area, licensed for service on 31st December in each year from 1929 to 1932 and on 30th June 1933.

Make & Type	1929	31st December 1930	1931	1932	30.6 1933
DOUBLE-DECK					
AEC Regent	—	4	4	10	10
Daimler Y-type	8	2	2	1	1
Daimler CF6/CH6	—	2	3	2	2
Dennis 4-ton	69	48	36	28	24
Dennis H/HS/HV	12	16	16	16	15
Dennis Lance	—	6	6	8	8
Guy FCX	2	2	2	11	11
Leyland LB	95	78	52	26	20
Leyland/City 4-wheel	1	1	1	1	1
Leyland/City 6-wheel	—	1	6	6	6
Leyland Titan TD1/TD2	22	72	106	127	129
Leyland Titanic	—	—	—	—	3
Maudslay ML7C	—	—	1	1	1
Straker A-type	1	1	—	—	—
SMC Sikh	—	—	—	—	1
TOTAL	210	233	235	237	232
SINGLE-DECK					
Bean	2	—	3	1	1
Dennis E	20	20	19	19	19
Guy BB/FBB	3	—	—	—	—
Guy OND/ONDF	1	3	8	—	—
Karrier JKL	2	2	2	2	2
Leyland Lion PLSC	17	16	14	11	10
Leyland Lion LT2	—	—	1	1	1
Leyland Titan TD1	—	—	1	2	2
Leyland Tiger	—	—	—	1	1
Maudslay ML3	2	2	—	—	—
TOTAL	47	43	43	37	36
GRAND TOTAL	257	276	278	274	268